SELLING EQUIPMENT LEASING

Selling Equipment Leasing

Michael Berke

amacom
American Management Association
New York • Atlanta • Boston • Chicago • Kansas City • San Francisco • Washington, D.C.
Brussels • Mexico City • Tokyo • Toronto

This book is available at a special discount when ordered in bulk quantities. For information, contact Special Sales Department, AMACOM, a division of American Management Association 135 West 50th Street, New York, NY 10020.

This publication is designed to provide accurate and authoritative information in regard to the subject matter covered. It is sold with the understanding that the publisher is not engaged in rendering legal, accounting, or other professional service. If legal advice or other expert assistance is required, the services of a competent professional person should be sought.

Library of Congress Cataloging-in-Publication Data

Berke, Michael.
Selling equipment leasing / Michael Berke.
p. cm.
Includes index.
ISBN 0-8144-5122-5
1. Industrial equipment leases—Marketing. 2. Lease and rental services—Management. I. Title.
HD9999.L4362B47 1994
381'.45—dc20 *93-49660*
CIP

Printing number

10 9 8 7 6 5 4 3 2 1

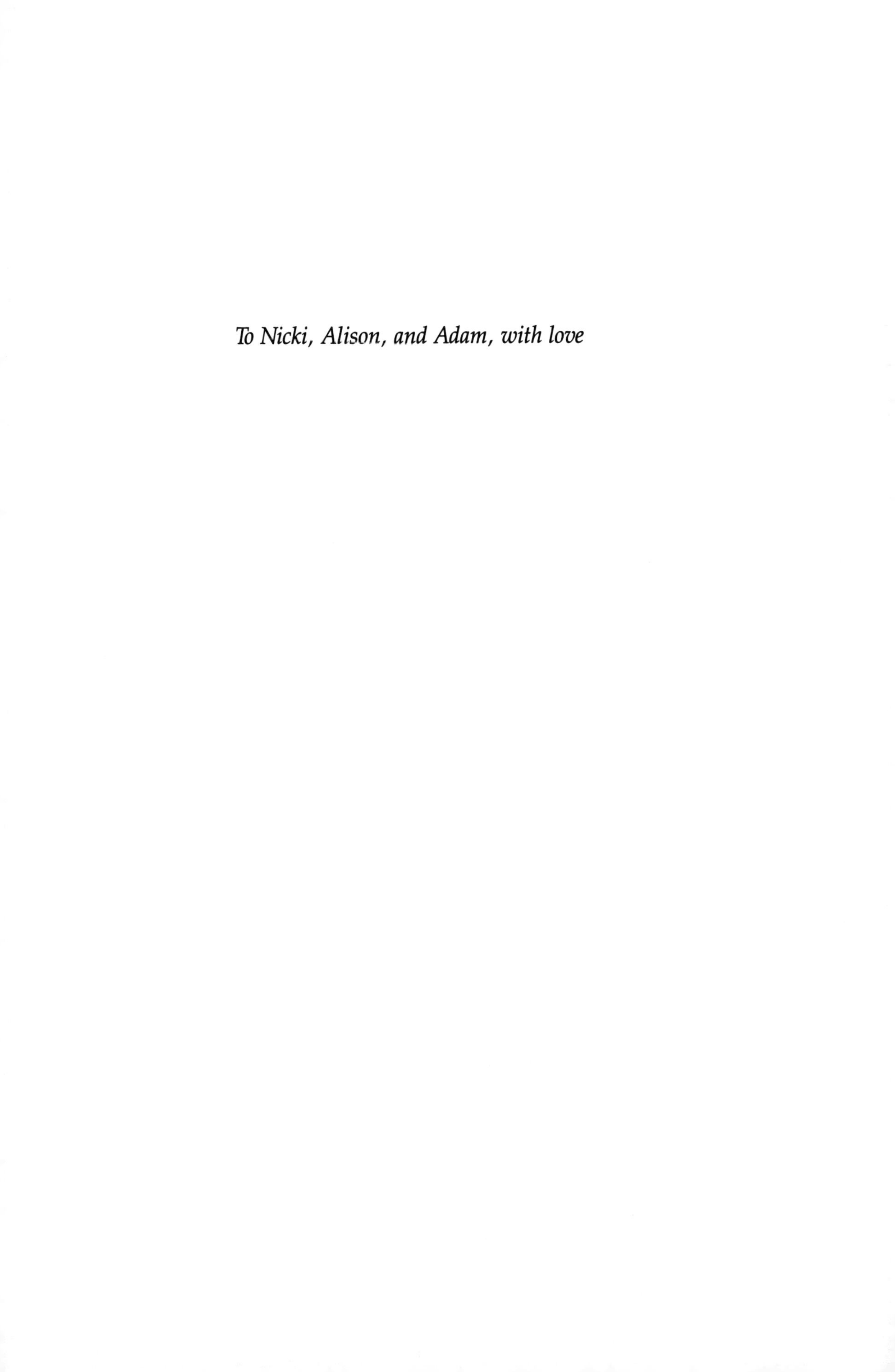

To Nicki, Alison, and Adam, with love

Contents

Preface

This book is dedicated to people who either sell equipment leasing services or plan to do so and to people who work in other areas of leasing and want to gain more insight into how leasing services are sold.

The reason for writing the book stems from the widespread popularity of equipment leasing as a financial tool, which has spurred the industry's rapid growth. Thousands of people have been actively engaged in the leasing industry for many years, and leasing's popularity continues to attract many more. However, equipment leasing is sometimes perceived as a much more conventional method of financing equipment than it really is.

People new to the business don't have enough experience to gain a broad perspective of leasing's capabilities. Many others who have spent considerable time in the industry with the same employer may have limited objectivity. Still others who have specialized in particular leasing markets may be constrained by a narrow focus. Whatever the case, a limited perspective reduces one's chances for sales success, especially in this particular industry.

The perception of leasing as a standardized alternative method of financing is an understandable one, because many leasing processes are well established. In fact, some practices have not changed since leasing's inception. When people are hired by an established company or join a new enterprise modeled on existing leasing businesses, it is natural to take the business operation for granted. Certainly, employees who join a successful business should consider much, if not all, of their job descriptions to be definitive. Any deviation from the description can affect job performance; what's worse, it can have a negative impact on the business itself.

In leasing, there are certain functions and processes that must always be performed precisely as described, because equipment leases are based on certain business standards encompassing financial reporting, credit ratings, accounting principles, government regulations, tax law, commercial law, business organizational structure, and even equipment specifications. These standards have been established outside the leasing industry and must be met in order to conduct a leasing business. Equipment leasing's basis, however, is the creation of financial products that benefit both customers and leasing companies while remaining within the guidelines. Creativity results from first understanding what the guidelines are and then designing financial services that optimize the benefits.

When you begin a leasing sales career—either as a newcomer or as an experienced salesperson from another industry—you may find yourself in a thriving enterprise, surrounded by people and processes that work in a certain way. You can be successful if you adapt to the environment by accepting the procedures for what they are, and also for what they appear to be. But you can be even more successful if you not only adapt to your environment but also know how leasing itself was created, what it is intended to accomplish, and why.

The importance of understanding the leasing industry in general as well as the particular environments of your own company and customers is evidenced by the emphasis on two aspects of the leasing business: *responsiveness* and *rates*.

If you were to listen subjectively to many leasing salespeople, you might quickly reach the conclusion that the only thing that matters is the leasing rate and the speed with which you can approve a customer for a leasing transaction. Both are important criteria, but neither scratches the surface of the leasing business. If you were to look at the same two criteria objectively, you would realize that both depend on who your customer is and what that customer wants to gain from an equipment lease. In fact, these two customer-related factors matter as much as, if not more than, anything your company can do.

Oddly enough, the emphasis on leasing costs and responsiveness is the result of leasing's popularity. Many other types of lenders that compete with equipment lessors do use *rate* as their primary offering. Banks, for example, use their ability to offer lower loan rates to lure business away from equipment lessors. Successful lessors take a lot of business away from banks, however, causing the banks to intensify competitive rate pressure.

There are also competitors within the leasing industry itself that succumb to competitive pressures, operate at lower levels of performance, or offer minimal services to their customers. Those leasing businesses that choose to price-compete with banks and other lessors can't sustain themselves for long; nor can those that provide inadequate customer service. Those that perform poorly will eventually fall by the wayside, but you must compete with them until they do.

Whether you are new to the industry or an experienced pro, your ability to compete is enhanced by how much you know about the leasing business. Knowledge increases your objectivity, and a broader perspective helps you get over the hurdle of working in a closed environment. A greater perspective allows you to better understand what lessors are supposed to do and to use that understanding to provide the services your customers want. Most importantly, knowledge and understanding help you earn a fair price for your leasing services.

Acknowledgments

Because this book reflects more than twenty-five years of my experience in the leasing industry, there are countless numbers of people who have contributed to its contents. The list includes salespeople, sales managers, credit and operations personnel, general management, bankers, commercial lenders, attorneys, accountants, prospects, and customers.

Many of these individuals provided examples of successful sales methods, procedures, and styles. Others demonstrated the importance of understanding, building, and maintaining relationships with those who provide support for the sales process. Still others, unfortunately, provided examples of what not to do.

More specifically, some particular individuals have helped to bring this book into being: Paul Gass, who hired me for my first leasing sales position and gave me my basic training; Cal Palitz and Harvey Granat, leasing pioneers who helped me to describe the background of the leasing industry; and Rene Lefebvre, who gave me guidance on particular aspects of lease accounting.

Many thanks go to AMACOM's Andrea Pedolsky for seeing the value of my work and encouraging it in the first place. Extra special thanks go to Carol K. Suddath, who tirelessly read, edited, and reviewed the original manuscript, helping to put it into readable form.

PART I

FOUNDATION FOR EQUIPMENT LEASING SALES

Equipment leasing sales don't simply occur, they are developed in stages. From the preliminary step of analyzing and evaluating potential markets to the identification and qualification of prospective customers to the implementation of sales strategies to the closing of leasing transactions, each stage of the leasing sales process must be completed diligently, thoroughly, and professionally if you are to succeed.

Before the sales process can begin, however, there must be a solid foundation from which to start. The foundation consists of the basic qualities that make leasing an increasingly popular method of equipment acquisition, the individual qualities of the organizations that provide the wide variety of leasing services available, and the personal qualities of the people who are responsible for producing leasing sales. Part I describes the components that are the basis for building this strong foundation.

The broadest area of the foundation for leasing sales is the leasing market itself. Understanding how, where, and why leasing fits as a financial alternative for businesses that seek to acquire equipment gives you a better perspective for working with prospective customers and for dealing with the competition. A review of the background of equipment leasing and financing (Chapter 1) illustrates that your product is more than just the provision of funds. Leasing companies can differentiate themselves from other types of lenders because what they offer is not simply a financing tool but a financial service that anticipates, flexes with, and adapts to the customer's changing needs. Approaching sales opportunities secure in the knowledge of how and why leasing has attained customer acceptability increases your ability to sell from a position of strength.

Although the foundation for leasing sales is the proven historical performance of leasing, your sales efforts depend directly on the capabilities of the organization you represent (Chapter 2). Your personal sales production is based on the specific products and services your company provides. The better you understand your organizational environment and the more you know about how leasing companies operate in general, the more you will be able to accomplish.

The last component of the foundation for leasing sales is what you add to the equation (Chapter 3). Technical skills, knowledge of the market, and an understanding of the leasing environment all help you achieve, but you must provide your own foundation for success by truly wanting to win. You must approach every opportunity prepared not only functionally but attitudinally to attain your sales objectives. Although all salespeople want to win, not all salespeople do everything possible to help themselves win. Combining a winning attitude with technical skill and a solid foundation puts you in the best position to prevail.

The three chapters in Part I set the stage for the specific material about equipment leasing sales that follows.

Chapter 1

Background of Equipment Leasing and Financing

A good place to begin understanding what leases are supposed to do is at the beginning. Some background from the history of the leasing industry and the concepts that built it will help broaden your perspective. The industry history is not intended to be a step-by-step account of specific occurrences but to provide a general overview of how and why leasing reached its current status. A broad perspective will help you approach your leasing opportunities by looking at them in total rather than focusing on only one or two criteria. That way, you can do a better job for your customer, your company, and yourself.

Leasing is now the most popular method of equipment acquisition in the United States and is even penetrating global markets. Today, leasing is a $120 billion industry and continues to grow. It is estimated that about 30 percent of all equipment acquisitions are made through some sort of leasing or financing arrangement.

The leasing market is driven by creativity. Entrepreneurial lessors search for new methods of packaging financing and take a broader look at the needs of customers than do traditional lenders. Although equipment leasing is a financial tool, it goes far beyond the basics of reviewing an applicant's financial condition to determine whether to extend credit. Lessors attract customers by anticipating trends in financial markets and by designing financing tools that facilitate and stimulate equipment acquisition. The marketing approach of lessors contrasts significantly with that of banks and other traditional lenders.

Lessors are, naturally, concerned about a prospective customer's ability to afford leased equipment, but they look beyond cut-and-dried financial information to find opportunities to provide financing. Lessors expand the credit evaluation process to assist applicants in arranging equipment leases. Typically, traditional lenders require prospective borrowers to compile their own financial information and then present it for credit review. Lessors work hand in hand with their prospective customers to help gather the appropriate information, providing expertise where it is needed. Often, assistance and expertise are lent by visiting the customer's place of business to get a better picture of potential financings.

Lessors help their prospective customers gather financial data by using a "credit packaging" process. The complete credit package includes supplemental financial information that helps define an applicant's credit strength. Lessors also obtain specific information about the equipment to be leased, its use, its benefits, and how the acquisition will help the customer in the future. The equipment and its value often allow lessors to structure lease transactions that could not be completed using other forms of financing.

Where Leasing Began

Business historians believe that the leasing concept originated in ancient Samaria around 2010 B.C. At the time, there were landowners who didn't use all their property to grow crops and laborers who didn't have land or farming tools. The landowners didn't want to sell the land, nor could the laborers afford to buy it. The landowners created a simple business arrangement: The laborers could grow their own crops on the idle land, using tools supplied to them by the landowners. The laborers' use of the land and tools was paid for by sharing the harvest with the landowners.

This arrangement established the basic premise of the leasing industry: The ability to use an asset is often more important than owning it. Ancient landowners conceived the idea of providing workers with resources that would pay for themselves over time; today's equipment lessors perform the same service. Equipment leasing has become more sophisticated through its evolution, but its underlying premise remains the same: Lessors provide equipment to businesses and allow them to pay for its use over time.

The Growth of Leasing in the United States

Although leases were occasionally transacted throughout the history of the United States, the leasing business as it functions today began to evolve in the late 1940s. At that time, businesses were generally limited to borrowing money from banks. Bankers relied solely on the financial strength of the borrower to determine whether to extend credit. The value of assets purchased with the borrowed funds was not a factor in the decision to grant a loan.

Businesses began to expand rapidly following World War II, intensifying the demand for equipment. A small group of aggressive nonbank lenders began to offer equipment leasing services to satisfy the need. Most of these early lessors were already in the business of financing equipment, offering installment sales and full-payout secured financing (described below). Leasing was a natural adjunct to their existing financial services.

With installment sales and full-payout secured financing, the borrower is required to repay the entire cost of the equipment, plus finance charges, over the term of the financing agreement. These "time sales" also call for down payments of 20 percent or more of the purchase price. At the end of the term, the borrower owns the equipment. Conversely, leases do not require down payments, and lessors often do not recoup the full purchase price and finance charges during the original lease term. The lessor still owns the asset when the lease expires and can then sell it to the lessee, lease it to another party, or sell it to someone else. Since lessors do not always recover the full cost of equipment during the initial lease term, leasing usually compares favorably with other forms of financing for businesses.

Businesspeople saw leasing as a way to acquire the use of needed equipment without the limitations imposed by bank loan agreements. By obtaining equipment this way, businesses freed their bank credit lines for other purposes. Since equipment leases were not "loans," the lessee's financial statement appeared stronger: Leased equipment did not have to be listed on the balance sheet; lease payments were expenses paid for equipment use and were not required to be recorded as fixed debt. Lease payments were treated as operating expenses and were listed in the business's income statement as a cost of operation.

Of course, the lessors also benefited from leasing arrangements. Because lessors were not banks and thus were not regulated by the government, they could charge a higher rate of return to offset the higher lending risks they were taking. Furthermore, there were tax advantages to be gained from the depreciation of the equipment they owned. Here again, leasing demonstrated its capability to trade off the benefits of equipment use against the benefits of ownership to create a win-win business arrangement.

Market Expansion

From a financial perspective, it is easy to see how both parties to an equipment lease gain economically. Lessors gain as equipment owners, earning income and reducing tax liability. Lessees benefit from the ability to increase productivity while paying for equipment as it produces. There is another aspect to leasing, however, that quickly became the stimulus for expanding the market.

Equipment sellers recognized that as a marketing tool, leasing had enormous potential to increase their sales significantly. During the late 1940s and early 1950s, lessors began to concentrate on ways to increase equipment sales through financial programs. They approached equipment manufacturers with leasing programs designed to offer a fixed-payment alternative to cash purchases or to eliminate a buyer's need to borrow from a bank. Expanding a business's financial capability to acquire equipment created additional sales, and focusing on maximizing the customer's capital equipment budget drove equipment sales even higher.

Equipment manufacturers themselves began to offer leasing programs, with IBM, NCR, Burroughs, Olivetti, and Singer leading the way. These companies saw leasing as a way to increase sales through "pay-as-you-go" financing programs; it also gave them the added advantage of being able to replace leased equipment with newer models in the future. By the end of the 1950s, the popularity of these programs made the leasing of business equipment an accepted practice.

Although business machines were initially the most common type of equipment leased, leasing began to take hold in many other industries. During the late 1950s and early 1960s, the industry began to boom. Leasing became the fashionable way to acquire all kinds of equipment. Leasing companies proliferated, with many becoming huge publicly owned entities. The rapid rise of the leasing industry caused significant expansion among existing lessors and provided the opportunity for new leasing companies to enter the market. Rapid expansion caused a new problem for lessors: There was no skilled personnel base from which to draw.

Growth of Leasing Companies

Here again, lessors took a creative approach to the growth of their own companies. Although leasing was indeed a financial arrangement, lessors were as much in the equipment business as they were in the finance business. Since lessees did not pay the full cost of the equipment and the finance charges during the primary lease term, lessors had to evaluate the *future worth* of the equipment if they planned to re-lease or sell the asset when the original lease term ended. Furthermore, they had to know how and where the equipment was sold, because leases depend as much on how equipment buying decisions are made as they do on financial circumstances. Realizing that they were in "financially focused equipment sales," lessors often went to the equipment industries to find new personnel.

Many salespeople were recruited from the major business machine companies as well as from the manufacturers and sellers of the various other types of equipment leased. Equipment salespeople were taught the fundamentals of finance by their new employers, but they were hired because of their knowledge of the equipment buying process. Expertise in the use and application of new equipment was even more valuable in the design and sale of equipment leasing services than was the ability to read and interpret a financial statement. Risks were evaluated by credit experts who reviewed the financial information that salespeople obtained from prospective lessees. Over time, new salespeople developed their own credit expertise through training and experience.

Equipment Ownership Incentives

Leasing differentiates itself from other forms of financing by increasing the criteria for credit review. The decision whether to approve a customer for lease financing involves consideration of not only the financial strength of the customer but also the type of equipment to be leased, the intended use of the equipment, and the value of the equipment itself. Lessors rely on the value of the equipment, its worth during the lease term, and its future resale value as part of the decision-making process. By including the value of equipment in the risk-assessment process, lessors can take more risks than can other types of lenders. In a typical leasing contract, the lessor is the owner of the equipment and is entitled to all the benefits of ownership.

In the early 1960s, an ownership benefit was added by the government's introduction of the investment tax credit (ITC), a measure designed to stimulate the economy by encouraging the purchase of new equipment by the nation's businesses. ITC was an allowance that could be deducted from a business's federal income taxes. Tax credit deductions were applied after a business calculated its taxes. The deduction was determined by multiplying the acquisition cost of qualifying equipment by the tax credit rate. If, for example, the tax credit rate was 10 percent and the equipment cost was $50,000, the tax credit allowance amounted to $5,000. In that case, the equipment purchaser would be able to deduct $5,000 from its tax bill, after its normal taxes were calculated, during the period that the tax credit applied.

Lessors were the purchasers of all the equipment that they, in turn, leased to others. When lessors included the value of ITC in their lease pricing, they were able to offer terms that were significantly lower than those of any other type of equipment financing. The introduction of ITC spurred huge increases in equipment acquisition and even greater increases in the percentage of equipment leased versus purchased.

Over the years, ITC has been instituted and repealed several times. However, the benefits resulting from ITC make it one of the major factors that attracted new customers to equipment leasing. Applying ITC to reduce lease payments demonstrated lessors' ability to design creative financing programs that significantly reduced the cost of equipment acquisition. Many lessees that were originally attracted because of ITC pricing incentives found leasing to be such a valuable financial tool that they continued to lease new equipment even after ITC was rescinded in 1986.

Equipment Specialization

By the late 1960s, equipment leasing was woven into the equipment buying process as a major method of acquisition. Many lessors were generalists, leasing any type of equipment that seemed reasonable to finance. Some lessors, however, began to specialize in particular equipment types. Computer, machine-tool, production, materials-handling, hospital and medical, construction, mining, office, aircraft, railcar, automobile, transportation, and printing-equipment specialists carved industry niches. Concentration on individual equipment types increased the lessors' knowledge of the equipment, its use, the typical customer, and the manufacturers and sellers, giving them the ability to be more creative while controlling the risks.

Banks and the Leasing Industry

Lessors relied heavily on commercial banks to lend them capital for their equipment purchases. To an extent, lessors were retailers of money, while the banks lent to them wholesale. Despite the examples that lessors set by proving that asset-based lending was a viable and profitable business, banks were still hesitant about lending directly to borrowers that were secured only by the financed assets. Compounding the issue for banks that were willing to negotiate equipment-secured loans was the reluctance of regulatory authorities to allow banks to risk depositors' funds in asset-backed financings.

In 1971, banking laws were amended to allow banks to form "holding companies." The holding companies were designed to serve as the owners, or "parents," of banks and could also own other types of financial service businesses. One of the first industries they entered was equipment leasing. The change in regulations caused panic among independent lessors; they assumed that banks, which were their primary source of capital, would force them out of the market. Lessors feared that because the banks had access to money at much lower costs, they soon would be unable to compete.

In fact, the opposite happened. Although some banks did enter the market, most focused their efforts on providing leasing services to their existing customers. Still new to the business, and realizing that they were not experts, many banks entered the leasing market cautiously, wary about extending credit to customers they did not know. A significant number of banks preferred to support established lessors, relying on the expertise of the lessors to build markets for them. The net result was that the leasing industry flourished rather than shrank.

The entry of the banking community into the market enhanced the image of the leasing industry. Businesses that had been reluctant to lease because they were uncertain about acquiring equipment through nonbank, third-party lenders now had evidence that leasing was an acceptable, perhaps preferable, way to acquire equipment.

Beyond enhanced image, the independent leasing community benefited because banks became closer to the industry. Whether banks chose to enter the market themselves or to support other lessors, their knowledge of equipment leasing concepts increased, making them more receptive to participating in leasing transactions.

Over time, some banks grew large leasing entities of their own, many of which, such as Citicorp, Bank of America, and Fleet Bank, are active lessors.

Geographic Location

Having carved a thriving market, the leasing industry continued an upward spiral through the 1970s and into the 1980s. Specialization became more important as competition increased along with popularity. During this time, specialization focused not only on equipment and customer types but also on geographic location.

Proximity to both the equipment seller and the equipment user significantly improves a lessor's ability to provide financial services. Leasing transactions often depend on the ability of leasing representatives to meet with potential customers and help them arrange their financings. As a result, local leasing companies and leasing brokers can offer services within particular geographic areas. The proliferation of these small, independent operators began to change the delivery of leasing services.

The leasing industry began to evolve into two types of operations. Giant, independent lessors operate nationally, along with large bank lessors and captive companies owned by major industrial concerns. These larger leasing entities provide lease financing to recognizable businesses, preferring to work with "rated" credits. The smaller, local, independent lessors concentrate on developing market niches that specialize in serving local businesses. Their size and closeness to the market allow local leasing entities to spend more time and effort in packaging transactions.

Automation and Communication

The continued growth of the leasing industry, fueled by growing customer acceptance and increasing competition, brought pressure on lessors to enhance their services. Equipment vendors relied on leasing companies to approve leases quickly so that they could deliver equipment, and end-user customers were anxious to receive their machinery. Automation and communication began to play a greater role within leasing company operations.

By installing data processing equipment, lessors were able to build databases to identify potential equipment vendors and end-user customers. Account tracking, lease processing, and receivables collection became simpler to manage. Reviewing and analyzing information about their own customers and industry data on financial performance by customer type allowed lessors to assess risk more accurately and to provide faster and better support to their customers.

The capability to manage large leasing bases permitted some lessors to specialize in the lower end of the equipment market. Prior to automated portfolio management, lessors had been unable to service small-balance leasing transactions profitably. Costs of selling, supporting, and servicing transactions of less than $25,000 had been prohibitive. This small-ticket leasing niche became its own huge new market.

Small-ticket lessors learned how to stay at the leading edge of technological development and to use technology as the cornerstone for their operations. Communication advances, such as networked telephone systems, fax transmissions, voice technology, and remote computer terminals enabled lessors to reduce costs while increasing responsiveness. Today, electronic advances have the greatest impact on transactions of $50,000 or less. For transactions of this size, financial information requirements are reduced, because many credit reviews can be completed without the lease applicant's written financial statements.

Databases are used to create systems for "scoring" credit risk. This process allows the lessor to evaluate the probability of creditworthiness. New lease applicants are compared by credit criteria, such as size, time in business, type of business, equipment required, credit rating, and credit references, to "models" that estimate risk. This capability keeps a lessor's response time to a minimum—sometimes just a few hours—and has made equipment leasing acquisitions similar to other types of low-balance credit arrangements, such as credit cards or automobile loans. Furthermore, well-designed automated credit evaluation systems allow as many as 65 to 70 percent of new applications to be assessed without individual credit review. As a result, credit personnel are able to allocate their time only to those applications that do not "fit" the system.

Indications for the Future

Over its history, leasing has demonstrated a continual ability to adapt to changing economic climates and to meet frequently changing customer needs. That ability stems from the realization that there is more to financing equipment than simply reviewing credit applications and quoting lease prices. From leasing's inception, when landowners recognized a synergy by providing land and tools for laborers, to today's development of an array of value-added services, lessors have strived to anticipate their customers' requirements. Since the past indicates probable directions for the future, the trends of automation and efficiency are likely to continue.

Value-added has become a buzzword for selling many products, and leasing is no exception. Customers and equipment vendors have come to accept leasing as a valuable tool for acquiring and selling equipment. The competition among lessors to deliver more services to attract new business is intensifying, and responsiveness in satisfying needs is a criterion by which lessors are measured. To compete in the leasing arena today, you must not only fully understand the product but also be able to guarantee its delivery. Merely having access to the leasing products that your prospective customers want is not enough in a competitive market. You are responsible for customer satisfaction. If you fall short, your competitor *will* deliver.

Chapter 2

Leasing Company Environment: A Marketing Perspective

Selling equipment leasing services presents a variety of challenges. Some businesspeople have never leased equipment before and may be unfamiliar with the benefits of leasing. These people have to be made aware of the value of leasing before they can become viable prospects. Sometimes sales prospecting will identify businesses that do use leasing services but currently use another leasing source. These prospects have to be persuaded to change leasing sources and to begin doing business with you. Whatever circumstances you find, however, sooner or later you'll reach the point in your sales presentation where you illustrate the specific leasing services your organization provides.

When you present your specific leasing services, you're actually describing how your leasing organization operates. The accuracy with which you describe the leasing operation is critical to sales success, because your operation is responsible for delivering what you sell. Leases and leasing programs are sold by salespeople but are delivered by the organizations that process them.

Lease Processing Functions

Leasing transactions are processed in stages. During each stage, specialists perform a particular function and move transactions along to the next step. Leasing processes are designed to produce and deliver the financial products sold by the organization and, most often, are structured to support the marketing objectives of the business. The steps of the leasing process correspond to the operating departments that are responsible for them:

- Marketing
- Sales
- Credit
- Contract administration/documentation/legal
- Accounts payable
- Accounts receivable
- Equipment inventory/remarketing

Most full-service lessors employ personnel to perform all the lease processing functions in-house. Independent local or regional leasing companies usually prefer to concentrate only on marketing and sales, but they sometimes perform limited credit functions themselves. Smaller leasing brokers generally limit their activities strictly to sales. When leasing companies don't handle the full operational process, they must have the absent functions performed by someone else.

A variety of funding sources and outside service providers are available to perform many lease processing functions. Sources are available for advertising, accounting, legal, data processing, specialized computer software, skill training, consulting, collections, and equipment remarketing work. The availability of these services helps leasing entities of all types and sizes to conduct business as they choose. Regardless of a leasing company's type and structure, however, every prospective leasing transaction it handles must be staged successfully through all the appropriate steps of the leasing process before the transaction can become "closed" business.

Company Environment and Organization

The lease processing method employed establishes the environment for conducting business. Salespeople are an integral part of the leasing environment, since they represent a business to its customers. As representatives, salespeople are responsible for seeking opportunities upon which the environment can capitalize. Consequently, the more salespeople know about their particular leasing environment, the greater their chances for success.

Although leasing businesses can choose from several alternatives for handling each of the lease processing functions, the functions themselves are performed similarly throughout the industry. Marketing programs, for example, must successfully attract vendors and/or end-user customers whether an in-house department is solely responsible for results or outside services are engaged. A prospective customer's credit condition is evaluated the same way whether inside analysts or those of a funding source conduct the credit review. Regardless of the type, size, or style of leasing environment, the individual lease processing functions are performed in a similar manner. Therefore, you will have a higher probability of sales success if you understand what transpires at each stage of the process in a typical leasing environment.

The Marketing Function

Marketing is the front end of the leasing process. The marketing department is responsible for the design and development of leasing products and services. During the design stage, marketing people must ensure that their efforts are consistent with the businesses's operating guidelines or that the operation can be adapted to support new marketing approaches. To help ensure success, experienced marketers generally create, design, and package leasing products after they have first determined the strengths of the organization. The identified business strengths can then be focused on carefully selected marketplace opportunities. If operational weaknesses that could prohibit success are discovered, marketers are responsible for pointing the problems out to top management for correction. Should management be unable to make corrections, marketers must adjust their plans accordingly by changing or adapting their strategies.

Marketing's scope generally includes the establishment of product pricing guidelines, leasing plan and program design, leasing services development, advertising, sales promotion, product distribution, and the business's selling style. Targeting customer types and the geography to be covered are also marketing functions, as is determining the sales method and describing the specific functions of the sales department. Marketing decisions also include the selection of the industries, equipment types, and cost ranges to be targeted. Marketers further determine whether sales efforts should focus on equipment vendors, end-user customers, or both. The overall marketing objectives and the specific leasing products to be offered establish the parameters for marketing plans or strategies.

Marketing strategies are most often formulated by gathering and analyzing information. Market research and analysis establish the basis for determining how best to maximize business results. Some marketing information is available without extensive research.

It is common, for example, for marketers to develop strategies that are formulated on the known business strengths of top management. If top managers have experience in particular aspects of the leasing industry, the natural strategy is to focus marketing efforts in that direction.

Management, too, tends to favor those aspects of the leasing business that it knows best. Top managers usually want marketing strategies that stress their preferences. Consequently, managers who want to emphasize credit quality favor marketing approaches designed to attract the most creditworthy customers. Managers who are more sales oriented and want to achieve significant production volume may believe that credit quality is less of an issue. As a general rule, high-volume marketing strategies expose a leasing company to more risk.

The primary focus of the marketing strategy, then, determines the type and depth of support needed from the rest of the operation. For example, leasing businesses that attract customers with high-quality credit and those businesses that instead pursue a high volume of customers need credit personnel with different skills. High-quality customers require less emphasis on credit review but often need more assistance in lease structuring. Businesses that attract lower-quality credit customers generally need credit reviewers who are experienced in individual transaction evaluation and can determine risk from a minimum of information.

The type of customer targeted also determines the type of lease funding needed. Higher-quality customers demand favorable pricing and ordinarily attract intense competition for their business. If a leasing company wants to work with top-rated customers, it must have funding available at prices that allow it to earn an acceptable profit from sales. As a rule, funding is more readily available for quality transactions, but funding supply alone is not enough. The *cost* of available funding is critically important to earning income. Lower customer credit quality usually means that higher leasing rates can be earned, but lower credit quality causes transactions to be less attractive to the providers of lease funding.

The marketing strategy also determines what types of lease contracts and documents will be used. Transactions involving costly equipment and large transactions that are negotiated with large customers generally call for finely detailed, individually drafted lease agreements. Small-ticket lease agreements may require only a universal, one-page document. Therefore, transaction size and type determine what kind of contract administration support is needed by the operation. Complex documents require expert preparation, negotiation, and review by skilled lawyers; simpler forms may be handled by trained administrators.

After leasing transactions are credit approved and the appropriate documents have been executed, the equipment must be ordered from the supplier. In some high-volume leasing operations, equipment orders are placed by contract administrators; in other smaller-volume operations, order placement is handled by individuals who regularly perform other functions. The equipment ordering procedure usually depends on the cost of the equipment, which influences the number and frequency of equipment orders. In small-ticket leasing, equipment is ordered frequently, calling for a routinized procedure. Larger transactions generally allow more time for equipment orders to be placed. When more time is available for ordering, the function can be handled by personnel who also perform other duties.

Leases start on the date indicated by the customer on an equipment acceptance certificate or form as the equipment acceptance date. As of this date, the stream of lease payments as described in the leasing agreement begin to become due from the customer. Collection of lease payments is handled by accounts receivable personnel. Most small to medium-size leasing businesses don't collect lease receivables themselves but rely on their source of funds, such as commercial banks or full-service lessors, to perform this function for them. Regardless of who collects the payments, marketing strategists must be aware of how the process works, because collection policies affect how delinquent customers are dealt with. Lease payments have due dates that ordinarily trigger an action if payment is not received in a timely manner. Whether customers who have missed payment due dates are sent a written notice, contacted by phone, or perhaps both, it is better for leasing companies to describe the collection policy and any late-payment fees at the sales or marketing stage rather than leave the issue unaddressed.

Beyond the above-described departmental functions that make up the leasing environment, other areas of the business affect the marketing process. Leasing transactions are written contracts that require the advice of counsel before changes can be implemented or when new documentation is to be drafted. At times, accounting or financial input is needed to assist marketing personnel in structuring lease payment plans. Here again, whether the support is provided internally or obtained from outside sources, it is a marketing function to ensure that leasing plans and programs are arithmetically, structurally, and legally correct.

Marketing responsibility includes the design of leasing plans and programs, the gathering and analysis of marketplace information, and the coordination of strategies with the other operating departments in the leasing environment, but these marketing plans must be implemented in order to achieve results. Most marketing plans are implemented by salespeople, because personal sales is the most prevalent method of selling in the leasing industry.

The Sales Function

Most small to medium-size leasing businesses don't create separate marketing departments, choosing instead to combine marketing and sales activities. But whether functioning independently or as part of a larger marketing operation, the sales department is responsible for working directly with customers. And whether the sales department employs a full support staff or the salespeople perform the work themselves, a significant number of activities are involved.

Typically, leasing companies produce brochures, sales and marketing pieces, literature, and promotional materials that describe and enhance their services. The sales department is responsible for ensuring that adequate supplies of current information are available and that any requests for information are handled promptly. One of the measures that prospective vendors and end-user customers use to determine a leasing company's responsiveness is how quickly and accurately requested information is provided. Quite often, leasing transactions are won or lost by the timeliness of a prospective customer's receipt of needed information.

Leasing plans and programs change frequently because they are based on money market conditions, competitive circumstances, and trends in the economy. When leasing plan or program changes occur, the information must be distributed to prospective customers, equipment vendors, and existing customers to advise them of current leasing terms and conditions. The distribution of updated information is also handled by the sales department.

Depending on the lease transaction size, lease documentation may also be a sales department responsibility. Ordinarily, small-ticket leasing documents are prepared by leasing sales personnel, by vendor salespeople, or sometimes by customers themselves. Lease documentation for equipment that costs less than $25,000 is generally a simple form that customers can execute with minimal assistance. When more costly equipment is leased, the paperwork is usually prepared individually for each transaction. Complex leases may require drafting by legal department personnel, by specially trained credit people, or by authorized contract administrators outside the sales department.

Many larger leasing transactions are "quoted" to prospective customers in a written proposal format. Proposals specify the exact lease payments, terms, and conditions being offered and are commonly used when either a prospective customer requests a written quotation or a prospective customer agrees to quoted terms before a leasing transaction has been approved by the leasing company. As a rule, lease documentation for costly equipment is not prepared until acceptable leasing terms and conditions have been agreed upon by the customer and the leasing company. Lease proposals are typically prepared by salespeople, with assistance from credit, legal, or other authorized personnel, depending on the circumstances.

Regardless of the method used for obtaining commitments from customers to leasing transactions, *closed* leases are the primary objective of leasing sales. A well-managed sales department is organized to ensure that its functions are properly prioritized. Top priority is placed on leasing transactions that will be closed, followed by transactions that can be closed, followed by activities that will lead to closed transactions.

Every sales department activity is focused on business development and production. Many activities are performed by the sales department itself, including telemarketing, personal sales calls, direct mailings, customer follow-up, account maintenance, and sales promotion. Since leases are financial transactions, however, sales are dependent on the agreement of personnel in other departments as to the acceptability of prospective leasing customers. The first step beyond sales in determining customer acceptability is the credit review.

The Credit Department

Every prospective customer must be reviewed for creditworthiness, regardless of the size or type of leasing transaction applied for. A credit review determines the prospect's ability to meet the financial obligations called for in a particular leasing agreement. The depth of the credit evaluation process varies, depending on transaction size, lease type, and the established credit criteria of the leasing company, but it is similar in basic concept throughout the industry.

Most leasing companies require prospective customers to complete an application form that asks for information about the lessee's business, including:

- The applicant's proper legal name, address, person to contact, and phone number.
- The applicant's type of business organization (proprietorship, partnership, corporation), number of years in business, and, if incorporated, the state and date of incorporation.
- The applicant's business bank, branch, branch address, account number, account officer, and bank phone number.
- The applicant's business trade references, including address, person to contact, and phone number.
- The equipment supplier's name, address, person to contact, and phone number.
- The equipment to be leased, including type, model, model number, serial number (if available), and equipment cost. (The equipment cost is the amount to be paid for the equipment by the leasing company, which is not necessarily the list price. At times equipment may be sold at a discount, or an allowance may be applied for equipment traded in.) A leasing agreement is based on the *exact* amount that the leasing company will pay for the equipment.
- A brief description of the leasing transaction, including lease term, lease payment, purchase option, and comments on the purpose of the equipment acquisition.
- If personal guarantees are required, or if the business is individually owned or a partnership, the home addresses and Social Security numbers of the principals. Depending on the transaction size, lease guarantors may be required to submit personal financial statements in addition to those of the business. Personal financial information is usually required when individuals operate a business as sole proprietors, as a d/b/a (doing business as), or as a partnership, or when the stock of a corporation is owned by an individual or small group of people.
- A section where comments or additional information can be entered to cover any special circumstances regarding the leasing transaction.

Completed leasing applications are used to begin evaluating an applicant's credit condition. A preliminary review of the application form provides basic information to guide the credit reviewer. The equipment cost and type, for example, indicate how much additional information, if any, will be needed for a complete credit review. Many leasing companies today do not require written financial statements for equipment that costs less than $25,000; instead they base their credit evaluations on reports supplied by outside credit rating agencies such as Dun & Bradstreet (for business credit reports) and TRW (for personal credit reports), along with account performance information gathered from the applicant's bank and trade references. Experienced lessors also rely on their own experience with customers that operate similar businesses, use similar equipment, and have leased similar equipment from them.

For equipment that costs more than $25,000 (or whatever maximum amount the lessor uses for an application-only review), the applicant's complete, accountant-prepared financial statements or federal income tax returns are generally required in addition to the application. When written statements are called for, it is common to ask for two or three years of financial reports so that credit reviewers can compare the applicant's performance from year to year and determine the direction of the business's performance. Analysts must determine whether sales and profits are increasing, decreasing, or remaining flat and whether the financial results are consistent with successful businesses of the same type and size. Analysts also want to see how much money is retained in the business as equity or net worth.

Equipment leases are long-term contracts, most often having terms of three to five years or more. Credit analysts must therefore try to estimate from information gathered today whether the business will be able to meet its entire financial obligation over the lease term. Since the future can't be predicted, assumptions about a prospective customer's ability to satisfy a lease obligation must be made from the manner in which a business has handled its credit arrangements in the past.

Because leasing can be used by virtually any business, the applications received by typical leasing companies cover a wide range of company sizes and financial conditions. The number and scope of leasing applicants, and the individual leasing preferences of those who apply, preclude most leasing companies from establishing rigid policies in making credit determinations. As a general rule for evaluation, most lessors use broad guidelines in establishing credit criteria.

General Credit Criteria

For the most part, leasing companies want to lease only equipment with which they are familiar. The length of a lease is limited to the equipment's useful life as determined by the leasing company. If sizable purchase options are to be offered to the customer at the end of the lease term, residual values will be gauged to the estimated future worth of the leased equipment. Leasing companies generally establish certain minimum criteria for an applicant's financial condition:

1. As a rule, leasing companies want the owner's equity or net worth of the applicant's business to be at least equal to—and ideally, significantly more than—the cost of the equipment to be leased, including the finance charges.
2. The working capital ratio (current assets in relation to current liabilities) should demonstrate that current assets exceed current liabilities by at least one and a half times.
3. The applicant's total debt (total liabilities) should be less than three times the net worth of the business.
4. Cash flow (net income, plus allowances for depreciation, minus the current portion of long-term debt) must be sufficient to cover any existing borrowings comfortably, plus the total of one year's lease payments for the new lease.
5. Most leasing companies do not lease equipment to businesses that have been in operation less than two years. As many as 85 percent of all new businesses fail before they are two years old, and because of their newness, these applicants can rarely supply sufficient financial information for review. Since credit evaluation stems from the review of historical performance, younger businesses that wish to lease equipment are at a decided disadvantage.

Although salespeople are not empowered to make credit decisions, they can significantly increase the probability of obtaining credit approval for prospective customers if they thoroughly understand the credit review process.

Working With the Credit Department

Salespeople find out very quickly about the interdependency between the sales and credit departments. Leasing companies must sell their services to succeed, salespeople must sell leases to succeed, and closed leasing transactions produce the income that permits leasing companies to succeed. But leases can't be closed unless and until they are credit approved. The credit department is responsible for analyzing leasing transactions and ensuring that prospective customers are creditworthy, yet the credit department can't perform its function unless leasing transactions are submitted for approval. Each of these functions, sales and credit, is dependent on the other for the production of leasing business.

The relationship between the sales and credit functions creates a system of checks and balances between the aggressiveness of salespeople and the company's need to control the quality of the business it transacts. Regardless of whether leasing transactions are credit reviewed in-house or by analysts from outside sources, leasing business production depends on the acceptability of prospective customers as credit risks.

Since salespeople strive to produce as much business as possible, there is often friction between them and credit reviewers. The friction is generally caused because salespeople are driven to close business quickly and credit people are trained to be conservative and methodical. By its nature, the granting of credit is a disciplined process in which every step must be completed within prescribed guidelines. Depending on the transaction size and type of lease applied for, the credit process can take considerable time to complete. Salespeople, however, frequently operate in an environment where time works against them. End-user customers want the leasing process completed quickly; they want possession of their equipment as soon as possible. Vendors especially want to know if leasing transactions have been approved so that they can be assured of an equipment sale. Both salespeople and vendors risk losing business to competitors until leases are approved and closed. Salespeople are generally anxious and uncertain until lease approvals have been granted and they can move ahead with the rest of the closing process. However, despite the impatience of salespeople, vendors, and prospective customers, the full credit procedure must be completed for each and every leasing application submitted.

Since the credit process is a step that can't be circumvented, and since the quality of business transacted is critical to the survival of leasing companies, salespeople must be prepared to conduct business within the guidelines. If a prospect isn't creditworthy, there is nothing a salesperson can do to improve the applicant's financial condition. When financial information is insufficient to meet the credit guidelines, the salesperson can't create the missing financial reports. And when an applicant can't or won't provide requested information, meet established credit criteria, or comply with the credit analyst's requests for additional information, there is little the salesperson can do.

Often, though, salespeople create problems rather than doing what they can to help accelerate the credit process or increase the probability of credit approval. Despite the fact that credit acceptability is an integral part of the leasing environment, salespeople sometimes take the position that credit people work against them, not with them. Instead of acknowledging that credit quality is critical to the leasing business, and certainly to the profitability of their own organizations, some salespeople view the credit process as a barrier to their productivity. Instead of cooperating with credit personnel, they become defensive about the credit information their prospects submit.

When salespeople take a defensive posture, they often counter credit analysts' requests for additional information about prospects with "internal" sales pitches. Salespeople tell stories to credit analysts about how tough it is to find small businesses that prepare complete financial information, or how the salesperson will lose his or her vendor relationship to competition if an application isn't approved without additional information. Or they inquire about the possibility of approval without having to go back and upset the prospect by asking more questions. Most often, the salesperson's paranoia is caused by fear that the prospect will be displeased about having to provide more financial information and will seek financing elsewhere. If a vendor is involved, the vendor may seek out another financing source to protect the equipment sale, should he or she become nervous about obtaining credit approval quickly. Considering a salesperson's potential loss of a transaction, or possibly the loss of a vendor relationship, attempts to persuade credit analysts to stretch the guidelines or to work with only the information originally presented are understandable. In the long run, however, salespeople who persist in "selling" leasing transactions to credit reviewers do themselves more harm than good.

It is true that every leasing credit submission is important. It is also true that vendor relationships are a valuable source of business and must be maintained with the highest level of performance possible. Nonetheless, the quality of business transacted affects the whole company. Although some credit analysts may be more conservative than others, and some may appear to be more inflexible than others, most credit analysts are simply trying to ensure that the organization's leasing portfolio contains transactions that will be paid as agreed by the customer.

A salesperson must respect the credit analyst's position and responsibility. Credit analysts review what has been presented to them; they do not prepare the information. Business owners and managers, not credit reviewers, are responsible for the performance of their operations. Leasing companies and credit reviewers earn their income from leases that are paid as agreed by the customer, not from assuming the risks of loss inherent in businesses with poor financial performance. Although lessors typically take more risks than other types of lenders might, it is not the credit reviewer's job to find ways to approve failing applicants or to create an additional sale for a vendor that is trying to sell equipment to a poor credit risk.

From time to time, even the best leasing salespeople find themselves in situations in which an applicant's credit information is obviously inadequate yet the applicant still appears to be worthy of a credit review. This scenario might arise, for instance, when new owners have purchased an existing company, consequently changing the business's management and decreasing the ability to rely on the business's financial history. Or there might be a case in which a lease must be closed before year-end financial statements are available in order to meet the equipment installation and vendor payment schedule. In these circumstances, a credit analyst has to make a decision based on only what is available from the applicant. When extraordinary circumstances exist, most credit reviewers realize that the business world is not perfect and make every effort to accommodate an applicant. The credit reviewer's willingness to try to accommodate, however, is predicated on extraordinary and understandable circumstances that are an exception, not a rule. When every applicant submitted by a salesperson has a story or excuse for its inadequacy, the credit reviewer's tolerance will be tested.

Despite the need to close business and the professionalism of most businesspeople, credit reviewers are human. When salespeople waste a reviewer's time or constantly submit substandard credit packages, the reviewer's patience and willingness to accommodate decrease. Furthermore, busy credit people naturally tend to work on the submissions that are the best prepared and most likely to be approved, because doing so increases the probability of success and saves time. Therefore, when you combine the professional benefits of submitting well-prepared credit packages for review with the personal satisfaction of being recognized as a skilled salesperson, it is obviously in your best interests to ensure that your credit submissions are legible, complete, accurate, clear, and understandable. Whether your credit packages are reviewed internally or by outside funding sources, you want your lease submissions to be on the top of the credit reviewer's pile, not the bottom.

Following credit review, approved leasing transactions must be documented. Lease documentation is the stage where the terms and conditions of lease agreements are drafted into a contractual form.

Contract Administration and Documentation

Written lease contracts are the documents that describe the specific agreements between lessors and lessees. In effect, lease contracts are the "instruments" that ensure lessors of their right to collect lease payments, purchase option prices, security deposits, advance payments, and any other monies due to them from end-user customers. This documentation also states the legal rights and obligations of all the parties to a lease agreement. Consequently, without properly executed documents, lessors are exposed to the potential loss of their right to collect monies due to them and also to the risk of losing their equipment.

As a practical matter in three-party leasing agreements, the lessee receives the equipment, the vendor receives full payment for the equipment, and the lessor receives a pile of paper. Since this paper is the only evidence of the lessor's rights under the leasing agreement, it is critical that the lessor's paperwork be contractually and legally correct. Most lessors strive to draft agreements that are appropriate for their purpose yet as simple as possible to use. Recognizing the importance of protecting their contractual interests, lessors still make every effort to provide user-friendly paperwork, further enhancing the image of leasing services as easy to use.

Much like credit criteria, contractual requirements vary with the lease type and the equipment cost. Many small-ticket lessors use simple lease agreement forms that contain a credit application, guarantee form, and equipment acceptance certificate as well as the lease itself. These simplified forms are designed to allow the prospective customer, vendor, or salesperson to submit an entire leasing package—from application to lessee-signed documentation—in one step. As equipment costs increase or leasing terms and conditions become more complex, documentation requirements generally increase as well. Leases for costly equipment often require individually drafted documentation.

Since lease agreements are legally binding, lessees often want to review the documentation themselves before final execution or to have the contracts reviewed by their attorneys. Smaller businesses ordinarily use outside counsel for legal work, and large corporations tend to employ staff attorneys. The extent of the customer's legal review usually depends on the size and type of the leasing transaction.

More often than not, customers view a small-ticket leasing transaction as a convenience and don't consult legal counsel about the documents. This is especially true when the leasing paperwork is handled by equipment vendors. When vendors present the customer with a leasing contract for a relatively inexpensive item, such as a photocopier or a personal computer, the customer's execution of the paperwork is similar to the signing of a purchase order. The lease document itself is ordinarily simple, the lease payments are small, and the lease closing is a natural step in the equipment acquisition process. Furthermore, small-ticket lessees tend to feel more comfortable about signing paperwork that is presented to them by the equipment vendor in the normal course of business than they would be in arranging a loan or financing with a bank or other lender. Leases covering more costly equipment acquisitions, however, are subject to closer customer scrutiny.

Even when prospective lessees don't engage an attorney to review leasing documentation for costly equipment, they are usually concerned about their commitments under the lease. Customers' concerns most often regard what action the lessor will take as a remedy in the event the lessee defaults on the agreement. Issues include whether the lessor has a right to assess an additional charge if a lease payment is late, when a late charge can be assessed, the amount of the late charge, the likelihood that the lessor might repossess the equipment, and any other liabilities the lessee might incur in the event of default.

Prospective lessees also inquire about their rights under the lease should there be a problem with the equipment after the lease becomes effective. Most finance leases contain a "hell or high water" clause that states that the lessor is *not* responsible for the selection, performance, maintenance, servicing, or any other aspect of the equipment or its operation. Finance leases, in effect, put the lessee in the same position as if he or she had purchased the equipment. Although the lessor is the owner of the equipment by title, the lessee is responsible for every aspect of the equipment's operation. The lessee is responsible for insuring the equipment against all types of casualty risk, operating the equipment safely, maintaining the equipment in proper operating condition, and—in the event equipment is returned to the lessor—returning it in operating condition, less reasonable "wear and tear." The lessee is also responsible for all taxes related to use of the equipment, including sales or use tax and any applicable personal property tax.

Regardless of how tightly or loosely leasing documentation is written, salespeople are responsible for thoroughly understanding the paperwork and for answering prospective lessees' questions. From time to time, prospects might request that certain language in lease contracts be amended. As a general rule, salespeople are not authorized to make any changes in written documentation. Changes in leasing contracts can be made only by authorized personnel—usually attorneys or contract administrators. After authorized contract changes have been made, however, salespeople meet with prospects to conduct the lease closing process, answer questions, ascertain that the proper individuals are signing the documents for the lessee, and ensure that all the paperwork is executed properly. Executed lease documentation is then submitted to the contract administration department.

A review of completed lease documentation is the final step before equipment is ordered from the vendor. Contract administrators for small-ticket leases, or attorneys for large transactions, review documentation to ascertain that the paperwork has been signed properly, that authorized signatories have executed the documents on behalf of the lessee, and that no unauthorized changes have been made to the contracts. Although contract administration is ordinarily a routine step, the process can delay the issuance of equipment purchase orders or the start of leasing transactions if problems arise.

Most problems occur when prospective lessees don't clearly understand how to execute leasing documents. From time to time, a lease signatory will change a document without authorization, sign documents in the wrong place (lessees often sign documents in the lessor's signature space), sign personal guaranties and include a corporate title after the signature (personal guarantors must sign as individuals, not corporate officers), or inadvertently fail to initial authorized changes (placing one's initials next to a language change acknowledges the change). Although these errors are not major, they do slow the leasing process. Even though a salesperson may not be at fault, the delay can cause the salesperson and the leasing organization itself to appear unprofessional.

The best way for you to ensure against improperly executed leasing agreements is to be certain that both vendors and prospective end-user customers understand where, how, and why contracts are to be signed. Small-ticket vendors can be trained to understand the lease execution process well enough to handle it themselves. End-user customers can be visited for lease closing or, if a visit is not practical, they can be sent documentation checklists containing completion instructions along with the contracts.

Here again, as in working with credit personnel, you must realize that contract administrators and attorneys are responsible for protecting the interests of the company, not for increasing sales. Vendors often want purchase orders released even though unauthorized changes have been made by a prospective lessee. End-user customers often promise to correct errors as soon as possible but want their equipment ordered before the corrections have been made. Knowledgeable lessors will not proceed until complete documentation has been properly executed by the lessee and they themselves have reviewed the documentation for acceptability. Experience has taught lessors that prematurely released equipment purchase orders can lead to disputes with the lessee, the vendor, or both. Some documentation errors can't be corrected quickly, and others may not be correctable at all. Understanding your organization's contract administration process and making an effort to ensure that documents are understood by vendors and prospective end-user customers are the keys to smooth lease closing and expedited purchase orders.

Once equipment has been ordered, the remainder of the leasing process is primarily administrative. Ordinarily the only steps that remain after purchase order placement are equipment delivery by the vendor followed by the written acceptance of the equipment by the customer. Salespeople often consider these two steps to be minor details, yet some critical mistakes can be made if serious attention is not paid to them.

Accounts Payable

Viewed on the surface, the accounts payable function appears to be a routine step in the leasing process. Once a customer has completed the required equipment acceptance certificate and returned it to the lessor, a check is issued to the vendor as payment for the equipment. From the vendor's perspective, receipt of payment for the equipment purchased is the most important step in the leasing process. Therefore, especially for small-ticket vendors, a lessor's invoice payment practices weigh as heavily in the vendor's continued use of a lessor's services as any other factor—maybe more so.

For many small-ticket vendors, a significant percentage of their equipment sales is made through equipment leasing programs. When vendors "sell" most of their equipment to a leasing company, the vendor relies on the lessor to remit payment expeditiously. Vendors often promote leasing because they are more confident of timely receipt of payment from lessors than directly from customers. Bearing this in mind, it is in your best interest to make every effort to ensure prompt vendor payment by doing whatever you can to expedite the accounts payable process.

Things that salespeople can do to help expedite the vendor payment procedure usually vary with the size, cost, type, delivery, and installation process of the equipment. The larger and more sophisticated the equipment, the more time it takes for delivery and installation. At times, knowledgeable customers take advantage of the anticipated length of the equipment installation to delay acceptance of the equipment. When customers delay equipment acceptance, they also delay the start of their lease payment obligations. Leasing salespeople can't, and shouldn't, push a customer into accepting equipment until the customer is satisfied with the equipment's installation, but salespeople can follow up to ensure that the lessee is aware that equipment acceptance is expected within a reasonable amount of time.

Follow-up calls to the customer for equipment acceptance certification can sometimes uncover problems that the vendor is unaware of and can quickly correct. When customers are waiting for vendors to make repairs or adjustments and using the equipment during the delay, they are under no obligation to sign an acceptance certificate. And if the customer is able to use the equipment with no pressure to accept it as satisfactory, he or she is not necessarily going to urge the vendor to rush the completion of repairs or adjustments. If you diligently monitor your transactions that are still pending the receipt of equipment acceptance certificates from lessees and pursue them, you can become a valuable ally to your equipment vendors. You can increase the probability of future vendor referrals to new prospects and gain a competitive edge.

Once equipment has been received and accepted for use by the lessee in writing, the lessor is able to start the lease. Started leases become effective as of the date of equipment acceptance by the lessee and can be added to the lessor's portfolio. The start date also signifies the beginning of the schedule of lease payments due from the customer. The lease payment schedule itself is listed in the lease document and illustrates the number of lease payments due, the period covered by each lease payment (week, month, half year, year, variable), the amount of each lease payment, and the amount or percentage rate of any applicable taxes to be remitted with the lease payment. The collection of lease payments is the responsibility of the accounts receivable department.

Accounts Receivable

The accounts receivable function is often overlooked by leasing salespeople for several reasons: As a general rule, salespeople do not interact with accounts receivable personnel on a regular basis, many smaller leasing businesses do not collect accounts themselves, and the accounts receivable function does not appear to affect leasing sales directly. In fact, although salespeople do not always recognize its influence, accounts receivable performance has a considerable effect on leasing sales. Credit decisions are based on the financial information presented by prospective customers and on the historical performance of similar businesses. If particular businesses, industries, or customer types have poor payment histories, that past performance will negatively influence credit decision making. Accounts receivable personnel work with customers that are delinquent in remitting lease payments, are in default of leasing agreements, or for one reason or another have not paid money due to the lessor.

Records of accounts receivable performance can clearly illustrate problems that might otherwise go unnoticed. It's not unusual, for example, for lessees that otherwise honor their financial obligations to delay or withhold lease payments for equipment that continually causes problems. Despite the fact that lessors are not responsible for the performance of equipment, and the fact that the lessee is obligated to remit payments regardless of how the equipment operates, lessees sometimes hold back lease payments as leverage to try to enlist the lessor as an ally in pressuring the vendor to repair or replace unsatisfactory equipment. As a practical matter, a third-party lessor has the right to collect lease payments and can pursue legal remedies for payment collection, but lessors do not want to expose themselves to collection problems that can be avoided. When lessee payment histories or equipment resale problems indicate that certain equipment types, models, manufacturers, or vendors are prone to collection problems, it is best to avoid them.

Accounts receivable records provide important data for marketers when they are designing new programs for particular industries; equipment, end-user customer, and vendor types; or individual equipment manufacturers and vendors. The lessee payment performance records, account histories, and lessee comments indicate whether otherwise hidden factors might cause problems in the future.

Leasing salespeople can also benefit from information about lessee payment performance. Time is a salesperson's most valuable asset; knowing in advance about equipment, vendors, and end-user customer types to avoid because of their tendency to be problematical is better than wasting time pursuing them. At times, however, there may be good reason for salespeople to solicit business that is typically considered problem business, because there are solutions. These might include validating that prior equipment problems have been corrected, creating a holdback of funds payable to the vendor as a reserve against potential lessee nonpayment, or eliminating particular models from a vendor's line of equipment. Before proceeding in this case, however, it is best to touch all the operational bases, including the determination of whether accounts receivable managers will veto such a business opportunity.

Part of the accounts receivable function is the remarketing of returned or repossessed equipment. Lessees do not always exercise the option to purchase equipment at the end of the lease term and return the equipment to the lessor. Equipment can also be repossessed by the lessor as a result of a lease default caused by lessee nonpayment or bankruptcy. When equipment is returned to the lessor, it must be remarketed.

Equipment Inventory and Remarketing

The probability of a lessor's need to remarket equipment is predicated on several factors, including the types of leases provided, the equipment types leased, the cost range of the equipment leased, the end-user customer types leased to, the equipment vendors serviced, the average useful life of the equipment leased, and the vulnerability of the leased equipment to technological obsolescence.

Typically, lessors that offer full-payout finance leases with minimal purchase option prices to lessees face the least exposure to returned equipment. Ordinarily, equipment is returned to finance lessors only in the event of an uncured lessee default leading to repossession of the equipment. Consequently, most full-payout finance lessors don't have much concern about equipment remarketing and rely on known vendors or equipment resellers to repossess and resell equipment for them on a case-by-case basis.

Lessors that offer leases with sizable purchase options, however, must establish a method for remarketing returned equipment as well as any equipment repossessed through lessee default. Small-ticket lessors generally offer leasing programs that provide the lessee with the option to purchase leased equipment for its fair market value at the end of the lease term. The norm is to assume that the residual equipment value is 10 to 15 percent of its original cost. Typically, most small-ticket equipment is purchased by the original lessee. Despite the high percentage of lessees that elect to purchase, however, some equipment will eventually be returned. Here again, the original equipment vendors and equipment resellers are the most likely purchasers of returned and repossessed equipment, but that is not always the case. When off-lease equipment can't be resold immediately, it must be stored by the lessor or another party until it is remarketed.

There are several methods for reselling off-lease equipment, including advertising, "retail" sales of used equipment, and direct marketing to typical end users. The more costly and specialized the equipment is, the more sophisticated the reselling process must be. Small-ticket lessors ordinarily resell equipment through remarketing adjuncts to their accounts receivable departments. Lessors with substantial portfolios may establish separate departments to handle remarketing. Specialized lessors that function in particular equipment markets may actively lease and resell costly equipment as a primary part of their business.

Market-focused lessors are prevalent in computer mainframe and peripheral equipment, hospital and medical equipment, vehicles, major printing equipment, scientific equipment, and costly production equipment. These lessors are knowledgeable about both the equipment they lease and the equipment markets. Their expertise permits them to structure leases with sizable purchase options because they know where and how to remarket or re-lease returned equipment. Market-focused lessors also rely on outside equipment and industry experts to help them.

Most established or standard equipment types are sold by numerous vendors, many of which belong to industry associations, form user groups, publish information, or provide data relating to the equipment they sell. Knowledgeable lessors often join vendor industry associations, subscribe to vendor industry publications, attend equipment seminars, and maintain files of publications and information regarding the equipment they lease. Besides these vendor networks there are many third-party equipment resellers, appraisers, and services that can provide lessors with equipment data. Third-party services supporting the automobile, medical, printing, photocopier, materials handling, and computer industries, for example, publish guides listing the typical resale values of vehicles and equipment by manufacturer, model, specifications, age, and condition, among other equipment-specific information. Market-focused lessors use these guides to help them make realistic assumptions about the future value of equipment and to help them structure equipment-based leasing products.

The equipment remarketing process can have a significant impact on leasing sales. When vendors request that a lessor provide fair market value purchase options, the lessor's operation must be able to manage the equipment leased. When competing in certain industries, salespeople can encounter competitive lessors that specialize in particular equipment types. Knowledgeable competitors may be willing to take more risks, offer larger purchase options, or be willing to commit to longer lease terms because they are comfortable with the equipment. Unless salespeople can convince their own decision makers to take similar equipment risks or can build a case for justifying the additional responsibilities inherent in remarketing returned equipment, there may be times when the salesperson simply can't compete.

Finance lessors are often unable to compete with equipment specialists because finance lessors typically structure leases to fully pay out the cost of the equipment during the initial lease term. When finance lessors do offer a purchase option, it is generally minimal. The full-payout structure of finance leases puts finance lessors at a competitive disadvantage in relation to equipment leasing specialists, because large purchase options and/or longer lease terms tend to reduce the size of lease payments. When a vendor insists on the provision of low-payment–high-purchase-option structures, or a prospective lessee believes that the leased equipment will be returned to the lessor at the end of the lease term, equipment leasing specialists have a decided advantage.

Despite the presence of equipment leasing specialists, the leasing market is large enough to support all types of lessors, and today the finance lease is probably the most widely used leasing structure. It is important for you to know who your competitors are and what leasing services you can provide. If your organization is not equipped to handle equipment remarketing, you are not competing against the specialist on a level playing field. If a prospective vendor or customer demands a purchase-option-focused leasing structure that your organization doesn't offer, you can't deliver. The key point is that there are leasing environments that specialize in particular equipment and take equipment risks that finance lessors may not. You must know exactly what lease structures your environment can and will provide for its customers and focus your sales efforts on prospects that fit the profile.

Thriving in the Environment

For customers, leasing is a user-friendly method of acquiring equipment. Lessors strive to make the leasing process as simple, efficient, and fast as possible to differentiate themselves from other sources of financing. What appears to be simple for the customers, however, isn't so simple for the lessors.

There are several steps to the leasing process, and each step has to be completed for every lease. Lessors must either perform each step themselves or ensure that there is a resource available to handle the functions for them. From lease marketing to equipment remarketing, the type, size, method, and scope of the leasing operation define the environment.

To maximize success, leasing salespeople must thoroughly understand the environment that they represent as well as the environments of any outside services that support their efforts. Competitors create their own environments. When salespeople try to match a competitor's products or services and the organization can't deliver them, time, effort, and money are lost. The greatest probability of individual success and of outperforming the competition comes from pursuing sales opportunities that best fit the objectives, capabilities, and strengths of your own organization.

Chapter 3

A Winning Attitude

Sales is a highly competitive profession. There are competitive alternatives for virtually all goods and services sold, and equipment leasing is no exception. The equipment leasing market is an intensely competitive arena. No matter what type of leasing services you sell, where you sell them, how long you have sold them, or what leasing entity you represent, you aren't doing your job unless you sell your product successfully. Whether you have just begun to sell leasing services or have sold them for many years, you are the person who interfaces with prospective customers. Despite the intensity of competition, you are the one who is responsible for ensuring that sales are closed.

You compete every day of your sales and business life. To win that competition, you not only have to continually prove and reprove that you know what you are doing, you also must want to win. Naturally, everybody wants to win, but not everybody does everything they can to help themselves win. No matter how much you do to help yourself, winning can't be guaranteed, but you can increase your probability of winning by leaving as little to chance as possible and by working at selling your product as hard as you can.

Your desire to win has an effect on every one of your selling opportunities and is sensed by your prospective customers. You must demonstrate a winning attitude.

Selling Yourself

All salespeople need a winning attitude, regardless of what they sell. In competitive markets, every order counts. In equipment leasing sales, however, there is an even greater need for a winning attitude because equipment leasing is a hybrid product. It is both a tangible financial product and an intangible service, and an intangible doesn't exist until you make it exist in the eyes of your prospects. When you deliver your sales presentation, you must convince your prospects that your leasing services are the best choice for them. To your prospects, you represent what you sell; you must impress them with your own quality, dependability, and reliability if you are going to convince them that your services can satisfy their needs best.

Leasing is a service that provides end-user customers with the financing they need to acquire equipment and enables equipment vendors to make more sales. In this sense, leasing is intangible. Leasing services can't be taken out of a box and used by the customer; services don't possess physical qualities, as do manufactured products. Yet in another sense, equipment leasing is tangible, because performance of services is measurable and comparable to others. But you can't demonstrate the services you sell until after you have persuaded a prospective customer to work with you. It is only after you have sold your prospect first on yourself and then on the idea of using your services that your organization can go into action and perform.

Selling the Packaging

Leasing companies are packagers of funds; they obtain money and shape it into sales tools for equipment sellers and acquisition alternatives for end users. The competitive difference between lessors is expertise in packaging. The ability to combine money and expertise is the resource that gives equipment lessors such great opportunities. If lessors are able to fund their equipment purchases, they can compete regardless of their size. It makes little, if any, difference to customers where the lessor's funding comes from—whether from individual transactions at lending institutions or from the treasury of the country's largest industrial organizations. What does matter is how that money is packaged. This means that whether you represent the largest leasing company or the smallest, you can still compete.

Packaging money is achieved through an operational process that is designed to service customer needs. By comparison, a manufactured item is a physical representation of its maker. A manufactured item can be seen, tested, and examined before purchase, but a lessor's processing capability can't. Credit application approval, documentation processing, and lease funding take place after a customer has selected a leasing company. The operational process of the lessor is, in a sense, the manufacturer and the product. Consequently, when you sell leasing services, your first step is to convince prospective customers that you will be able to satisfy their needs.

In the purchase of a tangible item—a computer, automobile, or machine tool, for example—the manufacturer is very important. Brand names are recognized, and buyers seek out the specific item they want. Many products are presold by reputation. Money does not have a brand name or authorized dealerships. No matter where money is purchased, it comes in the same color, sizes, shapes, and denominations. Money can be acquired from a myriad of sources.

Selling Future Performance

Leasing packages themselves are all similar on the surface. There is promotional material, a credit application, documentation, an operational process, and lease funding. When the buyer is purchasing money, the packager is not always critical. If it were, the industry giants and household names would have captured the market. Although Brand A leasing may be superior to Brand B leasing for a number of reasons, the ultimate acquisition by the customer is an amount of money.

Size and scope are not critical to a lessor's ability to compete. Although there are some vendor programs, leasing services, and end-user requirements that can be delivered only by large lessors, any leasing entity can function in the market within the range of its capabilities. At times a vendor may "test-drive" a lessor before entering an agreement to do business (by submitting applications to see how they are handled), and an end-user customer may offer the chance to compete (via a trial lease), but the opportunity to do leasing business usually occurs immediately. As a rule, the prospective customer doesn't see or try the lessor's operational process beforehand.

Leasing, then, is providing money in a packaged format that is more or less similar industrywide to a customer who is not brand conscious. If there is so much similarity in the leasing industry, and if money—the underlying raw material—is so widely available, what is it that differentiates one lessor from another? Why does a prospect accept one lessor when another might be larger, stronger, or more widely known? Why, if money is the end result of a leasing transaction, haven't the major lending institutions captured the market and frozen out smaller competitors? How do lessors get the opportunity to demonstrate their operational capabilities if they are not employed until after being selected by a prospective customer? The primary answer is, *the way that leasing is sold.*

Most leasing services are sold by sales representatives. It is the sales representative who describes the leasing products available, suggests the appropriate leasing plans and programs, reflects the leasing organization and the quality of its products, and builds the image of a tangible from intangibles. As a sales representative, you must be knowledgeable to be successful. You must know your company and its operation, its competitive strengths and weaknesses, and its markets.

Regardless of your technical skills, however, you are competing in an arena that is filled with similar offerings. You must be concerned not only with what you know and do but also with how you perform. In typical selling situations, your technical skills, supporting materials, and the company qualities you represent account for only a portion of the impression you make on a prospect. The balance is your own personal image. The image you present delivers its own message to prospects and may be the deciding factor between success and failure. Consequently, as a sales representative, you must use every available resource to favorably impress a listener.

Presenting the Right Image

Although you are interacting with them in a business context, the purchasers of leasing services are, first and foremost, individual people. Human characteristics are as important in most personal sales calls as the product being bought and sold.

People love winners. In a business populated with similar alternative sources, a salesperson perceived as a winner has a distinct advantage. The company represented by a winner has an advantage too, because prospects naturally assume that winners represent winners. Whether you represent a major lessor or a small leasing company or work independently, and no matter how many years you have sold leasing services, the impression you make positively or negatively influences the impression of the quality of the services you sell. Therefore, you must make every effort to ensure that you present yourself as a winner.

To illustrate how much we admire and enjoy winners, ask

yourself some simple questions: Which teams almost made it to the Super Bowl? How many second-place finishers in the Kentucky Derby can you name? What company is the second largest computer software developer in the world? These questions illustrate that few of us remember losers. But even people with little knowledge of sports have heard of Vince Lombardi and his Green Bay Packers. Folks who have never been to a racetrack are familiar with Secretariat, Seattle Slew, and Alydar. Whether people use computers or not, they would recognize Microsoft Corporation as the forerunner in software programs. Why are these names so memorable? They are all winners. Winners get recognition, respect, and publicity. Your primary objective is to present the image of a winner and then to perform like one.

Sticking to the Basics

For highly successful people, winning is a state of mind—an attitude. Vince Lombardi's famous quote, "Winning isn't everything; winning is the only thing," was a testimonial to his existence. In order to ensure that his teams won, Lombardi identified the key elements of winning and made them the cornerstone of his strategy. Lombardi realized that success derives from people learning their jobs, and most jobs are based on fundamentals. If a person has the basic skills required to perform in the first place, the rest is training, practice, and execution. He dwelt on the fundamentals of each football position until his players excelled and, most importantly, until the team excelled.

An analogy can be drawn between Lombardi's philosophy and the philosophy of many successful salespeople. Sucessful leasing sales result from thoroughly understanding the basics, practicing the basics, and repeating the basics. Every sales call is a new challenge, but regardless of the size of a potential sale, the quality and strength of a prospective customer, or the future potential of the opportunity, leasing fundamentals don't change. In every sales situation the prospect must be properly qualified, and the features and benefits of equipment leasing must be presented; the salesperson must clearly understand the prospect's leasing requirements, and the prospect must understand the leasing salesperson's presentation.

A common pitfall for seasoned leasing salespeople is carelessness caused by their time spent in the business. Although experience is one of the most valuable assets a salesperson can possess, years of sales calls can lead to haphazard sales presentations. Veteran salespeople sometimes forget that their prospects are not as well versed in leasing as they are. The basics can become so familiar to veterans that they may mistakenly assume that every prospect already understands leasing. Rather than insult the intelligence of a presumably knowledgeable prospect, salespeople sometimes skip over leasing fundamentals and quickly move on to more sophisticated issues. But when leasing fundamentals are glossed over for prospects who are less knowledgeable than they appear, problems tend to arise in the future. If major problems occur because a salesperson thought that the prospect knew the basics, leasing transactions or entire vendor programs can be lost.

Taking a page from Lombardi, you have to stick to the fundamentals in every situation. Sales presentations must cover every detail and include as much information as possible. If a truly knowledgeable prospect is encountered, that prospect's knowledge must be confirmed before moving the sales presentation on to other subjects. You are far better off explaining to a sophisticated prospect that you want to be sure to touch all the bases in your sales presentation than assuming that your listener already understands the fundamentals of your leasing program.

Competing in the Market

Salespeople work in a competitive arena, and many comparisons can be made between sales and sports. Basic talent is required to sell products, training is needed to learn the trade, and practice is necessary to reinforce skills. Success is based on the quality of execution. There are further similarities. Salespeople do not work alone; they are part of a team. Unless they know the functions of the other players, salespeople can't be successful. Sales managers are quarterbacks, leasing plans and programs are equipment, and sales plans are game plans. Operating personnel play different positions—whether in sales, credit, documentation, or accounts payable—and they are all integral to team success.

Salespeople are the most visible because they interface with the outside world. Salespeople are the reflection of what a leasing organization does, and they are responsible for its image. This premise is true whether they represent the largest or the smallest organization in the industry. A leasing sale cannot be completed without credit approval, lease documents, equipment acceptance, and lease funding. It doesn't matter whether a large group of people or only one other person handles the operational function. It is still a team effort. Because people identify with winners, your customers must be convinced that the team you represent is a winning team.

The game of leasing sales is played on a very large field, with many competitors. However, competitors are taken on one at a time. You don't win or lose sales to a group of other teams; you excel or fail against individual rivals. In leasing sales, your basic skills, training, and practice are focused on executing better than each of your competitors—not all of them. In some games you may have to beat several other teams, but there will be only one winner.

Successful sales begin when the prospect agrees to work with you and end when leases are funded—encompassing the entire operational process. You win when you understand how that process works and can clearly define the process for the prospect. Yet you can win only when the game is played on a field you've practiced on. Jack Nicklaus may be the greatest golfer who ever lived, but even he can't hit a baseball 250 yards with his golf club.

Representatives of small-ticket leasing companies work with operating personnel who know how to play the small-ticket leasing game. They process the applications sent to them and respond almost immediately. Leverage leasing specialists need time and expertise to design large off-balance-sheet financings. Should either of them wander into the other's ballpark and step up to bat, their teams will still be looking for the rule book when the game is over. Your probability of winning increases as your experience and skills in your own particular leasing market grow.

Learning What Others Do

Salespeople tend to focus their skills and training on resources that will improve their presentation quality, communication technique, and interpersonal skills. Although striving to improve is critical to success, there are other types of support that can increase performance as well. Your organization employs, or has access to, skilled personnel who are experts in other roles; there are outside experts at banks, accounting and law firms, and equipment suppliers. Learning how and why they do their jobs a particular way improves your understanding.

When you understand the other functions in your organization and can accurately describe to a prsopect how they work, your confidence increases. Each sales call you make has its own plan, designed by you. You have informed answers to the prospect's questions because you know how the whole operation works. Confidence is one of the key attributes of winners. When prospects agree to do business with you and your company, however, the operation has to respond by executing its responsibilities the way you described them. Winners are measured by how well they execute.

Winning With Vendors

The leasing business frequently involves designing and selling programs to be used by equipment vendors. When you're successful in selling your programs, you have a vendor sales force marketing not only its own product but yours as well. You then assume the role of sales manager for the leasing program. Your responsibility expands from closing a vendor account for your company to helping to manage other salespeople. You now have to utilize your skills to coach and support the vendor sales force, whose performance will depend on the training and support functions you provide.

The vendor salespeople have to understand how your equipment leasing program works. This requires demonstration, exercises, and reinforcement. You become a role model for the vendor's sales force by your participation in their sales meetings, training sessions, and sales calls on end-user customers. Together you develop strategies for different sales approaches and determine how best to work with the end-user customer.

You can provide ideas for introducing leasing to end-user customers, selling equipment by offering monthly payments, and overcoming budget restrictions. You can teach techniques for including leasing alternatives in written proposals. You can instruct the vendor sales team in telemarketing and demonstrate successful telephone strategies that illustrate the use of leasing sales tools. For example, instead of simply sending information to a prospect who requests it, the salesperson can take advantage of that conversation by offering a plan or program that highlights the convenience and cost-effectiveness of periodic payments.

Being a Good Risk

By helping to manage the vendor sales team, you assume a position of leadership. You become a coach. Leading is best accomplished by example, and effective leaders are admired and respected for their experience, training, and performance record. Professionalism, self-confidence, and a successful track record all give off certain "vibrations." When the vibrations are positive, vendors allow you to coach their sales teams. But that decision is not made without an element of risk.

When they let you, as a leasing company representative, work with their sales forces, vendor sales managers are relying on leasing to sell more equipment for them. They are investing valuable time when they invite you to attend their sales meetings, conduct training sessions, and instruct their people. The investments they make are at risk because if you can't perform, the vendors lose business. Vendors take even bigger risks when their salespeople make joint customer calls with you, and the biggest risk of all occurs when a vendor asks you to call on a prospect alone or to close a lease agreement. It's no wonder vendors want to be represented by winners.

Knowing the Guidelines

A vendor leasing program must be managed to minimize the risks. Risk can be reduced when everybody understands the guidelines. Every business has guidelines, and leasing is no different. The better and clearer the guidelines are spelled out, the better the leasing program will work. Overall guidelines are established by your company, but individual leasing programs have specific criteria. That's part of your responsibility as the leasing manager: You determine how vendor salespeople are to use your leasing program. The leasing program you give to the vendor sales force contains the particular plans or programs they can use when working with customers.

Most often, simple guidelines are better than complex ones. Simple guidelines are easier to follow, and there is less chance for misinterpretation or confusion. Although vendor salespeople may carry leasing program information with them when they work with their customers in the field, their first obligation is to sell their equipment. If you haven't made it easy for them to refer to leasing information, they simply won't use your program.

Taking Charge

Part of your job of training the vendor sales force is to explain the leasing program. What, for example, is the procedure for submitting credit applications? How long does it take to find out if an application is approved? Who is responsible for getting the lease signed by the customer? Where does an executed lease get forwarded? How does the equipment get paid for? The instructions may change from one vendor account to another, but in every case it is the leasing manager's responsibility to explain them.

Some experienced salespeople allow the hours, days, or months of hard work involved in landing a leasing program with an experienced vendor to go to waste. Rather than bore the vendor's sales force with details or requiring them to undergo lease training, the leasing salesperson simply provides information about how the program works and waits for the vendor's sales force to start producing leasing business. More often than not, however, the vendor's salesforce will not produce leasing business without training, reinforcement, and follow-up by the leasing salesperson.

Being Consistent

Vendor leasing programs succeed when they are consistent. Sales is a lot like baseball. The team that hits singles and doubles day in and day out will produce runs, and runs win ball games. Then, when the occasional home run is hit, it is really a bonus. Salespeople that swing for the seats every time tend to strike out a lot and need the homers just to get even.

Successful leasing programs produce business consistently. A productive vendor leasing program, or a productive leasing salesperson selling directly to end-user customers, is one that keeps everyday business flowing. Almost all leasing salespeople tend to want to chase the "mega-deal," to make an annual quota in one transaction or cover their production volume with one major vendor leasing program. More often than not, the home run doesn't get hit, and the salesperson strikes out.

A better method for ensuring success is maximizing the potential of business that can be produced regularly. Chances for success can be increased when existing vendor programs are serviced and maintained to their maximum potential.

Checking the Numbers

Leasing salespeople succeed in maximizing the potential of a leasing program when they go beyond simply training and coaching the vendor sales force. They look at vendor statistics to determine which vendors are winners and which are not. They find out who the best individual vendor salespeople are and what they do that the second-string and poor performers don't. Often the differences are the result of how the vendor salespeople use the leasing tools you have given them.

Speed and efficiency in leasing come from correctly filling in the proper forms and sending them to the proper place at the proper time. During the sales process, the timely introduction of a leasing application can result in a closed sale. At other times, that same form becomes just a piece of paper to be filed for future reference. Knowledge of leasing terms and conditions and the provision of clear, concise answers to a prospect's questions result in closed sales in the leasing business. Unfamiliarity, lack of training, and unclear answers result in errors and lost business.

Maintaining accurate, up-to-date records will help you manage the vendor's leasing sales. Reports and schedules can show you not only who the best individual salespeople are but also how the whole vendor sales force performs. You may have to go out on sales calls with poor performers to demonstrate some how-to's about leasing sales. A picture is worth a thousand words, and a live demonstration may be worth more than that.

Motivation

Winning professionals know that they can get the job done. They know their business and how to work with their organization. They know the guidelines better than anybody else. What's more, they really want to win. Their talent, training, and ability have made them confident. They want to be tested by the game, by their opponents, and even by their peers. When top performers are put in a sales situation, everything amplifies; as good as they are, they seem to get better. This is called motivation.

Top sales performers know what their talents are and they know how critical their talents are to their organization. But knowing what their talents are isn't what sets top performers apart. What sets them apart is that they use their talents every day. Top sales performers don't just know it, they do it. Top salespeople motivate themselves. They are the best at what they do, and they want the chance to prove it. Self-motivation is the driving force that keeps top performers rising to challenges, striving to increase their production, and seeking the resources that will allow them to become better.

Self-motivation is often mentioned as one of the things people notice most about top performers. Although it's true that top performers are self-motivated, what is most important is the direction of their motivation and the actions it causes them to take. People are motivated by hunger when they go out to buy a hamburger. People are motivated by a desire for entertainment when they go to see a movie. People are motivated by fear when they work until ten o'clock at night because they did nothing all day and are afraid of losing their jobs. Motivation itself is not enough. The focus of the motivation is what sets winners apart. The reason that winners motivate themselves is that they want to succeed. Their impulses are the triggers that cause them to draw on skills and abilities that will help them succeed. That is one of the reasons that people love winners and want to emulate them. Motivated people continually strive for success, and through their efforts they prompt others to try. Your organization will strive to help you meet your goals and be more willing to go the extra mile for you if you demonstrate that you are helping the organization succeed.

Winners improve at their profession by attempting to reach new heights. They learn new techniques and add them to time-proven basics. Nolan Ryan changed his pitching from total reliance on the fastball to finesse pitches as he got older and more skilled. Others take raw talent and employ it over and over again, until it becomes stale and ineffective. There is a big difference between a salesperson with fifteen years of experience and a salesperson with one year of experience fifteen times over.

Pride + Professionalism = Production

Winners have an intense sense of pride. Extraordinary accomplishment is certainly something to be proud of. Pride is reinforced every time a sale is made. Recognition from others also reinforces pride. A successful sale is the customer's acknowledgement of a job well done. For many salespeople, that is testimony enough to their ability. Some organizations award plaques, certificates, or other symbols of recognition for superior achievement, but individual pride is often more important than tangible rewards. Most salespeople are measured by production. Management gauges their results against an established quota or some other benchmark. But winners don't look at the objective at the beginning of the year and wonder how they'll ever reach it. What registers for them is that there is a managerially prescribed goal. Their personal aims may exceed the company plan. More often than not, they simply consider their quota as a production number that they know they will surpass at some point during the year. In a marketplace of value-added offerings, winners realize that *they* are the added value.

PART II

VENDOR LEASING SALES

Equipment vendors are recognized by leasing companies as the major conduit to end-user customers. Vendors have learned that leasing products and services provide them with the opportunity to close more sales, sell more costly equipment, and obtain the expertise of highly skilled leasing salespeople who often close equipment sales with or for them.

The two-way-street nature of vendor leasing programs creates a synergy wherein both the vendor and the leasing company increase their sales productivity by working together. The concept of vendors and leasing salespeople working together is a simple one: Vendors identify viable prospects who wish to acquire equipment, and leasing salespeople present attractive financial alternatives that facilitate the acquisition. The truth is, however, that real-world scenarios are never that simple.

As a practical matter, the attractiveness and productivity of successful leasing programs have made vendor leasing a highly competitive market for leasing companies. Additionally, a significant number of vendors have used leasing programs for many years and have become leasing experts in their own right, thereby intensifying leasing companies' need to excel. Experience has also taught more than a few vendors how to pressure, manipulate, and entice aggressive leasing competitors into stretching their guidelines in order to win or maintain a valued account.

As a result, there is a significant amount of information you must have if you are to succeed in the vendor marketplace. There are countless numbers of vendors that sell virtually every type of equipment for every purpose imaginable. Therefore, successful selling requires successful qualification—the process of evaluating and choosing vendors whose equipment types, cost range, and customer types match your leasing company's objectives and capabilities. It will do you no good to land a multimillion-dollar vendor account if your organization can't accommodate the equipment sold or the end-user customers that use it.

Qualification and selling go hand in hand in the leasing business. Successful leasing sales often depend on a series of *ifs*. The vendor that wants the lowest rates, for example, may be able to obtain them, *if* all its customers are impeccable credit risks. The vendor that wants low lease payments and high end-of-lease-term purchase options may be able to obtain them, *if* the equipment has a high resale value and the residual risk is acceptable to the leasing company. The vendor that wants immediate credit decisions may be able to receive them, *if* every leasing credit package is submitted in a thorough and timely manner. Most often, however, the vendor–leasing company relationship is not perfect. Vendor leasing programs are generally negotiated through a series of stages where trade-offs are made by each side with the intent of arriving at a middle ground that will produce the highest level of acceptable business production for both parties.

In vendor leasing program negotiations, the selling and qualification processes ordinarily interweave and, at times, overlap. Despite the fact that qualification and selling often occur simultaneously during an actual vendor sale, these two subjects have been treated separately in this book. Chapter 4 begins with a general overview of the vendor sales arena and moves through the steps of the vendor qualification process of finding the "perfect" vendor–leasing company match. Chapter 5 discusses the vendor leasing sale itself from inception to closing.

Chapter 4

Qualifying Equipment Vendors

Lessors are eager to build relationships with equipment vendors, because vendors provide direct access to equipment buyers. Every equipment buyer is a potential leasing customer, and no matter how capable they are, lessors can't sell their leasing services until they identify prospective customers.

To induce vendors to use their services, lessors create leasing plans and programs that are formulated on the operating features of the typical equipment sold and matched to the financial needs of the vendor's typical customers. By working together, lessors and vendors form sales partnerships. These sales partnerships create sales synergies. Vendors are able to combine equipment features and attractive financing for their customers, enhancing sales. Consequently, vendors have learned to use leasing as a sales closing tool, offering financing as a value-added service.

Vendors that provide access to financing are able to offer a one-stop-shopping convenience to equipment buyers. The probability of closing a sale increases when the vendor can handle all the buying arrangements, including financing. Furthermore, equipment sales are less likely to be lost when the prospective customer doesn't have to seek financing from other sources or shop for equipment suppliers that do provide financing. Vendors also rely heavily on leasing's ability to justify the cost of an equipment acquisition, since equipment is sold more easily when lease payments are matched to the customer's budget.

Because leasing can significantly increase the vendor's equipment sales, vendor-originated leasing sales can provide significant leasing opportunities for you—but the marketplace is highly competitive. The good news is that when vendors rely on equipment leasing as a sales aid, they provide the fastest route to leasing opportunity. Their salespeople are always prospecting. The more active the vendor, the higher the probability of increased sales for you.

The bad news is that your competitors know the value of productive vendors too. An active vendor is always an attractive target for competitors. What's more, vendors have become so dependent on leasing and financing to sell their equipment that many of them have become experts. This can put you in the position of dealing with prospective vendors that know more about leasing than you do. Last, a seasoned vendor salesperson may be able to take advantage of you and your company if you do not do a thorough job of qualification.

Focus for Effectiveness

Don't let stiff competition and vendor expertise keep you from pursuing vendors. The more a vendor knows about and relies on leasing, the more value you have—if you're able to provide what the vendor needs to sell products. As a place to start, the vendors you are seeking must be qualified. Vendors sell every type and model of equipment in use by every industry in the United States. That spells immense opportunity, but it also means a great waste of time if you don't focus your efforts. When you begin your qualification process, you need to ask yourself some basic questions:

- Which vendors should I pursue?
- What do I want to achieve?
- What leasing services can I deliver to help the vendors I select sell their equipment?

The answers to these questions can be used to help you develop your vendor qualification strategy and direct your sales efforts where they will be most effective. Focused vendor qualification increases the probability of success.

Vendor Organizational Structure

To help determine where to focus your sales activity, you should examine typical structures of vendor organizations and compare them to the way your company does its leasing business. Equipment is sold by many different methods. Simply contacting a vendor is of little value if you don't have some idea of where and how the seller operates. Depending on the type of equipment, its cost, and the frequency of sales and service, vendors organize their sales channels to end users for maximum efficiency. Products such as photocopiers and personal computers, for example, are usually sold through local outlets. Customers can walk into a showroom, select equipment off the floor, and take their purchases with them. Costly, highly sophisticated machinery such as radiology units or specialized production equipment, however, may be sold by a manufacturer's direct sales force, which has received extensive training in the operation of the equipment. These salespeople usually work out of the vendor's home office or regional facility and make personal visits to prospective customers. Some vendors employ salespeople at all levels of the sales channel: national sales at the home office, strategically located regional sales offices, and local sales branches.

The typical national vendor may be structured something like this:

National headquarters:	The vendor's national headquarters is the base for top management, marketing, and sales personnel.
Regional distribution centers:	Regional distribution centers warehouse products and may or may not sell directly to end-user customers.
Branches:	Branches sell to and service local end-user customers.
Independent distributors and dealers:	Independent distributors and dealers sell to and service end-user customers.
Local salespeople:	Local salespeople call on end-user customers.

Not all vendors are national, nor do all national vendors have regional or local branches. Some make retail sales only through independent distributors or dealers. Some dealers are franchised or become authorized to sell and service equipment. Most equipment is sold by independent businesses to local customers. These sellers may or may not offer service and supplies, and equipment sales are not always their primary business. Since the structure can be complex, your first step is to find out exactly how equipment is sold by your target vendors.

Vendor-Lessor Relationships

It is critical to match your leasing capabilities with the needs of the seller. There are several ways that lessors can perform, depending on their operational structure. If your company offers middle-market or big-ticket leasing services, you may prefer to seek individual transactions, an approach common for costly capital equipment units such as major hospital equipment, mainframe computers, large printing presses, machine tools, aircraft, railroad cars, and vessels. In these instances, the equipment suppliers and end-user customers are limited by the type, cost, and specific uses of the equipment, making identification of both simple.

If you are seeking a closer relationship with your vendors but are unable to arrange an exclusive agreement with them, your objective may be to become an "approved" or "accepted" lessor. Unfortunately, although approval offers a competitive edge against the majority of competitors, a given vendor often approves more than one lessor.

In small-ticket to lower middle-market leasing, your goal may be to develop an exclusive local account relationship with a vendor. These agreements can range from a strong "handshake," which is a verbal or loosely written outline of your relationship, to a detailed contract. In this case, the vendor employs your leasing plans and programs and agrees to offer them to prospective customers as part of his or her normal sales strategy. Vendors that enter such agreements ordinarily expect leasing terms and conditions that are more favorable than those available to the average vendor, in return for leasing exclusivity. Your company and the vendor work together closely, and you are often involved in the vendor's equipment sales planning and operational functions. By working together, you and the vendor can create special programs to emphasize certain equipment models, seasonal selling programs, and other focused sales strategies at various times.

A step up from the local account is the regional account. Similar to a local program, this arrangement establishes an exclusive program covering a larger geographic area. Coordination of the leasing program, consistency of support, and monitoring of leasing volume become more complex. Your company must be able to communicate with the vendor's remote offices, train sales personnel, visit customers, troubleshoot, and reinforce the program. Automation and data processing have greatly improved the ability of both lessors and vendors to enhance the performance of multilocational leasing programs.

At the top of the vendor ladder is the national account. Ranging through all ticket sizes, the national account is an exclusive arrangement between a lessor and a vendor to offer leasing nationwide (allowing for regional differences, where possible). Although this represents your biggest opportunity, it also involves a considerable commitment to program management and consistency. National programs require a local or regional support system for the program, extensive communication capability, dedicated lessor sales and operations personnel, timely supply of current materials and documents, and a sizable appetite for new business.

Whether the account is local, regional, or national, you can expect the vendor to request more accommodation than is normally sought in a simple, transaction-at-a-time relationship. You may be asked to provide "private label" documentation so that the vendor appears to be the lessor. The vendor may want more flexibility in terms and conditions, a wider range of credit approvals, and the ability to negotiate the costs of the program based on leasing volume.

For many lessors, a mix of vendor account types may be desirable. In certain industries, relationships with individual vendor salespeople may be sought and local and regional accounts pursued as well. Major national lessors may want vendor accounts at all levels of the vendor ladder through their national, regional, and local office networks. Whatever avenues you pursue to develop business relationships, certain characteristics of vendors and their utilization of leasing companies will help you decide where to focus your sales effort.

Vendor-Generated Individual Transactions

If your objective is to pursue individual transactions, you must identify salespeople who sell equipment that is of interest to you. Whether your prospecting for branch and local vendor salespeople is through field sales calls, telemarketing, trade shows, association meetings, conventions, networking of contacts, existing vendor and customer referrals, or a combination of all these strategies, you are trying to establish one-on-one relationships with individual vendor salespeople.

The benefit of this sales strategy is that it puts you in the best position to control the sales process; to individualize rates, terms, and conditions for end-user customers; to achieve a high close ratio; to have customer selectivity; and to manage time frames. And you will *not* be expected to offer much accommodation to the vendor. The downside is that to achieve significant results you must identify and establish working relationships with many salespeople, since there is no formal agreement to ensure a flow of new leasing applications. Without a vendor-endorsed program, loyalty of the vendor salespeople will be minimal, although success tends to build strong ties. Because vendor management is not working with you, you can lose out to competitive leasing companies that management may choose to support.

Approved Lessor Status

A step up the ladder is your acceptance by the vendor as an approved lessor. In this case, the vendor demands financial information about your company—trade references and financial statements—before accepting your purchase orders for equipment to be leased. Many vendors routinely require preapproval for any purchase made on an open-order basis. Unfortunately, another reason vendors may require preapproval is an unsatisfactory leasing experience in the past. Whatever the reason for preapproval, an approved leasing company has an advantage over competitors that are not approved lessors.

Vendors often have several approved lessors, meaning that you will have an edge over leasing sources in general but will not enjoy exclusivity. Vendors want to work with approved lessors, but they have no reason to actively promote any specific company. Approval, then, is similar to pursuing individual transactions, but it has its advantages. It gives you a measure of control over vendor salespeople and customers. It allows you to individualize leasing rates, terms, and conditions; select opportunities to pursue; and control time frames. There is little reason for you to accommodate any special requests by the vendor. The downside is that many accounts are required to produce consistently. There is some vendor loyalty and support, but continual sales efforts are required to maintain and grow relationships.

Local Accounts

A lessor's growth targets, lease volume projection, operating costs, and portfolio goals may require it to solicit vendor accounts that offer more leasing volume and closer relationships than those offered by individual transactions or approved lessor status. This brings us to the first level of a formal vendor leasing program: the local vendor relationship.

What the lessor wants in this arrangement is to become the vendor's exclusive leasing company, or the vendor's lessor of choice. The benefits include consistency of lease applications, high ratio of closed leases to application approvals, high lease-approval ratio, and strong vendor support of the program. Vendor salespeople will be *directed* by their employers to offer and promote the "house" leasing program.

This two-way-street relationship builds a kind of partnership between the lessor and the vendor, although there is rarely, if ever, a legal partnership. The leasing partner gains increased lease production, and the equipment partner gets the benefits of a favored account from a particular lessor. Instead of reviewing and negotiating each application, the rates, terms, and conditions are established for the entire leasing program (except in big-ticket or specialized equipment markets, because of the equipment cost, lessee type, or transaction complexity).

In the guidelines of the program, criteria can be set for different equipment and customer types, equipment cost ranges, lease terms, special circumstances, or any other specifics. Well-structured programs contain leasing plans that are clearly defined and easy and convenient for the vendor's sales personnel to use. For small-ticket to lower middle-market vendor leasing programs, lessors ordinarily produce cards, charts, or pamphlets listing rates, terms, and conditions of the program; formulas and instructions for calculating lease payments and sales and use tax; instructions for completing the lease application and documents (if permitted by the lessor); and promotional material. Background information is usually provided to answer any questions customers may have about the lessor.

Higher equipment cost, specialized equipment, or certain end users may require individualized lease negotiation by the lessor's salespeople. In these programs, the lessor provides enough vendor-controlled tools to permit "closing" of the customer by the equipment seller through signed applications, proposals, or some form of "customer only" commitment to enter an agreement. The lessor trains the vendor sales force in the mechanics of the program, the leasing process, general guidelines, do's and don'ts, and how to use leasing as a sales tool.

Designing and implementing an entire program can take a

great deal of time and effort, but the rewards of exclusivity and productivity make it worthwhile. When your selling effort is focused on one account, that account may require substantial support, but it will take less time overall than the maintenance of a diverse group of individual salespeople.

There is an impressive list of pluses when you have an agreement to do business with a local equipment vendor, but there are some minuses too. Quality vendors know their value and rightfully expect to receive the best possible return for their exclusive agreement to do business with you. In the individual transaction approach, you risk the loss of a single relationship—however painful that may be—if there is dissatisfaction or an unreasonable request that cannot be fulfilled. Here, the vendor can hold the entire program for ransom when asking you to stretch the guidelines. Although you don't enter into a legal partnership with your vendors, the vendors often perceive one and attempt to bend the boundaries of the program to meet their needs. This attitude is perfectly normal, since a vendor's primary mission in business is to sell equipment and to derive as much revenue as possible.

You must preserve the integrity of your own programs, plans, rates, terms, conditions, and profitability, even though your "partner" may be trying to stretch the limits through "accommodations" for customers. These accommodations can encompass pressure to approve marginal applicants; waive contractual requirements in lease agreements; issue purchase orders or payment for equipment before complete documentation (for example, guaranties, resolutions, landlord waivers, equipment acceptance certificates, financing statements) has been received; or grant requests for flexibility during the vendor's high-pressure month-end, quarter-end, or year-end periods. Whatever the type or frequency of vendor urging for accommodation, vendors feel free to make such requests because the increased volume and productivity of a successful program suggest that you are the beneficiary of the vendor's ability to provide leasing opportunities.

All vendors will, in time, ask you to stretch or bend your guidelines. You must be assured, before making any promises, that your organization is willing and able to deal with the situation. If not, you have to be able to decline vendor accommodations without losing the account. You can be certain that your competition will be on the sidelines, ready and willing to step in if you trip. Competitive pressure in productive accounts is always intense.

Vendors have learned to limit the terms of agreements, maximizing pressure and ensuring the highest level of performance. Although well-managed programs tend to be renewed or extended, negotiations to "rewin" accounts occur periodically. Productive vendor accounts are visible to your competitors, giving them the opportunity to submit requested, or perhaps unsolicited, proposals for leasing programs. Many vendors check the market from time to time, if only to see what is out there.

At times, competitors may perform when you can't approve an applicant for a valid reason, or they may accept a vendor customer's leasing transaction at rates below your minimum. This may occur because of differences between the competitor's guidelines and yours, or it may be an attempt to impress the vendor and replace you as lessor of choice. You must be aware of, and prepared for, penetration in larger accounts, because there will always be others trying to win away a valuable source of business. The larger the vendor, the greater the competitive attempt will be.

Regional Accounts

Regional vendors that offer leasing program opportunities usually sell equipment in the low to lower-middle price range. Office equipment and furniture and printing, production, hospital and medical, computer, and automotive repair equipment are examples of regional vendor types that appeal to lessors. Like large local vendors, regional operators offer high lease production volume as the main drawing point. These vendors control the leasing sale, ensuring a high ratio of closed to approved applications. Management is supportive of leasing programs and makes sure that the sales force uses and promotes them. The fact that vendors devote their own time, effort, and expense to implementing and reinforcing a leasing program promotes strong loyalty.

Conditions for conducting business are "programmed" to ensure manageability and consistency, making the point-of-sale process simpler for the vendor and reducing the amount of attention the lessor must give to individual applications. The leasing program sale is a focused effort to develop a major source of business, in contrast to seeking individual transactions. The level of perceived partnership increases for the vendor, ensuring protection of the program and enforcement of guidelines.

Regionality adds several requirements to the lessor's job. The ability to support the leasing requirements of a widespread vendor sales force is imperative. They will expect the same attention as if they were located centrally. Communication, information, materials, training, follow-up, and troubleshooting resources must be available in a larger geographic area. Systems must exist to consistently receive, act on, and complete leasing requests within agreed-upon time frames. For capable lessors, the regional vendor is a prized target. However, the negatives begin to increase in size and scope as well.

Despite additional support of the program by vendor management, controlling a diverse group of equipment salespeople is difficult. Time pressure for lease application approvals, release of purchase orders for equipment, and submission of invoice payment intensifies. The need to maintain accurate, complete, and current program guidelines of rates, terms, and conditions grows. These requirements are caused by the nature of the successful vendor.

Equipment suppliers are aggressive competitive forces in their markets, with highly pressured sales teams striving to meet goals and objectives of their own. Since leasing and financing are integral to product sales, the pressure on them transfers to pressure on you. Equipment salespeople have little or no regard for the policies or procedures of a leasing company when a sale is in jeopardy or their manager is demanding immediate results. You must perform in the time agreed on (which is always too long for the salesperson) or be prepared to manage and cope with the pressure applied by nervous suppliers.

Similarly, accurate and timely reports listing results of the leasing program, end-user customers, closeouts of existing leases, additional requests from existing customers, upgrades and trade-ins, along with any specially designed data become a considerable responsibility for the lessor. The most active equipment vendors may have their own administrators responsible for management of the lessee base. They require timely information for customer service and marketing research functions. Often, the lessor's information regarding customer accounts is more accurate and valuable than that of the vendor, causing frequent demands for portfolio information. Sizable relationships may even warrant vendor-lessor computer networks.

Here again, the sense of partnership takes on more weight on the vendor side. More success for the lessor produces a stronger position for the vendor in seeking accommodation and support. Maintaining unquestioned decision-making capability becomes more difficult, and pressures on the relationship increase with growing lease bases. Competition for regional accounts gets more intense, not only at the vendor's management level but also at the sales outlets, where local leasing relationships are being sought.

Leasing salespeople must be aware of the exposures and pitfalls that exist in order to determine whether they can maintain and grow regional accounts, before they spend the time and effort that closing them requires.

National Accounts

National accounts operate across the United States. Working from the bottom up, they are like a nationwide group of local vendors, tied together at the top. The description fits because, despite the scope of the supplier, individual sales produce the revenue. The decision to select a lessor is usually made by top management of the vendor, sometimes with input from the vendor's local personnel. The key to success in the national account marketplace is your ability to deliver a program that can be used and managed at the field sales level even though you are communicating through a centralized corporate channel. All the elements of local and regional leasing programs can be found in national accounts.

Lessors can become shortsighted in the structure and sale of a national account program if they focus on the "wish lists" of senior managers of the vendor organization. Although the leasing program sale can't be consummated without their agreement, these managers may be too remote from the leasing requirements at the lower levels of their organization to be able to identify the necessary elements. If a program is to work effectively, the lessor must be thoroughly familiar with how the leasing tools will be used. The program must be both effective for the salespeople working with end-user customers and administratively manageable to ensure that high-volume leasing can be processed efficiently.

The Achilles' heel of a national account program is the unwillingness of vendor salespeople to use an unwieldy or nonresponsive program, regardless of admonitions from senior management. Remember, a vendor salesperson's goal is to reach a personal sales objective through closed business, not to employ a leasing program put in place by corporate managers. Because of this real-world consideration, a lessor's delivery system must be capable of handling a sizable volume of lease applications and attaining a high ratio of approvals, within acceptable time frames. Anything less will make the program vulnerable to complaint and neglect from the real "customers": vendor sales personnel.

A lessor's insurance against neglect by the vendor sales force includes resources to train vendor personnel; the ability to provide timely and accurate program information; communication systems for immediate information on pending, approved, and closed business; the availability of leasing personnel to assist in the field; and automation that can provide vital and accurate customer-base information. Major programs require substantial resources if they are to perform properly, and there are many areas of exposure for a lessor. In the long run, it is the vendor sales force that has the deciding vote by supporting or not supporting the program. Therefore, competition plays a key role.

National account programs provide opportunities for competitors at many levels. Local outlets are always targets, regardless of an existing "house" program. Many branch sales managers are willing to use local or regional leasing alternatives if the company-endorsed program doesn't work for them. They won't hestitate to argue with higher management against the use of a company-endorsed leasing program if they believe that their sales production is suffering because of it. A national account's corporate managers are also targets for proposals and information regarding new programs, services, and leasing products offered by competitors, and the managers themselves stay abreast of trends in the leasing market. Since it is in the vendor's best interest to minimize the noncancelable term of exclusive leasing programs, there is the additional risk of short-term engagements.

You must know the characteristics of national accounts in order to evaluate the probability of landing and, more importantly, maintaining them as customers. The most desirable vendor qualities are found in a national account. The leasing volume, vendor management loyalty, and percentage of approved leasing applications are the highest. Programmed rates, terms, and conditions produce optimum results. There is sales promotion value in being the lessor for a recognized equipment supplier. Perceived partnership status reaches its most valuable stage, because the vendor partner incurs significant costs to help design, build, introduce, implement, and support the leasing program.

Because of this partnership, however, national vendor managers carry a lot of weight. The perception of providing vast opportunities for a lessor reaches its peak, increasing the expectation of accommodation from the lessor to its extreme. Despite the fact that you and your company are still assessing and bearing the risks of financing the end-user customers, a national vendor can bring intense pressure on you to extend your guidelines. Requests for special programs, lease rate concessions, documentation amendments, marginal applicant approval, or easing of paperwork requirements may be acceptable in isolated instances but can be disastrous in a major program. Amazingly, the communication channels (which can take weeks to transmit an adverse policy change or additional requirement) relay information instantaneously when it relates to an easing of conditions or an accommodation in costs.

Considering your vulnerability to this pressure, you must know (1) your capability to deliver the type of program the national account desires, (2) the probability of developing a program that will succeed despite potential contrary requests from vendor management, and (3) your organization's willingness and resources to deal with the circumstances. Time is your greatest asset, and you shouldn't waste it where the probability is not in your favor.

After comparing the pros and cons of vendor types and deciding that your organization will work best in one, two, or all of these markets, you need to look at the approaches to take when qualifying vendors.

Approaching Vendors

When seeking qualified vendors, the approach you take depends on the type of account you are interested in.

• *Individual transactions.* In individual transaction prospect development, the contacts you are seeking are the individual vendor salespeople. Despite the fact that many vendors use leasing programs, countless others offer no company-endorsed program at all. Salespeople employed by companies without "house" programs, individuals dissatisfied with the company program, and independent operators (usually sales agents or representatives) are all viable candidates. The best methods of finding them are telemarketing, cold calling at sales outlets, networking existing contracts, trade show visits, industry association meetings, trade publications, and the old reliable yellow pages.

Many local vendors have no objection to your visiting or participating in a sales meeting to persuade their sales personnel to work with you. Regardless of the method you employ to meet and communicate with equipment salespeople (it is a good idea to use them all), you don't have to go any further. If the salesperson is willing to work with you, you have achieved your goal.

• *Approved lessor.* In this case, you are still seeking individual relationships with salespeople, but you need vendor approval of your equipment purchase orders. You'll have to submit information or meet with a branch, office, credit, or regional manager or the business owner to establish your credentials before doing business. The key is to determine up front that you need more than the salesperson's acceptance to go forward. You don't want your purchase orders refused or to create delays in the equipment installation process that will alienate the salesperson and the customer.

• *Local vendors.* For most local vendors, whether they are a branch office of a larger company or an independent business, leasing programs are negotiated and approved by top management at the location. It is not enough to build relationships with salespeople, because they don't have the authority to enter agreements. Your selling targets must include the authorized decision makers.

You want your leasing program to be favored and supported by the salespeople that use it. Their guidance and input ensure that the leasing program includes the features they need to sell more of their product. But that's not enough. The management of a productive vendor may want its own components in the program. Your objective is to meet and include the decision makers as soon as possible. The larger the leasing program and the greater the reliance on it, the higher in the vendor's management structure you may have to go.

• *Regional vendors.* Productive regional vendors are often familiar with leasing programs and have experience in their design and implementation. Regional vendors may have been established as the result of growth of a local company, or they may be a branch of a larger entity. Unless they sell state-of-the-art or new product entries, they probably already consider leasing a necessary sales tool. A familiarity with the leasing process is a benefit because an in-depth education will not be necessary. However, their expectations are high.

Your solicitation of a regional vendor includes salespeople who will work with the program, local managers, and the regional management responsible for the entire sales process. To be certain that all procedural bases are touched during your selling process, you must evaluate the parties on the vendor side and determine which of them are most influential in leasing company selection.

• *National vendors.* National programs affect not only the sales of an equipment vendor but also many of its administrative procedures. Nationwide order-entry management, accounts receivable tracking, and order change and cancellation procedures are just a few examples. Systems must be established to enter and monitor voluminous paperwork, and funding must be available for a huge number of customers. In complex national programs that will require the eventual buy-in of the sales force and administrative and executive personnel, you are usually better off working with the vendor's corporate management, letting it guide you through the organizational maze.

When prospecting in the major account arena, you have to find and begin working with national managers as soon as possible. You wouldn't want to design the perfect program and invest your time and resources only to find that you have been dealing with the wrong people.

Productivity and Control

In any vendor-lessor relationship, from individual transactions to national accounts, the productivity of the vendor strongly influences control of the program. As productivity and leasing volume increase, the vendor's power to influence the lessor's decision-making process also increases. You can become dependent on the production of a major account. Despite the fact that there is no legal affiliation, the vendor can use its importance to gain your cooperation. This is not necessarily negative, but it must be considered in the qualification process. You have to realize beforehand that success breeds strength for the vendor and prepare for it; don't let surprises down the road weaken or destroy your working relationship.

A wise precaution is to involve your own decision makers as quickly as possible in major situations, to be sure that you have all the necessary buy-ins before you imply to the vendor that you can support an account. Remember, as the size and productivity of a leasing program increase, the control of the vendor increases.

So how do you maintain profit margins, portfolio integrity, leasing program terms and conditions, productivity, and control? By providing exemplary levels of service to the equipment vendor.

In the real world of equipment sales, vendors are in highly competitive markets of their own. Despite the intrinsic benefits of equipment financing and leasing, one of the strongest selling tools a vendor has is responsiveness to the desires of end-user customers. Even leasing plans and programs that offer the best rates, terms, conditions, features, and benefits have little or no value to either the vendor or the customer if the lessor does not perform up to expectations. Consequently, even though the vendor possesses great power to influence the lessor, a well-managed leasing program is hard to replace. A lessor's financial resources and expertise are invaluable, and they are further enhanced by knowledge of the vendor's business. Often, the lessor becomes as knowledgeable about the production and marketing of the equipment as the vendor, and the lessor's knowledge develops a power of its own.

It is not unusual for vendors to become dependent on well-managed leasing programs that deliver results. The lessor's response to application submissions, timely credit decisions, and issuance of purchase orders and invoice payment are key ingredients to control of the program. Providing easy access to information also enhances the lessor's value to the vendor. Equipment sales are won or lost by responsive, professional performance that prevents further shopping by the customer. For example, if sales depend on lease approval, your timely execution is critical to completion of the sale. Turnaround time from lease application receipt to completion of credit review varies according to the equipment and customer, but applications must be processed within the agreed-on guidelines.

Equipment leasing programs are designed to give the equipment salesperson enough tools to close the sale. A small-ticket leasing program may include everything from credit applications to the lease documents (subject to final approval by the lessor). For larger-ticket items, proposals or commitment letters may be used to confirm customer agreement. Vendor salespeople are responsible for handling financial arrangements, over and above the equipment sale. Leasing programs need to function simply enough for nonleasing experts to work with them quickly and conveniently. Vendor satisfaction is achieved from expertise in design and delivery of simplified programs and documents.

A vendor expects a high percentage of lease application approvals, so the lessor must be expert enough in the vendor's business to maximize the lease approval ratio. Lease approvals basically depend on the strength of the end-user customer, but the equipment also affects the credit decision. So does information received from the applicant, completeness of lease applications, background data, intended use of equipment, type of end-user business, and myriad other factors. Leasing programs become vulnerable when guidelines for customer qualification are not clear or are misunderstood. Training vendor sales personnel in the use of the program and preventing disputes or confusion are critical. Training, meetings, and frequent reinforcement are essential for the operation of an effective program.

Effective leasing programs are costly to operate and require solid financial expertise. That's why vendors themselves don't create their own leasing entities more often. Leasing programs require trained personnel (perhaps dedicated solely to the program), support systems, and materials to bolster performance and sales promotion. When vendors receive a satisfactory level of performance from a third-party leasing source, the thought of developing their own in-house operation diminishes. A lessor's strength in account control increases with its provision of support, people, and materials necessary to maintain optimum results.

Sometimes, when it wins a large account, a lessor may start taking the vendor for granted. The leasing salesperson who originated the account goes on to seek other objectives and lets the investment in time, money, and effort slip away. Vendors become displeased and either bring pressure to bear or go elsewhere. It should go without saying that follow-up is crucial. It is up to you to see that all promises are kept. Communication is a vital part of the follow-up procedure. Information must be current and accurate. Status reports on production, quality, and performance of the program provide vendor management with the data it needs to monitor activity and to confirm that it is receiving what it expected.

Access to Decision Makers

In any vendor program, the location of the decision makers is critical. Whether you are soliciting an account for the first time or have already developed a relationship with a vendor, you must have access to the individuals responsible for making decisions. In the case of individual transactions, salespeople are readily accessible. As accounts get larger (especially regional and national programs), you have to communicate with your vendors not only during the qualifying and selling cycles but also during the routine process of managing the account. If you cannot easily meet with vendor counterparts—the ones responsible for the leasing program—you are at a working, and competitive, disadvantage.

Location of Markets

Part of qualification is considering what will be required for future communication. How far did you travel to make the sales call? How often will you have to return if you win the account? What method of reliable communication can be established with a remote vendor for account maintenance? How vulnerable are you to local competition, if the vendor is not readily accessible? How many places will you have to visit, and how often, if the vendor has several locations? If you establish a method of communication to reduce personal visits, will it be effective?

Along with the need to visit vendors, you must also consider the location of the vendor's customers. Many vendor leasing programs, in all size ranges, require lessor sales support in the field. Some vendors sell their equipment in locations other than where their business is headquartered. If you're asked to assist in the field, where will the customers typically be? Can you readily get there? Do you want to be responsible for visiting these prospects? Are the costs of customer visits covered by the program? What exposure will you have if you cannot accommodate the requests in a timely manner? You're looking for a match in the location of your key vendor contacts and the vendor's customer base.

Vendor Qualification Checklist

Lessors are attracted to vendors because they offer instant access to leasing opportunity. By qualifying vendors, you are searching for equipment types that appeal to your organization, in cost ranges acceptable to your company, sold to customer types sought by your business.

The equipment sold, sales method, geography covered, strength and reputation, sales volume, and leasing experience are all fundamental to the decision-making process when evaluating the potential of a vendor account. These characteristics are also indicators of the probability of success, which increases when the strengths and expertise of your organization correspond to those of the vendor. Certainly, there are opportunities to enter new equipment markets or to stretch for valued accounts that can somehow be managed, but it usually takes a strong incentive to gamble in an unknown market.

The approval of your management must be obtained before

Exhibit 1. Vendor qualification checklist.

- ✓ What type of equipment does the vendor sell?
- ✓ How, and by whom, is the equipment used?
- ✓ What is the average equipment cost?
- ✓ What is the ratio of average cost by units sold?
- ✓ What is the average useful life of the equipment by type, size, and cost?
- ✓ How frequently is the equipment upgraded?
- ✓ Are parts and service readily available? From whom? From the dealer?
- ✓ How long has the vendor been selling this product?
- ✓ Is the vendor an authorized dealer? Can we get references at the manufacturer?
- ✓ Does the vendor maintain inventory?
- ✓ Can we get financial information?
- ✓ Is leasing currently used as a sales tool?
- ✓ Who are our competitors?
- ✓ What are the vendor's specific needs?

1. ______
2. ______
3. ______
4. ______
5. ______
6. ______

you go down the road of discovery, selling in markets that are outside of your organization's mainstream business. Since the vendor marketplace is so vast, a good way to focus your time and effort is to use a guide or checklist that lists the criteria for qualifying acceptable prospects.

Qualification checklists should contain the key qualities you are seeking in a vendor and basic questions to ask in your discussion with prospective vendors. Some questions may be of interest to all lessors as indications of a vendor's potential; others may be designed to derive information particular to you and your method of doing business. Checklist design should be an interdepartmental effort and include inputs from outside the sales area. Large programs may need the approval of credit, operations, documentation, and accounts receivable personnel.

A well-structured checklist presented in a professional manner (see Exhibit 1) impresses prospects and demonstrates that your organization is experienced, knowledgeable, and efficient enough to qualify its prospects rather than waste time and effort in the future. You can use the list as a guide for open conversation with the prospect rather than requiring its completion. You can also use it to be certain that all your questions are answered. This gives you a professional demeanor and dispels any perception that you are just going through administrative motions. Recording the vendor's responses to your interview builds a profile that will help you determine whether you have a match. Checklists also help you focus your efforts on the most attractive candidates. In time, the lists will become a database of reference material for sales projects in the future, whether or not you were successful in landing the accounts in question. Because the vendor market has such an enormous number of potential business opportunities, you are far better off pursuing those that have the highest probability of success.

Chapter 5

Selling Equipment Leasing to Vendors

Equipment vendors provide the fastest route to finding active leasing business, making the vendor market the most competitive arena in the leasing industry. But identifying viable prospective vendors and deciding to pursue them is only the tip of the iceberg. Regardless of what type of equipment vendors sell, or who their customers are, they are of no value to you unless you can convince them to work with you and your company. Because your primary job is to persuade vendors to work with you, you have to ask yourself three questions:

1. Why would a vendor want to work with my company?
2. What do I have to offer that sets me apart from the competition?
3. How can I use my offering to differentiate myself from the rest of the leasing competitors that are vying for the same business?

To begin answering these questions, you must realize that there's more to making a sale than simply presenting your sales brochure and asking for the order. It helps if you understand that every vendor environment—from the physical location to the vendor representatives that you meet to the "vibrations" that you sense—contains indicators of how the vendor does business and what will be expected of you. You can use these indicators to guide you in conducting your sales presentations.

Your presentations will be received based on the merits of the company that you represent. They will be perceived based on your audience's sense of with whom they'll be doing business. Since perceptions are so important in selling, you'll gain an advantage if you build your presentations on information that you gather from the vendor itself and the place where the vendor does business.

Observation

Vendors are inundated by leasing salespeople, advertising, and sales promotion. Alternatives are everywhere. Your mission is to persuade prospective vendors to do business with you, and you need every competitive edge you can get. One of those edges is to use the vendor's own environment and business style to give you some hints about how to conduct your presentation. Being observant gives you a strong sense of the type of person and operation you'll be encountering, so you can adapt your presentation accordingly. Take note of the following:

- *Your surroundings.* Are they neat, orderly, clean, impressive, expensive—or the reverse?
- *Your prospect's behavior.* Does your prospect seem casual or formal, attentive or preoccupied, open or evasive?
- *Your prospect's personality.* Will you be addressing an introvert or an extrovert? How does your prospect interact with others in the organization?
- *The activity level.* How often does the phone ring, either in the prospect's office or elsewhere in the environment?

The image you develop by absorbing all this information can be used to pace and manage your presentation to match the prospect's style and business conduct.

The level of activity going on around you is a strong indication of how productive the vendor actually is. Many vendors try to impress you with their value as a reliable source of quality leasing customers, using their implied value as a negotiating tool. But if the surroundings don't match the information you are being given, that is an indication to intensify your qualification questions.

First Impressions

When you first arrive at a vendor's location, you observe the prospect's interaction with others in the environment and gauge the activity around you. You also make some value judgments about the physical surroundings. When you actually meet your prospect, you must immediately state who you are and why you are there. A brief description of your purpose, and a thank you for the time allowed, sets a business premise for the meeting.

As much as 65 percent of the effect of your personal presentation is sensed. You make assumptions about your prospect's business from outward appearances, and the same judgments are being made about you. Your materials, handouts, proposals, promotional items, and stated features and benefits make an impression on the listener, but your conduct and appearance in delivering them are also important.

If you don't have enthusiasm, why should your prospects? If you aren't confident about your ability to meet needs or to deliver, why should they expect satisfaction? A prospect has to be convinced that you believe that your products and services are the best for the purpose. You must convey the professionalism and capability of your company. You can't promise delivery of a sophisticated financial product if you appear disorganized, unsure, or uncomfortable.

The Sales Presentation

The sales presentation begins with your credentials—a brief description of your organization, some background about the company, and the services it offers. If you have qualified your prospect properly, you already know some things about the prospect's business. You should know what type of equipment the vendor sells, have a general idea of the equipment cost range, and have an indication of who the typical leasing customers are.

Armed with this qualification information and the hints you've picked up through observation, you are now prepared to present the key points about your services that apply directly to the prospect's business—the major reasons that establish you and your company as the best choice for providing leasing services. What these reasons are depend on the prospect's business type, size, sales territory, equipment type, and equipment cost.

A good way to choose the appropriate benefits to highlight is by imagining your list of leasing services as a warehouse, the shelves of which contain your products. Select only those items that will be of most interest to the prospect, and then present them one at a time. For example, your list might include these benefits:

"We are a local leasing company and cover the same area you do."

"We are a national leasing company and cover the United States."

"We are specialists in leasing [*vendor's equipment*]."
"We provide full leasing sales training for your salespeople."
"We work with your salespeople in the field to assist them in closing leasing transactions."
"We have been in business for [*number*] years."
"We work with many vendors in your business."
"We use simplified lease documents."
"We generally make credit decisions in [*number of hours or days*]."
"We pay vendors for equipment in [*number of hours or days*]."
"We have toll-free phone lines for our vendors."
"We will participate in joint advertising promotions with you."
"We can tailor [seasonal/step-payment/skip-payment/unique plans] to meet your customers' needs."
"We offer municipal leases."
"We allow up to [*percent*] of the costs of [software/intangibles/delivery/installation/training/*other software costs*] to be included in a lease."
"We give you all the forms, documents, and promotional material that your salespeople need to use the program."

Including references to areas that are the same as, or similar to, the prospect's business helps build a premise of familiarity. If you have vendors and customers in the same business as the prospective vendor, it's important to point that out.

While you are describing the products and services that apply to the prospect, pause in your presentation to provide more detail when it is requested. There's no reason to continue the list once the prospect indicates that you've presented something of special interest. After covering the point of interest, you can return to your list if the prospect would like to hear more.

During the sales presentation, you are trying to identify the prospect's specific needs. This identification process requires as much listening as it does presenting. Your occasional pauses for feedback from the listener confirm that you are being understood and that there is interest; they also dispel the notion that you are spouting a list of prepackaged propaganda. Pausing for confirmation prevents you from rambling and from offering services in which the listener isn't interested or that your own company wouldn't consider acceptable for this particular prospect. There is no value in continuing to provide information that is of no use or interest.

When you receive acknowledgment that a point has been made, proceed.

While you're probing for information, you should be able to pick up on indications of the prospect's interest, and these should become points on which to concentrate. Examples of prospect interest are statements such as:

> "I'm glad to see you have been servicing customers in this area for several years; that means you're familiar with. . . ."
>
> "My people need a lot of support in the field. Your willingness to go out with them on customer visits could be a big help."
>
> "Since you specialize in our industry, your credit people should feel comfortable with our typical leasing customers."

When you receive this kind of response, you can start to narrow the focus of your presentation to the subjects of most interest to the prospect. By pursuing the listener's thought process, you get the opportunity to build rapport, leading to a more open discussion. Sharing common ground and language with the prospect builds the base for comfortableness and provides the opportunity to identify specific needs.

The Vendor Profile

Once you establish a rapport, you can intensify your probing about the prospect's business operation. Rapport creates a communication channel for asking further qualifying questions. The answers enhance the vendor profile you developed during the vendor qualification process, as described in Chapter 4, and further illustrate how leasing is or is not used in the vendor's business. The stronger the sense the vendor has about your experience, credibility, and knowledge of the particular business, the more likely you are to obtain quality information.

Your profile should consist of notes and comments about key areas of the vendor's operation. While developing the profile, you can simultaneously begin to outline a checklist of suggestions and solutions for the vendor's application of your products and services. But you must proceed with caution. The applications you suggest must be readily deliverable by your company. You can't listen to a list of needs and offer solutions you can't provide. The "perfect world" desires of qualified vendors are usually flexible enough to be adapted to the normal operating procedures of most equipment lessors.

Sales Call Management

During your sales presentation, rapport building, and vendor profile development, you established your image as an expert. You can now use this expertise to "manage" the sales call. You want to channel the vendor's thoughts toward the specific products or services that you have determined will work best, as they are provided by your company. Once you have established the advantages of using your leasing services, you can begin to direct the focus of the meeting to the key points that need to be covered in order to design an appropriate leasing program.

Advantages of Leasing

There are many advantages of equipment leasing for end-user customers, each of which offers a financial or equipment-related benefit. During your presentation of leasing benefits, one or more of them may be of specific interest to the prospect and become the focal point of your discussion. For example, leasing:

- Conserves working capital.
- Eliminates large down payments.
- Can allow off-balance-sheet financing.
- Can provide tax benefits.
- Preserves bank lines of credit.
- Offers long-term financing.
- Provides an additional line of credit.
- Improves cash flow.
- Overcomes budget restrictions.
- Avoids restrictive covenants.
- Provides 100 percent financing.
- Hedges against inflation.
- Hedges against obsolescence.

The list is quite impressive. As far as the vendor's customers are concerned, any one or all of these items could have a positive impact on their business operations. Yet most equipment vendors —and through them, customers—tend to focus on the lease payment as the place to begin leasing discussions. Vendors can be shortsighted about the ultimate value of using leasing to sell more equipment. Many of them insist on making the lease payment the first topic of discussion in a sales situation. What's worse, many leasing salespeople fall into this trap.

In managing the sales call, your job is to defuse the vendor's initial preoccupation with price in order to determine which advantages of leasing will have the most appeal to end-user customers. It is not surprising that vendors get sidetracked by overemphasizing lease payments; after all, lease payments are easier to sell than cash purchase price, they are easier for customers to budget than cash purchase price, and most businesses think in terms of months, quarters, and years. But lease payments are *not* universal. They represent only one part of the rates, terms, and conditions that make up a vendor program. Before you can carry on an intelligent discussion of pricing for a leasing program, you have to add lots of information to your vendor profile. There are many factors that affect lease payment.

1. *Lease structure.*

- *Full-payout finance leases* allow the lowest end-of-term purchase alternatives to the customer but have the highest payments.
- *True leases* have the lowest payments but the highest end-of-term purchase costs.
- *Noncancelable rentals* have the shortest terms and most flexibility but the highest overall usage costs.

2. *Risk.*

- In *nonrecourse* programs, the lessor assumes full credit risk.
- In *partial* or *full recourse* programs, the vendor shares the risk. If your vendor is willing to share risk with your company, you may be able to be more flexible.

3. *Equipment resalability.* There are costs incurred in recovering, refurbishing, and reselling reacquired equipment. If the vendor agrees to remarket returns and repossessions, lease costs decrease. Vendor remarketing may be either mandatory or "best efforts."

Mandatory remarketing agreements require the vendor to resell returned equipment within a certain amount of time, usually ninety days or less. The relatively rapid resale protects the equipment selling price and ensures that the equipment has its best chance of actually being resold. If the equipment is not resold, however, the vendor must repurchase the equipment itself. Vendor repurchase prices are negotiated in advance, when the leasing program is designed. Mandatory remarketing assures the lessor that at least a minimum price will be repaid if the equipment is repossessed.

When vendors agree to use their best efforts to resell returned equipment, they are not bound to any specific resale terms or time frames. Lessors are more secure with best-efforts remarketing agreements than without them, but there is no real assurance that the equipment will ever be resold.

4. *End-of-term lessee alternatives.*

- *Predetermined purchase options* allow the lessor to establish a value for the future worth of equipment.
- *Fair market purchase options* are valued in the future, when the equipment is actually sold. Since the lessor can only estimate what the equipment will be worth at the end of the lease term, fair market value purchase options significantly increase the lessor's risk.

5. *Advance payments from the customer.*

- *Advance rentals* are prepaid by the customer and reduce the lessor's cash outlay.
- *Prepaid purchase options* and *down payments* also reduce cash outlay.
- *Security deposits* reduce cash outlay if they are nonrefundable, but they have less value when the deposits are subject to return.

6. *Lease term.* The longer the lease term, the higher the risk.

7. *Equipment cost.* The higher the cost, the higher the risk.

8. *Program support.* The cost of funds, promotional material, forms, documents, communication systems, personnel, automation, and training are all components of leasing programs. The allocation of the cost of these components between vendor and lessor affects pricing.

Each of these elements is a structural part of a leasing program. Beyond the structure, you must consider the everyday operation of the program. And the biggest factor in the operation is the end-user customer.

Customers

Vendors often give you a description of their business, sales strategy, and target customers but don't provide enough detail to enable you to develop a clear picture of what to expect when leasing applications begin to arrive. Vendors are apt to confuse their customers' perceived financial ability with their creditworthiness for long-term financing. Vendors would have you believe that all their customers are exemplary.

The customer is a determining factor in your ability to be responsive. Different end-user industries have different standards for conducting business. Company size and time in business play a part. What is an acceptable risk in a Fortune 500 customer is not always satisfactory for a smaller applicant.

Geography is also a consideration. Customers located outside of your general trading area may be less desirable. Working on large transactions in remote locations can affect the quality of information and the cost of doing business.

Vendors selling the same product in the same area do not necessarily attract the same *quality* of customer. You need to know the makeup of the typical applicant, how much information will be available, and how you will obtain it before you can move ahead intelligently. As part of the customer evaluation, you also need an accurate description of the equipment. For example, both Mobil Oil and Fred's Mobil Station may buy computers, but there's quite a difference.

Equipment

Equipment determines the types of customers you are likely to see. Large printing presses are generally acquired by substantial printers. Personal computers are used by everyone. A value-added marketer of personal computers may have a customer base of successful physicians who acquire specialized software programs with the system; "clone" computer sellers may sell to start-up companies. These examples illustrate that general equipment headings do not always indicate enough about the end user to establish a definitive fit between the end user and your preferences.

Equipment also weighs heavily in the type of lease that can be offered. Expert medical equipment lessors may be comfortable offering fair market value purchase options for x-ray machines but have no future use for hospital beds. Average useful life of the equipment also influences the lease type. A drill press may survive for twenty years, but a state-of-the-art scientific analyzer may be obsolete in twenty-four months. Equipment has life cycles. Some models may be nearing the end of their cycle while new models are being introduced. You may want to build your program to offer only full-payout leases for older equipment to offset the risk of remarketing obsolete equipment.

If you are offering true leases, operating leases, or cancelable rentals, you should be concerned about average resale values and how the equipment is installed, removed, serviced, and upgraded. If the equipment is new to you, get the names of recognized equipment resellers, wholesalers, and appraisers that deal in the equipment. These industry experts can give you independent opinions and data about the estimated future value of the equipment you will be leasing. They can also advise you on trends in their industry, and provide information about the historical performance of equipment types. Expert guidance gives you ideas for further questions to ask your prospective vendor.

Some experienced vendors may ask you to provide lease structures that they have not used before. Although experimentation and creativity are excellent ways to explore new methods of selling equipment and can often attract new customers, you may not want to build your leasing program on speculation. Similarly, vendors that are unfamiliar with leasing may have no real idea of their customers' leasing preferences. In these cases, use your leasing experience to guide you in designing the program. Even if you agree to experiment with vendor-suggested leasing structures, be sure to include leasing plans that you know to be successful with similar equipment. Your experience and the input received from experts within or outside your organization can tell you what actually occurs at the end of the lease term:

- *Do most of your customers buy the equipment when leases expire?*

- *If your customers ordinarily buy the equipment, are fixed purchase options preferred?* If fixed purchase options are preferred, do most of your customers prefer large end-of-term purchase prices such as 5 or 10 percent or more of the equipment's cost, or do they favor paying one dollar?

• *Are your customers willing to prepay the purchase option price?* If customers find prepayment acceptable, it is a good way to reduce the size of lease payments.

• *Do your customers typically "trade up" the original equipment for new models?* If leases are terminated before their expiration date (lease buy-out) to allow the lessee to upgrade equipment, the balance of the original leasing contract must be paid in full, including the purchase option price. Even after applying trade-in values for the existing equipment, the lease buy-out may be too high to make an upgrade attractive. Large purchase option prices cause the buy-out to be even more costly.

The best time to approach these issues with the vendor is when you originally design the leasing program—not two or three years later when there is a sizable portfolio of leases. In the case of trade-ups, you can work with the vendor at the outset by promoting lease structures with minimum purchase options. This will help reduce the cost of trade-ups later on. Neither you nor the vendor want to disappoint existing customers and lose future sales because your original design was shortsighted, causing equipment trade-ups to be prohibitively expensive.

Leases that offer the lessee the choice of purchasing the equipment—for either a sizable predetermined option price or its fair market value—must also allow the lessee to return unwanted equipment at the end of the lease term. You need to know the probability of equipment return, because your organization will have to resell it or re-lease it to earn your originally projected income. If you find that equipment is likely to be returned, you must be certain that you have a profitable method of remarketing the items.

Aside from equipment purchase or return, leases generally allow the lessee to renew for a period of time after the original lease term expires. Here again, the time to address the renewal alternative is when you are designing the leasing program, not after leases have begun to reach their expiration dates.

If a substantial part of the lease structure is based on the equipment providing part of your eventual income, you have to know about its future value. The same equipment may have different values when used by different customers. For example, a forklift used inside a building for four hours a day will have more value than one used in a lumber yard seven days a week and left outdoors.

How the equipment is serviced, by whom, and how often also affects its value, as does parts availability.

As you continue to discuss the details, your understanding of the type, purpose, and use of the equipment by the customer solidifies. Your vendor profile now contains enough information to tell you who typical end users are and, specifically, what types of equipment they acquire from your prospective vendor. Your suggestions for lease structure alternatives can be based on known criteria. You are also better able to counter requests that are unreasonable because of equipment or usage factors. The next step in your profile is to determine how the acquisition decision is made.

The Acquisition Decision

Equipment is acquired by different customer representatives. The principal of a small company may handle all equipment acquisitions personally. In larger businesses, department heads working within budget allocations may select certain types of equipment. Some equipment acquisition is done or influenced by specialists in an organization.

There can be different opinions about the best type of lease and end-of-term alternatives as reviewed by hands-on operators, budget allocators, and business owners. Your profile may indicate that several alternative lease structures are necessary in order to appeal to the requiremens of different customer representatives.

Competitive Alternatives

Most vendors have some experience with leasing. Competition may be present or may have existed in the past. The solutions you propose will be compared to other alternatives or experiences. You must be certain that your solutions are clearly understood and based on accurate information developed in your profile.

Vendor comparisons to alternatives are not always specific enough. For example, your proposal may offer low fixed purchase options, while a competitor's employs fair market value purchases. If this is the case, your lease payments will naturally be higher. You may require fewer advance payments, security deposits, or prepayments from the end user, which also increases the size of payments. Whatever the case, if there is a discrepancy between your alternative and the competition's program, you must be certain that comparisons of all terms and conditions between programs are exact.

Your vendor profile is now full of important information. Although your prospective vendor may have been urging you to immediately provide pricing information, you have managed to build a sizable but not yet complete profile. The vendor can now see, however, that:

- Affordable, competitive lease payments are a major concern, but not the only concern.
- Payments are not the selling point to focus on.
- Payments are the last issue to discuss, not the first, because first someone has to sell the equipment.

Vendor Salespeople

Your leasing program will be used by vendor salespeople to close equipment sales. Vendor salespeople are experts in their own equipment, *not* in equipment leasing. Leasing programs are designed to be used by them as sales aids and closing tools. As a general rule, the simpler the leasing plan, the more equipment it will sell.

Lease structure covers a wide range of variables. You can devise plans that offer leasing alternatives to satisfy every conceivable combination of customer and equipment criteria. The vendor can have the answer to any customer request. The problem is, there is no simple way to implement such an approach.

Your objective is to provide an alternative to end-user customers that will close *more sales*—not every sale—for the equipment supplier. To do this, you have to take the vendor profile and look for common customer characteristics. Your plan should include lease structures that appeal to the majority of your vendor's end-user customers, not every end user. Special circumstances can always be handled individually.

Whether your leasing program allows the vendor salesperson to complete the transaction, provide a proposal, or indicate estimated costs, the process must be simple. Vendor salespeople are not going to use reference libraries created by lessors to transact business. A cash sale is the equipment supplier's only objective. If your programs are too unwieldy, the supplier will take cash or turn to your competition.

Cost-Effectiveness

The lease alternative that sells the most equipment is the one designed to maximize the equipment's cost-effectiveness. Cost-effectiveness is determined by what the equipment does, how the equipment is used, and by whom it is used. Regardless of the budget size of an end-user customer, a simple premise is applied to justify the acquisition of equipment: Will the equipment acquisition make or save money for my business?

A spreadsheet of some sort will be created by most end users to look at the cost of acquiring and operating new equipment. Most often, the analysis compares the monthly, quarterly, and annual costs with the money earned or saved. Leasing breaks the budgeting into equal payments and crystallizes cost comparisons for the customer. The easier the equipment seller can demonstrate the payment and help determine the cost per period, the easier analysis becomes. Most often, the assistance in cost justification provided by the seller moves the leasing process along and shortens the justification cycle. This, in turn, shortens the equipment selling cycle.

That's another reason why vendor focus on specific payments is less important than imagined. The *availability* of payments, provided they are reasonable, is far more important than a "fine tooth comb" comparison. If the vendor is helped through your expertise, support, and availability, more equipment will be sold than through negotiation of minimal differences in payments. Your job is to get vendors to use their equipment expertise to create desire for the product and to rely on your expertise to facilitate the sale.

Trial Closes

From the initial identification of the vendor as a prospect, your objective has been to establish a relationship. The size and type of vendor and your method of doing business determine what kind of arrangement you want. Whether you are interested in certain transactions or in the development of a major program, you are calling on the vendor to achieve a particular goal. As you move through the stages of your presentation, you need to periodically ask for the order.

Although you may not expect immediate agreement, trial closes tell you about your progress. The vendor's response may result in agreement, or it may indicate that more discussion is needed or that you are doing fine so far. Periodic attempts to close also remind the vendor that you are serious about doing business and expect a favorable conclusion. At points along the way you can confirm that certain issues have been agreed and move on to the next step. Use comments such as:

> "What you have said, Mr. Vendor, is that if we can provide a true lease program, you are ready to go ahead with us."
> "You agree then, Ms. Vendor, that the three-year finance lease program is the plan that you will use."

These are efforts to get agreement from the vendor and to close your business arrangement. You can rarely suggest closing early in your discussions without getting some type of objection. Objections can have many forms and degrees of strength.

Vendor Objections

Objections can be sincere problems that the prospect has with your proposed offering. They may also be negotiating strategies or screens to avoid other issues. Whatever the strength or reason for the objection, your job is to overcome it or to clearly determine the importance of the issue.

Objections are opportunities; they are not rejections. You are not being told that the vendor has no desire to work with you, but simply that you need to satisfy particular issues. The issues have to be clearly understood, so it is good practice to restate them. Objections are often indications of misunderstanding or uncertainty, causing hesitation. Clarification allows you to proceed.

You also get the opportunity to reaffirm why your program, organization, business style, experience, quality, or other attributes are the best for the situation. With each objection you answer, you get another chance to ask for the order: "So, you're saying, Mr. Vendor, that if we are able to . . . you will go ahead with us." (Common objections and questions are covered in detail in Chapter 12.)

Asking for the Order

For some reason, failure to ask for the order ranks high among the causes cited by sales managers for poor production among their salespeople. Comments such as "Knows his stuff, but not a closer" and "Works very hard, but not a closer" are all too common in sales. Most of the time, not closing is a result of not asking for the order. Yet that is why people sell in the first place, *to close.*

Order closing is a building process, from the initial identification of a qualified prospect to selling your product to asking for the order. At times, you may become comfortable in selling situations, go through the stages of sales presentation, and allow the opportunity to complete the sale slip by because of a sense of finality if the prospect says no. Perhaps backlogs are small, and you don't want to scratch a prospect off the list. While you're still in there pitching, you think, you can include the "open" items as "pending" business. This self-deception does not help you reach quota! What's more, everyone knows that *getting the order* is the focal point for the sales profession.

Whenever you contact a prospect, there is a purpose for the call. In telemarketing, personal visits, or any other sales-related contact with an equipment vendor representative, there is always an objective. It may be a qualifying interview, a request for an appointment, a sales meeting to offer your services, or anything in between. *The objective is to achieve your goal.*

- Getting the information is a goal.
- Getting the appointment is a goal.
- Arranging the sales meeting is a goal.
- Achieving the goal is, getting the order.

As you move through your trial close efforts, manage objections, and come closer to your objective, you must begin to make closing statements, such as these:

"Well, Ms. Smith, I'm glad to see that all your questions have been answered. Simply sign this agreement and we're in business."

"We are very pleased that you have chosen us as your leasing company. We can begin working with you this afternoon."

"Since we will be working with your salespeople every day, we would like to schedule our first training meeting for Monday morning at 8 a.m."

"We can provide you with information to be included in all your written customer proposals explaining how our leasing program works."

"I can take all your lease applications with me and begin working on them this afternoon."

Success

Vendor leasing sales offer the greatest opportunity because of the repetitive business they produce. They also possess the strength of equipment sales forces that have continual access to new leasing business. As a result, the vendor sale is not an easy one.

Strong vendors usually mean experienced vendors and many leasing competitors. Success, though, is readily attainable. If you take a focused, organized approach to your selling strategy and complete your vendor profiles before you negotiate, you increase your chances of success. Knowing what to expect, preparing your organization properly, and leaving as little to chance as possible also improve the probability of keeping the vendor account after you have it.

PART III

END-USER CUSTOMER SALES

For leasing salespeople, leasing companies, and the leasing industry itself, sales are everything. Because nothing happens until somebody sells something, the most important material in this book is that which addresses selling to end-user customers. The end-user customer is the factor in the leasing equation that pays the bills. Regardless of what strategies are employed to identify prospective customers, what methods are used to solicit sales opportunities, what strengths a leasing operation possesses, or what resources are available to support end-user customers, there is no business if the end-user customer is not sold.

Much like the previous subjects discussed, sales to end-user customers are accomplished in stages. Despite leasing's flexibility and its ability to fulfill a virtually boundless variety of equipment acquisition needs, not every leasing company or every leasing prospect can meet the qualifications of every leasing situation. Therefore, leasing sales must begin with a careful and accurate qualification of prospective customers, as described in Chapter 6.

Much of the qualification process focuses on determining the prospect's credit strength. Simply stated, the stronger the prospect's credit condition, the more flexibility a leasing company has in delivering its most attractive rates, terms, and conditions. Today, however, the vast majority of businesses in the United States are small, privately held, and owner-operated enterprises. Since these types of businesses usually don't prepare financial information as completely or as often as larger or publicly held operations, leasing salespeople must know how to obtain the information required for credit review and evaluation.

Furthermore, leasing sales also depend heavily on the equipment to be leased. The equipment generally predicates the type of lease that can be structured, the lease terms, and the end-of-term alternatives that can be made available. Beyond creditworthiness and the equipment in question, prospect qualification establishes the basis for negotiating with a prospect. Proper qualification sets the guidelines for a salesperson to suggest the appropriate leasing solutions and to offer the products and/or services that are most likely to be accepted by a particular prospect.

Using the prospect qualification process as the foundation, Chapters 7 through 13 cover the specific stages of the sale:

1. Developing a prospective customer profile and prospecting plan
2. Identifying viable prospects and creating a prospect file
3. Soliciting prospects
4. Identifying the prospect's needs
5. Making the sales presentation
6. Overcoming objections
7. Closing the leasing sale

Although you may decide to review only certain aspects of the information, you'll benefit more by reading all the material from the beginning. Despite the fact that each of the subjects discussed in this part of the book is an independent aspect of the leasing sale, each can influence, or be influenced by, the others. The leasing sale, for example, should not begin with a discussion of pricing. A significant amount of information must be gathered, weighed, and analyzed before a proper price can be determined for a leasing transaction. The same is true of leasing structures. Before an appropriate leasing structure can be designed, many components of the transaction must be considered.

Taking a staged and orderly approach to each of your sales presentations adds an element of thoroughness and control to your efforts. Touching all the bases helps ensure that you present the leasing alternative that has the highest probability of both meeting the needs of your prospect and resulting in a transaction that is acceptable to your own organization.

Chapter 6
Qualifying Customers

Leasing salespeople have an almost limitless opportunity to sell their services. But closed sales depend on the equipment to be leased, how the equipment will be used, where the equipment will be used, and, most important, who will use it. If salespeople don't solicit creditworthy lease applicants, their time has been wasted.

The Importance of Creditworthiness

Regardless of the sales strategies you use to identify prospective lessees (vendors, end users, or both), the lessees must be acceptable to your organization. The lessee will ultimately be obligated to fulfill the financial and contractual obligations of the equipment lease. Therefore, once a prospective lessee indicates the desire to lease equipment from you, or when you believe that a lease can be consummated, the next step in the leasing sale is to qualify the prospect.

"Qualification" is performed in order to evaluate a prospect's ability to fulfill the financial obligations called for in a lease and to determine the acceptability of the equipment that the lease will cover. Both factors affect the probability of a leasing contract being fulfilled as agreed.

Leases are long-term financial contracts whose terms will be met in the future. A prospective lessee's financial strength and the value of the equipment leased make the difference between eventual profit or loss for the lessor. This being the case, lessors give careful consideration to each leasing applicant and the equipment to be leased before deciding to grant credit approval.

Although salespeople do not make credit decisions, they are responsible for obtaining the information that will be used for credit—and equipment—evaluation purposes.

Obtaining Financial Information

The cost of the equipment to be leased usually determines how much information you need to obtain from the applicant for a credit review. Today, most small-ticket leasing companies do not require applicants to submit financial statements for leases of less than $25,000–$35,000, although in some instances the amount may be higher. Small-ticket lessors generally rely on bank and trade references, along with reports obtained from independent credit rating agencies and their own experience, to make their credit determinations.

For larger transactions, however, accountant-prepared financial statements or, at times, federal income tax returns are required from the applicant. In all cases, bank and trade supplier references are needed and, depending on the type of lease being considered, additional data may be called for.

The financial information received from the applicant and the results of reference checks, along with reports supplied by credit rating agencies (e.g., Dun & Bradstreet, Moody's, or Standard & Poors for businesses; TRW, Transunion, Equifax, or Chilton for individuals), are used to assess an applicant's creditworthiness. With the exception of small-ticket leasing, salespeople are responsible for obtaining financial information from applicants or for ensuring that it is obtained by a third party, such as a vendor. In small-ticket leasing, a completed lease application that includes the name, address, phone number, and individual to contact for the applicant company; identification of the equipment; and names of the vendor, vendor salesperson, and individuals to contact for bank and trade reference data is generally sufficient for credit review. More often than not, small-ticket leasing application information is gathered and submitted by the equipment vendor. Whatever information-gathering method is used, it is this input that is the basis for evaluating the risk involved in the transaction.

Market Focus

Credit approvals depend on the quality and depth of the information presented for review. Generally, the larger the transaction size, the more information must be obtained. The more you know about the applicants that you pursue, the better equipped you are to gather meaningful information. Market focus helps you do that.

Market focus stems from the logic that a lessor with expertise in specific equipment types, end-user customers, or both has an advantage. Risk is evaluated differently when a lessor understands the operation, value, and remarketing potential of equipment. Decision making is improved by an understanding of the individual businesses and overall industries of end-user customers. Market focus also addresses geographic areas, equipment price ranges, lease structures, end-of-lease-term alternatives, services provided, and marketing strategies.

If you are located on the East Coast, for example, your company may not fully understand the economy or customs of the West Coast. Midwesterners may not feel comfortable divulging information to southwesterners. Whatever the case, you have a decided advantage if you are working in a familiar area.

If you represent a small-ticket lessor, your organization must be able to perform quickly with only limited financial information from your applicants. Small-ticket lessors make their credit decisions on broad-based characteristics of business types and their experience with them rather than on the individual circumstances of a particular applicant. The operating procedure in small-ticket leasing is to build large bases of small transactions, spreading risk over a large number of customers.

If you sell big-ticket leasing services, your credit decisions require the expertise of knowledgeable analysts. An individual big-ticket lease presents a sizable risk all by itself. A press used by a local print shop may cost less than $25,000, but a six-color unit for a major installation can have a $2 million price tag. A big-ticket lessor could face the loss of $2 million if an individual lessee defaulted on a lease agreement. A small-ticket lessor would distribute the same $2 million to eighty lessees or more, giving the default of an individual lessee much less impact.

In recent years, the availability of leasing programs that include the financing of "soft costs" has expanded significantly. Equipment itself is "hard" collateral and has a value of its own. If a leasing contract is defaulted, equipment such as machine tools, printing presses, or x-ray units can be repossessed from a lessee and sold or leased to someone else. There are many types of equipment, however, that require additional "soft" accessories or features before they can be operated or whose operation would be enhanced by their addition. Computer software, chemicals or reagents for medical diagnostic machines, and photocopier drums and toner units are typical illustrations. When equipment requiring soft items is to be acquired, the soft items must be acquired as well.

Some lessors that specialize in particular equipment types have learned how to package these additional items into their equipment lease offerings. Lessors that finance soft-cost items along with leased equipment are able to provide additional benefits to their customers. In these types of leases, however, risk is greatly increased because the lessor is financing items or services beyond the equipment itself. If your company offers these additional services, you must expand your qualifying process to address the increased responsibility and increased risk.

In order to compete effectively and prevail, you must be certain that your vendors and customers fit the requirements of your company. Your efforts take you not only into the vendor environment but, for larger transactions, into the businesses of end-user customers as well. You are the interpreter of what you discover, and as an interpreter, you must gather information about your prospective customers and put your findings in writing for review during the credit process to help determine whether your prospective customer meets the criteria for approval. The key to maximizing successful results is the amount and depth of the information you present for review. What, then, are the financial characteristics of the typical lease applicants you will encounter?

Financial Reporting Practices

Regardless of the market focus of your operation, the creditworthiness of your applicants is the primary issue for lease approval. Your first challenge is to obtain sufficient financial information to evalute the applicant's ability to meet the lease obligation. How easy or difficult this is depends on a number of factors.

Business Size and Type

As a rule, the larger the customer, the more financial information there is readily available. If you are dealing with large publicly held companies, published financial statements that have been audited and certified by outside accounting firms are easily obtained. Frequently, reports ordered from independent credit-rating agencies include enough information, reproduced from the applicants' financial statements, to make additional investigation unnecessary. Many public companies regularly provide their financial statements to these agencies, or the agencies obtain the information themselves from the Securities and Exchange Commission, which requires all publicly held companies to report their financial condition at least quarterly. The agency reports, along with reference data from banks and trade creditors, generally supply enough input to allow many financings for public companies to be approved.

Large privately held organizations usually have audited financial statements but are not required to release them to the public. They will ordinarily provide them to you, however, in order to gain credit approval. Some companies do not go to the expense of an audit because the business does not require large borrowings or extensions of credit. These companies are required to complete federal income tax returns, however, and tax returns can be substituted for financial statements in credit reviews. Since financial statements from privately held companies are not readily available, outside credit-rating agencies may not have much information either. Consequently, bank references, term lender input, and trade information become more important in evaluating this type of prospect.

Depending on the equipment cost, the nature of the lease request, and the equipment type, obtaining sufficient financial information about large public and private companies is usually no problem. Credit-related questions can normally be answered through a number of different sources. According to government estimates, however, 85 percent of American businesses are not in these categories. They are small businesses.

The typical American business is a small manufacturer, service provider, or supplier, many of which are family owned and operated. Financial reporting for these businesses is as limited as the law and their management practices allow. You must gather enough information from what is available to enable your credit people to make their decisions. Owners of small businesses are not going to expand their financial reporting processes just to lease equipment. Many small businesses have no use for audited financial statements in their normal course of business. Audits are costly and time-consuming; they require an outside accountant to perform many procedural tests, including confirmation of balance sheet accounts and detailed analyses of revenue and expense accounts, to determine the accuracy of information. Credit reviewers obviously prefer audited financial statements, because an independent certified public accountant (CPA) has certified the accuracy of the information.

Unaudited financial statements are much more common for small businesses. The simplest type is a compilation statement, in which an outside preparer arranges the financial information according to accounting guidelines. No accuracy tests are performed, and the information listed is simply that which has been supplied to the preparer by the management of the business. A review statement is one step up from simple compilation. When a financial statement is reviewed, the preparer performs certain minimal tests for accuracy but does not attest to the validity of the information. Sometimes, compilation and review statements are prepared by people who are not CPAs, further decreasing their value. Consequently, when you receive compilation or review statements from a prospect, the credit reviewer often asks you to obtain federal income tax returns as well. Many credit reviewers assume that if the information listed in the financial statement matches that in the tax return, it is accurate. They also derive some comfort in knowing that tax returns have been submitted to the Internal Revenue Service, suggesting full disclosure by the taxpayer.

Outside Factors

Financial reporting is organized according to the practices of the particular industry. For small-business credit evaluations, banks and trade suppliers base their judgments on how applicants compare to similar businesses of the same age and size. If you sell small-business leasing services, you must be supported by a credit process that is equipped to function in the same way, because you will encounter the same obstacle of insufficient financial information for in-depth review.

Small-business financial reporting is also influenced by outside factors. Tax and business laws affect the structure of the business. Some businesses are proprietorships with a single owner, others are partnerships with more than one owner, and still others are incorporated. Incorporation provides protection from certain types of liability and converts ownership into shares. Shares may be owned by one or more people. A closely held corporation, whose shares are owned by an individual or a small group, may be entirely dependent on the financial strength or expertise of the people involved. Without obtaining their personal endorsements, a lessor may have no control over the assets financed and no guarantee of repayment. Personal financial information must be added to the credit package when you are dealing with individual owners, partnerships, or closely held corporations.

Generally accepted accounting principles (GAAP) also influence how a small business reports its income. Timing of financial reporting—by selection of fiscal year-ends—can result in dramatically different pictures of the same company, depending on the period covered by the statements. Many seasonal businesses end their business years during their slowest season to accommodate the time required for year-end reporting. When seeking credit, a seasonal business may present an interim statement that reflects peak production. Interim information by itself is not sufficient, because year-end adjustments can often significantly alter the financial condition of the company. A typical adjustment might be a year-end bonus or dividend paid to the owners, which reduces the capital in the business. When an interim statement is offered by a prospect, you must obtain additional year-end statements and interims, covering two or three prior years, for comparison purposes.

Financial statement comparison is used to determine the trend of a business. Trends indicate the direction in which the business is going. Year-to-year increases in sales and profits encourage credit approval, but the reverse does not. For this reason, leasing companies generally require financial statements for two or three year-ends as part of a credit request submission, as well as a recent interim statement if the year-end statement is more than six months old.

Industry practice affects the financial structure of a business. Some industries tend to expand business operations by treating additional facilities as branches or divisions of the parent; others establish separate entities or subsidiaries, owned by the same parent or individuals. Some grow through franchising new locations, bringing in new owners. Some industries use all these methods of growth. It is important that you discern whether you are working with one business divided into different parts or different businesses that appear to be a single company, because you must be able to determine who owns the company.

Credit reference information can be affected by suppliers and trade creditors that support their customers by extending payment terms. These longer periods for payment correspond with the business's collection of accounts receivable—money owed to a business by its customers. Extended payment terms are a marketing strategy used by trade suppliers to stimulate more business. When analyzing applicants, you must be aware that these conditions exist so as not to be misled by what seems to be slowness in trade payments.

Term lenders and lessors can affect the financial reporting of businesses. The structure of lease agreements and loan repayments can lead to discrepancies between what a business's obligations appear to be and what they actually are. When financial statements or tax returns do not include details of loan or lease payment amounts and the timing of payments, a cedit reviewer may develop an inaccurate picture of the company's financial status. For example, bank borrowings are often structured as demand loans. If the borrower defaults in the repayment of this loan, the lender can demand immediate repayment of the full unpaid loan balance. Since a default can trigger the immediate repayment of the entire loan balance, a demand loan obligation must be recorded on the borrower's financial statement as a current liability. Current liabilities are obligations that must be paid within one year. Unless a default occurs, however, the borrower is actually responsible for only the payments due for the year, which would be considerably less than the entire loan balance. Therefore, you need the history of a borrower's demand loans to determine that in the past, they have not, in fact, been paid out within one year.

Considering all the potential influences on the financial reporting practices of businesses, interpretation and expertise play a significant role in credit evaluation. When you are qualifying prospective customers, it is crucial to obtain as much information as possible for the credit review.

The Lease Application

Most lessors use an application form (asking for basic information about the prospect) and, for larger transactions, require additional financial reports or tax returns. The application is usually a preprinted form requesting:

1. The legal name, address, and phone number of the applicant company
2. Person to contact, title, and phone number
3. Form of organization
4. Time in business
5. Type of business

6. Bank and trade reference contacts, addresses, and phone numbers
7. Equipment to be leased (new or used, type, make, model, and serial number)
8. Equipment cost
9. Equipment supplier and salesperson
10. Location where the equipment will be installed
11. Lease term requested
12. Lease payment amount
13. Type of lease
14. Name, home address, and Social Security number of the principals, if necessary

The application may also require that the last two or three years' financial statements or federal income tax returns for the business be attached, depending on the transaction size. Applications from proprietorships, partnerships, and closely held small corporations generally must include personal financial statements for the principals.

You are likely to receive the majority of your applications from small businesses that report their financial condition in a format that is in their own best interests, in light of industry and regulatory practices. The result is that the surface information you receive will probably not be sufficient. Worse, the information that is received may not be acceptable, resulting in a credit decline. In these cases, you have to dig below the surface.

Building an Applicant Profile

Since you are faced with the problem of requiring financial information that prospective customers do not necessarily have or that is insufficient because of their business practices, you have to find other ways to supplement their applications. You can't always offset absent or insufficient information, but you can increase the likelihood of approval by presenting as complete a package as possible.

Reasons for Equipment Acquisition

The need for the equipment is a good starting point from which to build a profile of the applicant. Knowing the purpose of the acquisition can help you to fill in some of the blanks. Businesses ordinarily want equipment for one of three reasons: to expand the business, to replace existing equipment, or to capitalize on an opportunity. During your interview, ask the prospect to tell you about the equipment.

Checklist of Questions to Ask if the Business Is Expanding

- ☐ Are there new customers?
- ☐ Are new products being introduced?
- ☐ Have contracts been received for additional production?
- ☐ Is the business speculating on growth that the new equipment will allow?

Expansion is a strong, positive purpose for equipment acquisition. Discovering the reasons—with specific references to additional customers, products, or markets requiring the equipment—enhances the application and increases the probability of approval. Discussing expansion with the prospect also gives you the opportunity to uncover more information. Perhaps there is a business plan or projection that can be added to the submission to strengthen it.

Businesses often acquire equipment to replace an existing unit, a fact that can be advantageous in many cases. If an applicant doesn't quite measure up on paper as being able to handle an additional obligation, it may be that the company is *already satisfying* the obligation. The new equipment may be replacing not only older equipment but also its financing costs. When the old equipment is removed, so is the obligation to pay for it. This situation is common when equipment is leased or financed. Since replacement equipment may present significantly less risk than an additional piece of equipment, your prospect qualification must include specific questions about the replacement.

Checklist of Questions to Ask if Equipment Is Being Replaced

- ☐ What equipment is being replaced?
- ☐ How long have you had the existing equipment?
- ☐ Why is the equipment being replaced?
- ☐ How was the existing equipment acquired?

- ☐ If the equipment was financed, what are the current payments?
- ☐ When will the payments terminate?

Replacement equipment may provide some other benefits to help weaker applicants. The equipment being replaced as the primary unit may remain to serve as a backup or to handle production overflows. If it is free and clear of encumbrance, it might be available as additional collateral, giving you more security in the lease. If it is being traded in, it might reduce the new equipment cost and risk to a more comfortable range, resulting in approval of the lease.

When equipment is acquired to capitalize on an opportunity, the circumstances require a full explanation.

Checklist of Questions to Ask When Equipment Is Acquired to Capitalize on an Opportunity

- ☐ What is the opportunity?
- ☐ How will the company benefit?
- ☐ Why will the company benefit?
- ☐ When will the company benefit?
- ☐ What contingency plans are there if the situation doesn't work out?

With the answers to these questions, the application will include a more complete picture of what the prospect hopes to accomplish and give your credit people significant information to consider.

Details of Business Operation

There are more blanks that can be filled in. Credit people become concerned when businesses don't provide enough "hard" financial information to analyze. The situation is compounded because the credit analyst doesn't meet the principals or see the operation. Credit people may try to approve as many applicants as they can, but they have no incentive to stretch. Salespeople, not credit people, are responsible for production. Knowing the professionalism (and understandable conservatism) of credit analysts, you must become their eyes and ears. Asking the prospect to tell you about the business gives you more information to support the lease application. Providing additional details when the application is originally submitted can go a long way toward making your credit grantors more comfortable in issuing approvals.

The questions you ask should be simple, yet designed to draw out how the business operates.

Business Operation Checklist

☐ *Who operates the business?* The ownership of a business and its operation are two different things. A hands-on owner-operator usually has more at risk than an investor-owner. The investor may risk money but not necessarily livelihood. Ask:

"What ties the operators to the business?"
"Are the operators employees who may leave at any time?"
"Do the operators have some form of equity in the business now, or will they in the future?"

The risk of the owner can sometimes make a credit package stronger.

☐ *How long has the same management been in place?* Lease applications can come from older companies with new managements. Ask:

"Who are the new managers?"
"What are their backgrounds?"
"Why should they succeed?"

Founders retire, businesses get sold, managers get replaced. Stability of management and promotable, experienced subordinates strengthen businesses.

☐ *What does the business do*? Businesses do not always function precisely as their names or appearances imply. A company may be the only supplier of product to a major buyer, which is different from servicing a wide customer base. Depending on the specific circumstances, a single-customer business is a greater risk. What happens if a business loses its only customer?

☐ *Who are the typical customers*? The size, type, and quality of a business's customers have a significant impact on its operation. Ask:

"Are the customers in seasonal businesses?"
"Do customers remit payment promptly?"
"Are the customers local or remote?"
"How long have most customers been customers?"
"Is an accounts receivable "aging" [*a list of how much is owed to the business, by whom it is owed, and for how long it has been owed*] available?"

☐ *What is the distribution of customers*? Ask:

"Are there many small customers?"
"A few large customers?"
"A mix of customer types and sizes?"

☐ *Who are the direct competitors of the business*? Ask:

"How many competitors are there?"
"Where are they located?"
"How long have they been competing?"
"Are competitors larger or smaller?"
"How do competitors compete (price, quality, service)?"
"How effective are competitors?"
"What is the reputation of competitors?"

☐ *How does the business rate against its competition*? Ask:

"Is its product better?"
"Are products or services more or less expensive?"
"How high is customer recognition?"

☐ *What are the competitive weak points of the business*? Ask:

"What is being done to correct them?

☐ *Who are the business's primary suppliers*? Ask:

"What are their terms and conditions for invoice payment?"

☐ *Who are the business's term lenders and/or lessors*? List them with details of existing agreements, including:

- The original amount financed
- The original term of each loan or lease
- The number of payments remaining for each loan or lease
- The amount of each loan or lease payment
- The expiration date of each loan or lease
- The end-of-term alternatives for each loan or lease
- The specfic equipment leased or financed by each loan or lease

Ask:

"Is there a trade-in value against the equipment to be acquired?"
"Can any owned equipment be used as additional collateral, if necessary?

☐ *Is there a prepared business plan or projections? Who prepared them?*

Step by step, you have expanded the profile. You now have a complete and accurate picture of what your prospect's business is, how it operates, and what the equipment acquisition will accomplish. It will take time to compile and organize the information and prepare your write-up. The credit review process will also take time. You have to be assured that the prospect will allow you to complete your packaging and credit submission and review before going to the competition. You may also have a nervous vendor pressuring the situation, trying to close the equipment sale. For as long as it takes, you must control the situation.

Gaining Control

Control is the ability to establish, direct, and orchestrate the conditions of doing business. There are situations in which control is accepted by one party because of the relative position of another party. Examples of this type of control include an attorney's or accountant's relationship to a client, or an expert's control of a novice. In these instances, the person in control has some power, skill, authority, or function that the other party needs, respects, or admires.

Control may also exist in instances of perceived power, skill, authority, or function. Since, in most sales scenarios, you don't have the strengths possessed by the prospect's banker, lawyer, or accountant, you must appear to have them if you want to control the leasing process. Your control, then, derives from the appearance to others of power, expertise, substance, and professionalism. These appearances, in fact, have become reality. While you were persuading the prospect to discuss the operation of the business with you —discussing financial condition, equipment utilization, and management practices—your role underwent a subtle evolution. You moved from the position of salesperson to the position of financial consultant or advisor. Your development of the applicant's financial profile was far more like consulting and advising than selling.

Act Like an Expert

The change in your role has great value. Lessees are in the "money market" infrequently. Vendors and their salespeople are in the money market more often, but they aren't experts. You're in the money market all day, every day. You are an expert. Your expertise has a value, your exposure has a value, and your access to money and information has a value. These values add up to control. Your control is further enhanced by the other party's positive perception of your attributes and capabilities.

The way you deal with prospects and their financial needs displays your positive attributes. By identifying the areas of strength in a company through your questions and providing a profile of the company that will enable it to obtain the equipment it needs, you are providing a valuable service. Your request for specific information has been guided by your knowledge of what it takes to structure an approvable transaction when the prospect's financial reporting system is inadequate. Although your motive may have been to complete a leasing sale, the prospective lessee is the beneficiary of your expertise. In fact, it is likely that the support you bring to the situation is not available from any other source.

Bankers and term lenders generally review only what has been provided by the applicant. Their decisions are more dependent on hard financial data than on the business in total. Their risk analyses tend to be conservative. They leave it up to the borrower to present the company "story" and uncover any hidden values or strengths that are not readily apparent in financial reports. Often, business owners simply do not realize what those values are, how to identify them, or how to present them—but you do.

The prospect's perception of your positive attributes is also influenced by your personal qualities. Your self-confidence in dealing with the prospect has an effect. Do you seem comfortable in your role as financial consultant? Does your prospect get the feeling that you have done this before and been successful? Are you efficient, businesslike, and focused? Are you enthusiastic? Enthusiasm is contagious. People tend to cooperate with an individual who is upbeat, positive, and helpful. Your company pride instills a feeling of confidence in the prospect. When you are sincerely sold on your own organization, the prospect's desire to conduct business with you is heightened.

Product knowledge makes a strong impression. Financing is critical to the operation of any business. If you convince the prospect that you know your product—the provision of financial alternatives—your perceived value increases. Although your primary objective is to fullfill a leasing requirement, the listener gains knowledge about financing in general from you. You touch on many aspects of business financing when you present your leasing solution. Comparisons may be made to other methods of acquisition, financial reporting styles may be discussed, credit packaging and the philosophy of term lending may enter the conversation. The listener is more inclined to want to do business with you when your knowledge is perceived as an additional resource.

The prospect's interest and comfort level increase even more if you prove to be knowledgeable in his or her industry as well as your own. End-user industry knowledge allows you to communicate in the prospect's language. This shows that you are familiar with his or her business and suggests that others in the industry are your customers too. Your perceived positive attributes are greatly enhanced when listeners sense that you have been there before. Your comments gain more respect, and your statements carry more weight. Experience is a powerful tool. The more experience you and your company are perceived to have, the stronger your position becomes. Your consultancy becomes validated when prospects feel that they are dealing with people who have earned their stripes.

Presume Control

You can use the elements of perceived positive attributes as a selling strategy and employ their strengths to manage the customer qualification meeting. Your objective is to develop as thorough a financial picture of your applicant as possible. You have lists of questions regarding equipment, business operation, management, and financial resources that must be answered, and you need time to accumulate and submit the information. It is imperative that you control the process.

If you are perceived positively, you can take an approach that assumes that you are managing the meeting with the prospect, and thus performing as the controlling person. Your ability to achieve control is determined not only by what you do to obtain the information you need but also by how you do it. The prospect can sense your capabilities by your behavior. If your behavior presumes control, you will probably achieve it. Otherwise, you will be controlled.

Let's compare the language patterns of "controllers" and "controlees":

Controller: I need some more information before I can proceed.
Controllee: If you get some time, would you please fill out this leasing application?

Controller: I'm sorry, I can't go ahead without. . . .
Controllee: I'll talk to my boss about it.

Controller: The reason we require that form is. . . .
Controllee: Maybe I can talk legal into waiving it.

Controller: I will speak to you in a few days to update you on the transaction.
Controllee: I will have an answer for you faster than anyone in the industry.

Controller: Let's take a few minutes so that I can explain our contracts to you.
Controllee: Everybody signs the same forms.

Controller: Since your business operates as a . . . we will need the guarantee of. . . .
Controllee: I'll see what I can do about waiving the guarantee.

Controller: I have a real concern over financing this software because it is intangible.
Controllee: We're very flexible.

Controllers not only obtain information but also earn the professional respect of the prospect by their businesslike approach and their self-confidence in knowing what needs to be done.

Use Control

You have built an image during your interview with the prospect. You've used positive attributes to gain confidence and respect. Your product and industry knowledge, financial consultancy role, and meeting management style have given you control of the situation. Your questions have been answered, and the prospect has agreed to provide you with any items or information that must be gathered. If the lease application could be approved right now, you'd be ready to close. However, you don't have approval authority. The information has yet to be reviewed for creditworthiness by others, and that will take time.

Consequently, your objective now is to use the control you've gained to freeze the transaction until final approval can be granted. You must prevent the prospect from further "shopping," from consulting the competition, and from seeking other alternatives. There are several approaches you can take to prevent the prospect from straying.

Freezing the Transaction

During the customer qualification process, the terms and conditions of lease alternatives are discussed. While functioning in a consultancy role, you provide guidance by assessing and analyzing the information received and suggesting lease structures that will suit the customer and that have the highest probability of approval. But now your role has changed once again. You now function as a "lender" and, perhaps, as an "attorney," in the sense that you may present, describe, and discuss certain documents or proposals.

To some extent, a negotiation takes place during the qualifying interview. Your questions about the prospect company are designed to match its strengths against its desires in lease structure. You outline the terms and conditions of a proposed lease agreement during qualification and become more definitive as you uncover information. These terms and conditions discussed with the prospect can be used as a transaction *freezer*. The best way to accomplish this is to proceed with the lease agreement. Documentation can be completed, executed by the prospect, and confirmed by a check covering any required advance payments. This approach is common in small-ticket to lower middle-market leasing, where sales personnel are permitted to prepare all the paperwork. It must be clearly understood that the lease is subject to final approval at the sole discretion of your company. By signing the lease, however, the prospect is making a commitment. Although the applicant understands that the lease does not have final approval, the process of discussing the business in detail, providing background information, and executing a contract usually discourages the applicant from further shopping.

Not all lease contracts can be prepared by sales personnel. Larger transactions, specialized equipment applications, company policy, or other factors may prevent you from fully completing a lease agreement. In these instances, proposals that are subject to final lessor approval can serve the same purpose. Complete terms and conditions are described in letter form, to be accepted by the applicant. Here again, the prospect commits to an agreement, although a final approval has yet to be granted. By executing the proposal, though, the prospect has made a decision to go ahead with you. Receiving a check covering any advance payment or deposit required from the applicant binds acceptance.

Similarly, some lessors employ lease application forms that contain space for entry of the terms and conditions of the transaction, equipment description, and any other pertinent data. An acceptance block is included for the prospect's signature. Execution of the form and payment of advance monies due also imply closure.

Receiving signed paperwork and advance payments or deposits from the applicant is the best freezing technique, but this isn't always possible for a number of reasons:

- The applicant may have doubts that final approval will be granted.
- The applicant may want to research other alternatives.
- There may be a company policy preventing the applicant's release of funds.

If possible, you should still pursue a signed lease or proposal. Even if you don't receive payment to bind the agreement, you will have an advantage when the application *is* approved. And, having signed an intent to proceed, the prospect may not shop further.

The purpose of seeking written acceptance of an agreement is twofold. You want to obtain commitment from the applicant, and you also want to gain enough time to obtain final credit approval. You don't have a solid prospect commitment without written acceptance. However, there are alternatives that may get you sufficient psychological commitment to allow adequate time for the credit approval process.

Once you reach a clear understanding of what the final terms and conditions will be, you can request a handshake as a binder. Although your position is not as strong as it would have been with a signed document or proposal, a sincere handshake may be enough to stop shopping. If you still sense some concern, a handshake with a time limit may make the applicant more comfortable. Solicit an agreement to go ahead if you are able to provide final approval within a certain number of days. Of course, this is by far your weakest position, so you must be certain that your credit package contains enough information to allow your credit people to respond by the agreed-upon deadline.

Many equipment leasing decisions involve more people than just the individual with whom you have been interacting. These others may not be brought into the picture until after alternative sources of financing have been researched and a decision has been made to proceed with one. The introduction of the other people in the process is often an indication of a decision to go ahead with you. This group may include an equipment manager; a controller; a chief financial officer; an outside accountant, attorney, or financial consultant; a partner; another employee; or an advisor. The equipment vendor may also be included to discuss ordering, installation, or payment procedures. Large installations may involve a building manager or landlord.

Bringing others into the equation requires an investment of time by the prospect. It also means an investment of time by the third parties. A willingness to make this investment, though short of a commitment to do business, is evidence of a serious intent to finalize an agreement. If third parties are not naturally involved, however, you shouldn't go looking for them.

Advantages Over Other Lenders

Throughout the qualifying process, you employ individual skills to gain control, manage the meeting, and freeze the situation until the approval process is complete. Positive personal attributes, company knowledge, industry knowledge, and product knowledge all contribute to your success in meeting your objective. The ability to put these strengths to use gives you a definite advantage over other types of term lenders.

You usually have direct access to the customer at his or her place of business. Whether it's by an actual sales call or by telemarketing, the qualifying process is performed personally with the applicant. Telemarketing is often employed for smaller-ticket transactions, but it can be just as effective in larger transactions. Whatever the method, it is your assistance to decision makers that differentiates you from other lenders. Most other forms of commercial lending don't allow for personal interaction to the same extent. More often than not, the prospect presents the application and supporting material with little or no help from other types of lenders.

If assistance is provided by other lenders, it is often strictly credit focused. Rarely is an attempt made to develop the strongest credit profile possible for the applicant. Your approach is to function as a facilitator, to give every application the highest probability of success. By contrast, term lending philosophy is more often: "Show me why I should lend you the money."

As we have seen, you perform more like a consultant than a credit analyst or seller when assisting the applicant. During the qualification process, you provide valuable input and direction to help the prospect identify company strengths. You use your knowledge of the applicant's business to support the credit submission by describing all the merits of the acquisition. You uncover and highlight hidden assets of the company, when possible. Your consultancy role expands to include financial assistance in selecting the proper lease structure for the situation. The prospect merely seeks needed financing; you provide much more.

Whether you are working directly with end-user customers or selling leasing programs to vendors, you are best able to assist in the acquisition of equipment by focusing your expertise on the business of the customer. You also use your knowledge of the typical end user when you train vendor salespeople to qualify their prospects. You train them how to ask the right preliminary questions, use specially tailored application forms, and employ below-the-surface qualifying techniques. Basic training in customer qualification lets the vendor salesperson direct prospects to equipment that they can afford; it saves time by focusing efforts on the strongest candidates, thereby accelerating the approval process.

The Disadvantages

Although it's true that leasing companies have many advantages over other types of lenders, there are also some drawbacks. Most leasing salespeople do not have credit or financial backgrounds; training and experience increase their skills but fall short of in-depth knowledge. Sophisticated credit analysis, complex forms of business organization, and evaluation of long-term risk require greater expertise. In these cases, term lenders with credit experts who interface with the customer may have an advantage.

Leasing salespeople are likely to have experience in other types of sales or to have sold equipment themselves. Although this knowledge is invaluable in selling leasing, these salespeople may not fully understand all the operational processes of their own company. Until they are completely familiar with each department, their qualification of a prospect may be inadequate. They may still be able to make the sale, but the time frame for gathering all the information required for approval may be lengthened, additional callbacks may be required, and the likelihood of upsetting the applicant is increased.

Once a need for equipment has been identified, a prospective customer wants to move ahead as effortlessly as possible. The vendor selling the desired equipment doesn't want any obstacle to the sale. Despite your best intentions, the prospect may become impatient with the qualifying process. If other alternatives exist, such as open lines of credit at a bank or other lender, the customer may elect to take the simpler route.

Time pressures are *always* hurdles for you. Prospects get anxious, and equipment vendors simply don't want to wait. Regardless of their experience or knowledge of the time it takes for information gathering, it is not unusual for either or both parties to attempt to accelerate the process. Whether or not viable alternatives exist for the prospect or the vendor, you may be told that they do, simply to coax you into moving faster. At times, this pressure can cause you to perform an inadequate qualification or to present an incomplete package for credit approval. In doing so, you significantly decrease the probability of success.

Compounding the problem is a salesperson's inherent difficulty in saying no. Salespeople try their best to be accommodating. When prospects or vendors ask you to move more quickly, to work with less than you know you need, or to attempt to influence approval for them, you are put at a serious disadvantage. Your credit system has valid reasons for requiring that certain criteria be met. If you're not firm in your requests for information, you risk disappointing the prospect and yourself.

Stages of Customer Qualification: A Review

When you first meet prospective customers, you are performing as a salesperson. Your identification of a leasing opportunity requires qualification of the prospect. Most larger organizations supply sufficient financial data with little or no effort on your part. Smaller applicants may not have the financial reporting capacity to give you the depth of information you need, so you have to go below the surface to obtain it.

In your development of financial background, you assist the prospect in presenting the best possible picture of his or her company and move into the role of consultant or advisor. This role allows you to use your expertise to control the qualification process, exhibit your expertise, and manage the situation. As details of leasing terms and conditions are discussed, you again change roles to function as "lender" or "attorney." In this capacity, you seek commitment from the customer to go ahead with the transaction, and you must earn adequate time to compile, package, and submit the credit profile for approval. Successful completion of the lease agreement results in a satisfied customer and vendor, validating your expertise and offering opportunity for the future.

Quite simply put:

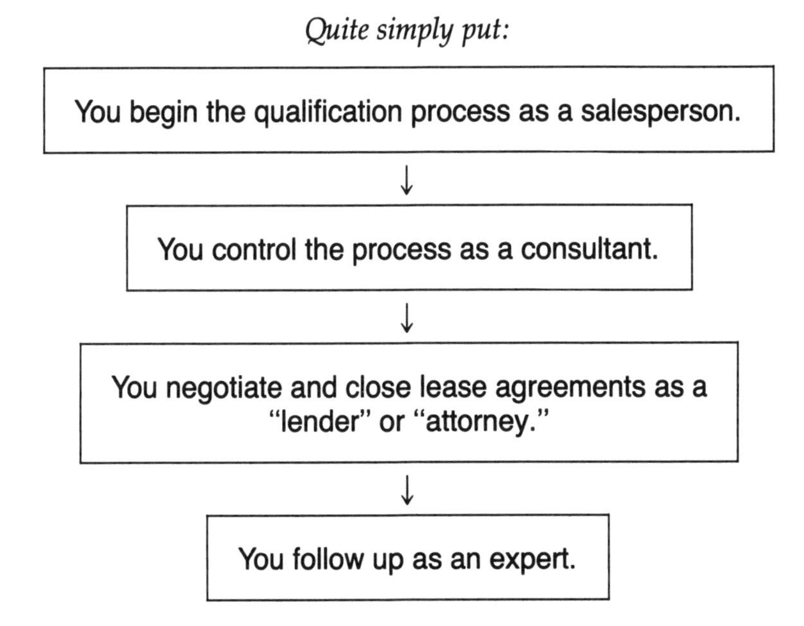

Chapter 7

Stage 1—Developing a Prospective Customer Profile and Prospecting Plan

Regardless of how well you know the benefits of leasing, the leasing marketplace, or the particular leasing services provided by your company, knowledge isn't enough. Knowledge will help you sell, but knowledge alone won't close sales.

Success in closing sales depends on how skillfully you apply your leasing knowledge when you are selling. Above all, closing sales depends on your ability to convince prospective customers to do business with you. Even if your organization's capabilities are the best in the leasing industry, they are valueless unless you sell them, and the target for your sales efforts is the end-user customer.

The Customer Profile

The first step in originating leasing sales is to determine who your most likely customers are. An effective way to identify viable prospective customers is to develop an end-user customer profile, which is a description of the characteristics possessed by the types of businesses that typically need or are known users of your particular leasing products and services. Viable prospects are only those businesses that need what you can provide.

Leasing Products and Services

You begin developing a prospect profile by compiling a list of the leasing products and services that are available from your organization. The process of making the list is similar to preparing an inventory of items for sale. Listing your inventory helps you visualize the characteristics of the business types that are most likely to need what you have to offer. A picture of viable prospects begins to develop as you compile your list, because your inventory readily applies to particular types of equipment and to particular types of end users.

The development of an end-user customer profile is especially helpful if you are new to leasing sales, if you are changing sales positions within your organization, or if you have sales experience but are taking a position with another leasing organization. However, developing end-user customer profiles can be just as helpful to seasoned salespeople who have represented the same leasing organization in the same capacity for some time. Even the most experienced salespeople can get too comfortable or begin to stagnate when they repeatedly sell the same products and services in the same way. The process of developing a prospect profile serves as a refresher and reminder and can highlight products or services that the salesperson may have forgotten, overlooked, or ignored. Periodically preparing a prospect profile also serves to stimulate new sales ideas for existing products, or it can lead to the creation of new ways to apply old ideas.

The following list can be used to remind you of items that may be provided by your organization and should be included in your inventory.

Inventory Questionnaire Checklist

- ☐ Does your leasing organization function as a broker; local, regional, or national leasing company or lessor; bank affiliate; independent, captive, and/or full-service lessor?
- ☐ In what way does your organization set itself apart from other providers of financial services and/or from other leasing competitors?
  - Responsiveness
  - Particular leasing expertise
  - End-user industry specialization
  - Specialization in vendor's equipment
  - Vendor/end-user customer industry expertise
  - Credit packaging
  - Creativity in structuring leases
  - Flexibility in leasing terms and conditions
  - Simplified documentation requirements
  - Attractive lease pricing

☐ What are the strong points in your leasing operation?
- Equipment leased
  - —New equipment only
  - —New and used equipment
- End-user customer types leased to
  - —General business
  - —Production/manufacturing companies
  - —Service businesses
  - —Wholesalers/retailers
  - —Professional practitioners
  - —Printing businesses
  - —Packaging businesses
  - —Materials-handling businesses
  - —Banking businesses
  - —Finance businesses
  - —Insurance companies/insurance agents
  - —Research and development companies
  - —New businesses
  - —High-technology businesses
  - —Hospitals/clinics/medical laboratories
  - —Medical/dental practices
  - —Communications companies
  - —Automotive repair/automotive aftermarket
  - —Restaurants/retailing
  - —Construction/contracting
  - —Schools, colleges, universities
  - —Entertainment businesses
  - —Leisure time/sports businesses
  - —Municipalities
  - —Federal govenment
- Lease/financing types offered
  - —Finance leases
  - —True leases
  - —Operating leases
  - —Equipment rentals
  - —Tax-oriented leases
  - —Conditional-sale contracts
  - —Municipal leases
  - —Federal government leases
  - —Sale/leasebacks

☐ What lease structures does your organization offer?
- Skip-payment leases
- Step-payment leases

- Seasonal-payment leases
- Variable-payment leases
- Thirty-, sixty-, ninety-day no-payment leases
- Master lease programs
- Range of lease terms

☐ What end-of-lease-term alternatives are available to the end-user customer?
- Fair market value equipment purchase options
- Fixed-price equipment purchase options
- Five percent of the equipment's original cost
- Ten percent of the equipment's original cost
- Fifteen percent of the equipment's original cost
- One-dollar equipment purchase options
- Prepaid purchase options
- Other fixed-price equipment purchase alternatives
- No equipment purchase options

☐ What geography does the organization cover?
- Local
- Regional
- National

☐ What additional vendor/end-user customer services does the organization provide?
- Equipment maintenance financing
- Photocopier "meter click" financing
- Medical reagent (supplies) financing
- Computer software financing
- Equipment transportation/delivery financing
- Equipment installation/operator training financing
- Vendor inventory financing
- Floor-plan financing
- Equipment trade-in/trade-up programs
- Progress payments to vendor against equipment purchase price
- Prefunding against vendor's leasing production
- Vendor salesperson training
- Vendor/lessor joint advertising
- Vendor salesperson sales contests
- Remote vendor computer terminals
- Lease production/customer reports and information to vendors
- Acceptance of faxed lease applications

- Lease-application-only credit requirement up to a certain dollar amount (i.e., written financial statements not required)
- Inbound 800 numbers (phone, fax, both?)
- Preapproved customer lines of credit or credit card programs
- Lessee asset management/tracking reports for leased equipment
- Equipment remarketing services
- Equipment maintenance services
- Used equipment inventory
- Short-term equipment rental

The list you prepare from these items, plus any additional features or strengths of your organization and its offerings (see "Value-Added Services," below), is your inventory of leasing products and services. Your inventory should also contain applicable items that can be incorporated into vendor sales approaches.

Value-Added Services

The experience gained by equipment-focused lessors over the past several years has led to the development of many value-added or add-on services for both equipment users and equipment vendors.

Soft-Cost Financing and Variable Billing

It is now common for lessors that lease photocopiers, fax machines, business machines, and personal computers to finance many of the soft costs of equipment acquisition and operation. Soft costs include items such as equipment maintenance financing, computer software programs, disposable supplies, operator training, delivery costs, and installation charges.

Some highly sophisticated lessors provide "meter-click" plans wherein leasing costs are derived by charging a basic fixed lease payment plus a "unit charge" that is assessed each time the equipment's usage meter "clicks." Usage meters are common in photocopiers, mailing machines, and computer printers.

Other types of equipment are also conducive to the provision of value-added leasing services. Medical diagnostic equipment, for instance, often requires the purchase of chemical reagents along with the equipment. Some lessors finance the chemical supplies that are purchased with the equipment and provide for the periodic replacement of chemicals during the lease term.

Lessors need only develop the technology to bill the customer for the costs of ancillary items purchased periodically during the lease term and to track the collection of those variable billings. If you represent a lessor that provides variable-billing services, your company probably has an existing market for those services. However, if you are not specifically limited regarding the types of prospects to whom you can offer variable-billing services, you may have an opportunity to create new markets.

Progress Payments

Value-added services can be provided for costly equipment that is manufactured to particular customer specifications or equipment that requires a significant amount of time to install. Many suppliers of specially built or installed equipment demand that periodic progress payments be made by the purchaser during the equipment's construction or installation period. Progress payment schedules typically require the equipment purchaser to remit payments in advance, against the equipment's purchase price. A typical progress payment schedule might be:

With the original order:	50 percent of the equipment's purchase price
When the equipment is ready for delivery from the manufacturer:	25 percent of the equipment's purchase price
When the equipment is delivered to the customer:	15 percent of the equipment's purchase price
When the customer accepts the equipment for use:	10 percent of the equipment's purchase price

Equipment manufacturers require advance payments, first to deter purchasers from simply canceling the equipment order after construction has begun. As a rule, a customer that cancels an equipment purchase order after making progress payments is subject to the loss of some or all of the monies paid. Second, manufacturers require progress payments because they don't want to take the credit risk created by customers that are unable to pay for the equipment immediately. A third reason for suppliers to require advance payments is that many machines are manufactured outside the United States. The equipment dealer has to pay for the equipment either when it is shipped from the foreign manufacturer or immediately upon its arrival in the United States. Dealers don't want to take the risk of paying the manufacturer for equipment without the customer's prepayment of as much of the cost as possible.

Some customers don't have the cash available to remit progress payments to the supplier. Others don't want to remit the payments because they don't believe that interim equipment financing is their problem. Still other customers don't want to arrange short-term loans through their bank lines of credit to cover the costs of progress payments. Since customers may object to or be unable to remit progress payments, many machine tool, production equipment, and major equipment lessors now arrange progress payment financing in conjunction with a long-term lease.

Leasing companies that offer this service generally provide progress payment financing by arranging a short-term promissory note or loan to the customer. The lessor's loan is an unsecured advance of funds to the customer; if the equipment is not delivered for any reason, or if the customer cancels the equipment order, the leasing company has no collateral to protect its advance payments to the equipment supplier. The long-term lease agreement itself can't become effective, and the equipment can't be secured by the lessor, until the equipment has ultimately been received and accepted for use by the customer.

When the lease finally does become effective, the lessor's loan to the customer is repaid from the proceeds of the long-term lease funding. The funds become available to repay the lessor because the equipment supplier has already been prepaid in accordance with the progress payment schedule. When progress payment leases are funded, the remaining balance payable to the vendor is normally only a small percentage of the equipment purchase price. This amount is paid with the remaining proceeds of the lease funding.

Naturally, the only prospects that are acceptable for progress payment financing are those businesses whose creditworthiness merits an unsecured loan directly from a leasing company or those businesses whose credit standing permits a leasing company to arrange an unsecured loan on behalf of the business from a bank or other short-term lender. Although progress payment financing generally requires the customer to pay an appropriate short-term interest rate for use of the money lent, leasing companies provide progress payment financing more as a customer accommodation than as a revenue-producing service. Progress payments require customer credit evaluation, paperwork, and time to arrange. Since leasing companies are not banks and are not in the short-term loan business, they can rarely charge sufficient rates to make progress payment financing profitable. Instead, progress payment financing is generally viewed as an opportunity to arrange long-term lease financing, from which the leasing company can then earn its income. If you are able to offer progress payments, you can pursue users of machine tools, production equipment, heavy industrial equipment, and chemical processing, plastics, paper, packaging, and printing equipment.

Services for Equipment-Intensive Customers

Leasing companies that are highly automated can provide other types of value-added customer services, such as customized billing. Customers that have many items on lease, for example, can be billed individually for each item, they can be billed in "batches" by grouping leased equipment according to the particular departments where it is located, or they can be billed for all leased items together. Customized billing helps the customer track and manage all leased assets, regularly schedule equipment replacement, account for individual leased items, and monitor and control equipment utilization.

Similarly, the availability of master lease financing allows customers to arrange a universal lease to cover all their projected leasing needs for a period of time in the future. A master lease is an agreement between the leasing company and the customer that is negotiated now, even though specific items of equipment will be ordered and delivered later on. This way, individual lease negotiations and executions are not necessary each time additional equipment is needed. When equipment is added to a master lease, the individual payments and any other information relevant to the added equipment are included into the contract via a lease schedule that becomes part of the master agreement. Most master leases contain provisions that allow the leasing company to adjust the leasing rates, terms, and conditions when new equipment is added.

If your organization provides customized billing, asset-tracking systems, or master lease capabilities, your services are applicable to equipment-intensive customer types, such as large manufacturers or service organizations, major hospitals, production companies, and businesses in high-growth, technologically focused industries.

Services for Small-Ticket Customers

Many leasing companies have created value-added services that are geared to prospects that need relatively inexpensive equipment. These services include application-only credit review for equipment that costs less than a particular amount. For example, financial statements are not required for equipment costing less than $25,000 or even more by many small-ticket leasing companies. Some lessors accept lease applications that are submitted by fax transmission, and most leasing companies provide toll-free 800 numbers for customer service.

Additionally, some small-ticket leasing companies have found that many new leasing applicants could be approved for larger equipment acquisition amounts than they apply for. The leasing company's willingness to lease additional, or more costly, equipment to particular leasing applicants or to qualified existing customers has led to the creation of preapproved line-of-credit programs. These preapproved leasing programs give customers the ability to lease additional equipment in the future without having to reapply for credit.

Although most of the small-ticket value-added services have been created to accommodate end-user customers, many of them are attractive to vendors as well. Some leasing companies, for example, offer their line-of-credit services directly to equipment suppliers. Certain leasing companies offer short-term financing to cover the vendor's inventory purchases or to pay for items that the vendor will sell from a showroom floor. Inventory and floor-plan financing provides significant financial benefits to equipment vendors, and some lessors offer these services as a method of capturing the vendor's leasing business in return for the extension of short-term financing.

Prefunding

In recent years, a limited number of leasing companies have introduced a variation of vendor inventory financing that, in effect, prefunds the vendor's leasing production. In a prefunding program, if an equipment vendor generates a consistent amount of leasing business over a given period (typically monthly), the leasing company will prefund the vendor with a portion of the cost of the equipment projected to be financed during that period. Prefunding gives the vendor early use of the money rather than having to wait until leases are funded later on. The attraction of prefunding is greatest to vendors in the photocopier industry, where the majority of leasing sales are usually made during the last few days of each month.

Naturally, prefunding programs present enormous risks to the leasing companies that offer them. Prefunding programs ordinarily include a contract between the leasing company and the vendor that states the terms of the vendor's obligation to repay the prefunded amounts (which ensures that the vendor will strive to provide the lessor with viable leasing transactions). The programs may include fees payable to the leasing company or discounts on the cost of equipment purchased for lease. Nevertheless, the prefunded amounts are unsecured loans from lessors to equipment vendors. There is always the possibility that a vendor will not provide a sufficient number of acceptable leases to allow the leasing company to recover the amount prefunded. There is also the possibility that the vendor may not be able to repay the lessor's advance immediately. There are also the general risks inherent in any unsecured loan to any business.

Variable Lease Payment Programs

Many leasing products have been developed that accommodate particular needs of both the vendor and the customer during the equipment sale. Some leasing companies structure transactions that allow for delayed payments from the customer. In effect, the customer is given a thirty-, sixty-, or ninety-day "no-pay" or free rental period at the beginning of the lease term. During this time, the customer is able to break in the equipment, receive operator training, or program a new machine. If the new equipment is replacing existing equipment, and the existing equipment is also financed, this "grace period" means that the customer does not have to make two financing payments, provided the existing equipment is removed before the no-pay period elapses.

Other plans address the needs of seasonal businesses such as resorts, schools, or tourism-related operations by allowing for a moratorium on lease payments during slow business periods.

Your inventory list should now be complete. Generally, the larger the number of items it contains, the broader the range of customers you can pursue. But the type of leasing organization you represent also affects the size and scope of your potential market.

Therefore, the next step in developing your prospect profile is to identify your leasing organization's operating method.

Leasing Organization Type

Leasing organization types include captive leasing companies, bank and financial services affiliates, and independently owned leasing entities. Independent leasing businesses may be specialists or "niche players" that focus on specific markets, or they may be general equipment lessors that lease a broad range of equipment types. Within the categories of leasing organization types, there are entities of all sizes and structures, including local, regional, and national operations; full-service leasing providers; lease brokers; and lease packagers.

Certain types of leasing organizations specialize in particular equipment and/or end-user customer types. For example, most captive leasing companies are owned by equipment manufacturers or sellers and are engaged primarily in supporting and enhancing the parent company's equipment sales. Bank leasing affiliates tend to provide financial services only for customers of the parent bank, or they may limit their territorial coverage to only the specific trading area covered by the parent. Some bank affiliates do, however, function as full-service leasing companies and provide leasing services on a local, regional, or national basis. Specialists lease only particular types of equipment, which naturally causes them to concentrate on particular types of end-user customers. Some lessors offer lease types that expose them to greater risk of potential return than do others. True or operating leases, for example, include substantial option prices should the customer decide to purchase the equipment at the end of the primary lease term. If customers have no further need for the equipment or are reluctant to pay a high price to purchase it, they simply return the equipment to the lessor when the lease term expires. Consequently, most lessors that offer leases that do not fully recoup the cost of the equipment during the primary lease term prefer to lease only equipment that they can readily remarket. Lessors that offer equipment for short-term rental also generally limit their inventories to specific equipment types.

Lessors that do not specialize and lease many types of equipment to a wide range of end-user customer types are known as general equipment lessors. Even generalists, though, typically establish some guidelines as to how and where they focus their sales activities. Most often, a generalist's sales criteria include:

- A concentration of sales coverage and customer service activities in a particular geographic area (local, regional, national).
- Parameters for the cost range of the equipment leased (small-ticket, middle-market, big-ticket).
- Sales production through end-user sales strategies, vendor sales strategies, or both.
- Limitation of the number of leasing products and services offered. (Most generalists limit their leasing services to the provision of full-payout finance leases.)
- Establishment of lease pricing guidelines.
- Establishment of lease structure guidelines.
- Establishment of guidelines for purchase option alternatives. (Ordinarily, generalists prefer to offer only one-dollar options to purchase equipment, but some generalists occasionally offer larger purchase options for particular equipment types.)

Generalists typically lease a wide range of equipment types and tend to rely more heavily on a prospective customer's financial strength than on the value of the equipment to be leased. General equipment lessors do not ordinarily stress specialization in any particular equipment type, but they exclude equipment and end-user customer types with which they feel uncomfortable.

The Prospecting Plan

Once you have compiled an inventory of leasing products and services and a list of your organization's policies for conducting business, you then combine the inventory and the business policy information to develop a personal prospecting plan. The best way to organize a prospecting plan is to enter your information in a chart format that contains a complete description of your organization's capabilities and its criteria for customer acceptability (Exhibit 2). The description can then be matched to the characteristics required of the prospective customers you are seeking. Your most viable prospects are those businesses whose leasing needs match the services you offer.

If your chart, for example, indicates that your leasing products and services are designed for users of equipment that has a high

Exhibit 2. Personal prospecting plan.

Leasing Products and Services Offered	Prospective Customers
Competitive advantages Business types leased to Equipment cost range Lease types offered Lease structures offered End-of-lease-term alternatives Geographic area covered Additional vendors/end users Customer services offered [*plus any other leasing products, services, or business policy criteria*]	[*In this column, list the businesses that are most likely to need the products and services listed in the left-hand column.*]

resale value but doesn't specify any particular type of equipment, your prospects might include users of machine tools, production equipment, printing presses, hospital and medical equipment, and plant machinery. If your chart indicates the availability of shorter lease terms and equipment trade-in or upgrade programs, your prospects might include users of high-tech equipment such as computers, scientific equipment, and state-of-the-art technology.

The preparation of a prospect profile and prospecting plan before you begin your sales efforts can save you countless hours later on. By simply organizing the material in advance, you will be able to see your market more clearly, better define your most likely prospects, and program yourself to pursue opportunities that have the highest probability of success.

Chapter 8

Stage 2—Identifying Viable Prospects and Creating a Prospect File

The charted prospecting plan you developed in Stage 1 now includes the characteristics that are typical of the prospects you are seeking. Your next step is to find them. In some cases, you may have the advantage of an existing customer list, prospect list, or other resource to start you off with a base of potential prospects. As a rule, the more specific your lease prospecting plan, the more readily identifiable your prospects will be. This is particularly true of prospecting plans prepared by salespeople who represent leasing companies that specialize in equipment such as hospital, medical, and dental equipment; computer mainframes; scientific equipment; laboratory equipment; specialty vehicles; printing equipment; production equipment; electronic test equipment; or any other type of equipment that is traditionally acquired by certain types of end users.

If you sell for a general equipment leasing company, however, your prospect profile probably allows for a broad range of potential end-user customers, giving you a vast potential market. The generalist's guidelines for prospect acceptability are most often bound only by criteria such as:

- The range of lease types provided by the organization
- The organization's terms and conditions of leasing agreements
- The organization's criteria for lease term minimums and maximums
- The end-of-lease-term purchase option alternatives the organization provides
- The equipment cost range financed

- The geographic location of the end user
- The exclusion of particular equipment or end-user customer types

Although every well-managed leasing company establishes guidelines for the application of its products and services and maintains criteria that must be met by its customers, general equipment lessors ordinarily sell to a wide cross section of the leasing market.

Having a vast market is a significant benefit to you as a salesperson, but it also presents some problems in prospecting. Theoretically, you could pick up the phone or get into your automobile and present your services to virtually any business you contact. If you reached the right prospect at the right time, you would have an opportunity to make a leasing sale. The term most commonly applied to such broad-based, undirected, sales calling is "shotgunning." In fact, in any sales prospecting effort, the more people you contact, the greater your chances for success. You can, however, increase the probability of finding the most viable prospects by adding some control and direction to your prospecting approach. Although you certainly want to contact as many businesses as possible, you also want to contact those that have the highest probability of needing your services.

Acceptable Equipment Types

The first step in identifying viable prospects is to consider the equipment that is most commonly leased:

- Computers
- Photocopiers/fax
- Business machines/office equipment
- Telephone systems
- Manufacturing equipment/production equipment
- Printing equipment
- Hospital/medical/dental equipment
- Machinery/machine tools
- Automotive repair/aftermarket
- Office furniture
- Construction equipment
- Store fixtures/restaurant equipment
- Communications equipment

- Heating/air-conditioning systems
- Construction equipment
- Agricultural equipment

Within and beyond the above list, there are certain types of equipment that are commonly leased but are handled predominantly by specialists. Specialization is common in computer mainframes, aircraft, airline ground-support equipment, vessels, locomotives, railcars, oil rigs, mining equipment, vehicles, and broadcast equipment, for example. There are also submarkets within the general headings, including CAD/CAM equipment and phototypesetting within the computer category; robotics, fiberoptics, electronic test equipment, and circuit board testing equipment within the manufacturing heading; and woodworking equipment and machinery for chemical, plastics, and pharmaceutical manufacturing within the production and manufacturing category.

If you represent a leasing generalist, you are usually limited only by those equipment types that your organization specifically doesn't want to handle. Some lessors, for example, may avoid or exclude equipment that is used in retail stores. Although there is nothing wrong with the retailing business itself, a significant number of new retail stores open each year. Start-up businesses are harder to finance than existing businesses because of their newness; a high percentage of them are declined for financing. Furthermore, the equipment ordinarily used by retailers—shelving, fixtures, telephones, and computers—all tend to have very low resale values. Low equipment resale value tends to increase the lender's risk. Rather than spend the time and money to solicit businesses whose lease approval ratios may be low, some lessors prefer to consider only those retailers that they encounter indirectly, as opposed to actively soliciting them. Since your sales success is predicated on identifying prospects that have the highest probability of lease approval, you must avoid your organization's dislikes and concentrate on its preferences in customers.

Information Sources for Identifying Prospects

When you have compiled a list of equipment types that are acceptable to your organization, the next step is to identify a base of viable individual prospects. There are many sources of information for compiling a prospect base, including:

- The yellow pages
- The chamber of commerce
- Business listings and advertisements in newspapers, magazines, and periodicals
- Business newsletters
- Industry directories
- Industry associations
- Business clubs
- Business/industry trade shows
- Business consultants, attorneys, and accountants
- Equipment suppliers
- Friends and relatives

Despite the higher probability of finding viable prospects through a prospecting plan, sales is also a networking business. If you are entering sales for the first time or if you are changing employers or changing your sales responsibilities with your current employer, it's a good idea to inform everyone you know about the change. A simple announcement, card, or letter can be sent to friends, relatives, neigbors, schoolmates, former employers, former and existing customers, business contacts, associations, groups, clubs, and anyone else you can think of to inform them of your new position. The contacts themselves, or people they know, may lead to sales opportunities for you. You can also prepare a press release or announcement for local newspapers, trade journals, and local advertising publications that may give you some free publicity in their business announcement sections.

The yellow pages is a good place to start compiling your prospect base. The primary benefit of the yellow pages is that the names, addresses, and phone numbers of virtually all businesses are listed by category. A drawback is that you have to contact each business individually to learn more about its specific function and leasing needs and to identify the name, title, and function of the decision makers involved in equipment acquisition. In some cases, you can learn more about businesses if they have display ads in the directory. Large advertisements in the yellow pages generally indicate larger businesses, and the ads themselves often provide more detailed information about the advertiser's business. Yellow page directories can also be ordered from the telephone company for regions outside your local area.

Local chambers of commerce publish information about the businesses in their area. The information is generally provided free of charge and includes the names, addresses, and phone numbers of the chamber's members. An advantage is that the names of key officers are usually included in chamber of commerce publications.

It is a good practice to read the business section of your local newspaper every day as well as the financial sections of national publications such as *The Wall Street Journal*. Business magazines and publications are also excellent sources of information. Articles, advertisements, classified ads, news releases, and news items can indicate the introduction of new products or new businesses, business expansion, and business relocation. Businesses that are expanding or relocating often need additional equipment, as do businesses that are hiring additional personnel. Although leasing for new businesses can be difficult if not impossible to arrange, you may find that a "start-up" entity is actually owned by or affiliated with an established business that will guarantee the lease obligations of the new business.

Many large businesses publish newsletters that discuss new products, plans for expansion, employee promotions, job changes, and relocations of personnel. Ordinarily, nonemployees can't be included on the newsletter distribution list, but you can often obtain newsletters in the lobbies or waiting rooms of the businesses you visit or from individuals you know who are employees. The information found in newsletters can indicate opportunities to lease equipment and identify additional contacts for you, but there is also another advantage. If you keep abreast of current information about a particular business, you will be thought of as an informed and concerned salesperson by the employees of that business. Your care and concern can help enhance your image and differentiate you from your competition in a positive sense.

Publications and directories are produced within most major industries. Trade publications include current industry events, personnel items, new product information, advertisements, articles, and general information. Industry directories often contain the names, headquarters locations, and phone numbers of businesses in the industry; businesses that support or service the industry; and information about subsidiary or branch locations of the individual businesses listed. A good way to find out which publications would best serve your purposes is to ask customers, vendors, salespeople, and others you meet within particular industries which publications they read. Ask why they read them. You will frequently find copies of industry publications in the reception areas of businesses you visit. You can gather general, specific, and subscription information from the publications themselves.

Major industries also have trade associations. Trade associations produce written material about their particular industries and also publish membership directories. Some associations require that you become a member before they will provide information to you, and some are closed to nonindustry membership. If you conduct substantive business within a particular industry, however, joining the industry association can be a benefit. Association membership helps reinforce your dedication to the industry in the eyes of your prospects and customers. It provides you with current industry information and also helps differentiate you from nonmember competitors. Another benefit of your association membership is access to trade shows.

Business and industry trade shows are excellent places to conduct business and to network within an industry. Trade shows are attended by both sellers and end users of specific types of equipment. Trade shows are also beneficial because they afford you the opportunity to learn how particular equipment operates, how the equipment is sold, and how the equipment is used. New products are often introduced at trade shows, and significant information can be gathered about equipment that already exists. At times, equipment vendors that exhibit at trade shows are open to the idea of having you work with them in their trade show booths. Your attendance as the vendor's leasing provider can help the vendor accommodate prospects interested in financing an equipment acquisition, and your participation can strengthen your relationship with the vendor's salespeople and customers.

A key to trade show sales success is the follow-up immediately after the show. If you actively network at a trade show, you will meet a number of people, but those people will also have met many other salespeople. You must follow up quickly and diligently on the contact information you gathered. You must remind those people about your meeting, and you should do it as soon as possible after the show is over; you must pursue the specific issues discussed with them; and you must persistently follow up with those people in the future. Persistence and diligence in trade show follow-up is necessary regardless of how long you have been engaged in sales. Trade shows can be places where experienced salespeople meet old friends, network among them, and stimulate business activity. Once a trade show is over, however, it is back to business as usual for the attendees. If the opportunities discovered at trade shows are not followed up expediently and persistently, once you are out of sight, you will be out of mind.

Beyond businesses that are viable as prospects, there are individuals who may be able to introduce you to prospects. As third-party providers of business services, consultants, attorneys, and accountants are often aware of a client's plans to expand or to acquire equipment, or of a client's possible need for equipment leasing services. When you encounter third-party service providers, it is a good practice to ask them if you can be of help to their clients. Inquiring about referrals is especially opportune when you are successfully completing a lease agreement for one of their clients. Referring clients to a professional leasing salesperson also helps the service provider by demonstrating that he or she is concerned enough about the client's business to try to be of additional help.

Preparing, Organizing, and Maintaining a Prospect File

The two keys to successful prospecting are identifying as many prospects and compiling as much information about them as you possibly can. The most valuable time you spend as a salesperson, however, is the time spent with prospective customers. Therefore, the time for compiling and organizing information about your prospects and preparing prospect lists for solicitation is before or after the prime selling hours of the day, on weekends, or at times when, for any reason, you can't actively interface with prospects.

The information you gather that identifies prospects for solicitation must be prepared, organized, and maintained in a format that is easy for you to work with. A simple way to prepare prospect information is to enter the data on an index or file card or, ideally, in an automated database. A separate card, file, or contact sheet should be prepared for each individual prospect. The contact information should include:

- ☐ Date contacted
- ☐ Full legal name of the prospect
- ☐ Address of the prospect
- ☐ Phone number of the prospect
- ☐ Person(s) to contact and title

- ☐ Name of individual who referred you to the prospect (if applicable)
- ☐ Prospect's business/industry
- ☐ Prospect's credit rating
- ☐ Equipment type used by the prospect
- ☐ Equipment vendor
- ☐ Equipment unit cost or the cost range of equipment typically used
- ☐ Lease term
- ☐ Lease payment or rate
- ☐ Purchase option
- ☐ Special conditions (if any)
- ☐ Competitor(s)
- ☐ Account status (active, closed)
- ☐ Date for follow-up
- ☐ Notes

Depending on how you originate your prospect information, you may not have enough data to complete a contact sheet for every prospect. If, for example, you gathered your preliminary data from the yellow pages, you may be able to enter only the prospect's name, address, business or industry, and telephone number. In addition to the demographic information that you gather about a prospect's business, it is also a good practice to include a mini credit-rating notation for each prospect. You can accomplish this by assigning a letter or number code to individual prospects whenever you are able to obtain sufficient credit information about them. For example, you may rate excellent credit risks as an A or a 1, with lower ratings noted as B or C or 2 or 3, and so on. This will give you an indication of prospects' leasing potential from a credit viewpoint when you contact them.

Of course, you will have little or no credit information about prospects you identify from many of your reference sources. When you use telephone directories, business listings, publications, advertisements, classified ads, or similar resources to identify prospects, you rarely find more than the name and business type of the businesses listed. If you obtain prospect information from credit-rating agencies, however, you can request that the rating agency include at least the agency's own credit rating for the individual prospects identified. If your prospecting lists include existing customers or prospects that previously applied to your company for leasing but did not become customers, you may be able to obtain enough information from your own credit department to assign a credit-rating code to those businesses.

Since you will not have enough information to complete a contact sheet for every business on your prospecting lists, you will have to fill in the remainder of the input after contacting the prospect and gathering as much additional information as possible. The point is, you must have an organized way to enter, track, and manage all the information you gather about prospective customers and a system for following up with the prospect in the future.

If you use index cards or file cards to record information, you can batch the cards for follow-up by date and time. A simple way to establish a callback tracking system is to set up card files or file folders for each prospect and then index the files by date and time for future contact. Each time you schedule a call, task, meeting, or event for the future, you can put your follow-up information in the "future contact" file or folder. It is a good idea to retrieve your records for follow-up far enough in advance to allow you to prepare any materials, obtain additional information, or complete any other task that is relevant to your follow-up contact with a particular prospect.

When you batch your calls for follow-up by date and time, you are building a backlog of prospects to contact in the future. A routinized procedure for contact follow-up, supplemented by additional new leads gathered from your everyday prospecting efforts, helps ensure that you have a sizable backlog of prospects to solicit each day. There is only so much quality sales time in a day, and that time must be put to its most productive use. You may find, for example, that you are able to reach decision makers early in the morning or late in the day, when they are not totally involved in their primary function of operating their businesses. Whatever your particular case, and whatever the characteristics of your prospects, you must maximize the number of people you can effectively contact.

The same is true of making field sales calls. Make every effort to group your field sales calls by geography. When you know that you will be traveling a significant distance from your office, make as many appointments as possible with prospects located in the same area, maximizing the value of the commute time. Informing a prospect that you will be coming to his or her area at a particular time establishes a good reason for visiting a prospect with whom you have had difficulty arranging a meeting. Preparation and planning go a long way toward helping you maximize the value of your time.

There are other time management techniques and resources that can help you sell more efficiently. Many automated database and contact management programs are available from a variety of software manufacturers or suppliers. The account tracking and contact programs operate in standard personal computers, including lap-top and notebook models. Considering the importance of organizing and maintaining your current contact base and future backlog, an automated system may be a worthwhile and cost-effective investment. If you use an automated contact tracking system, you can automatically schedule calls, meetings, tasks, and follow-ups and program sufficient notice time for advance material preparation as well. Additional benefits of a computerized database include built-in word-processing programs and telephone and fax modems that include automatic dialing features, all of which can save you time and effort.

The contact information that you gather is your database for soliciting prospects. The larger your database, the higher the probability of sales success. Regardless of how many prospects you identify, however, the prospects are of no value unless you can turn them into customers. Every prospect that you discover must be solicited for sales opportunity.

Chapter 9

Stage 3—Soliciting Prospects

There are several methods you can use to solicit prospects, including direct mail, telemarketing, and personal visits. Each method has its own strong and weak points, and you will probably use all the methods from time to time.

Direct Mail

Direct mail is prospect solicitation through the distribution of written promotional and sales-focused materials. Mail is an effective sales method because you can send information to large groups of prospects frequently and inexpensively. Mailers can be designed for general distribution to your entire prospect base, specially written for specific prospect types, or directed to individual prospects.

You can make up your own mailing lists from your prospect base, or you can purchase mailing lists from other sources, including mailing list suppliers, trade associations, and industry organizations. Credit-rating agencies, such as Dun & Bradstreet, can design mailing lists by particular criteria, allowing you to select the specific parameters for your target prospects. For example, you can select the prospect's geographic location, number of years in business, business type, sales volume, net worth, income, and number of employees.

The negative side to direct mail is that it is one-way communication. You get responses only from those prospects that are interested enough by what you send them to respond. Furthermore, direct mail is such a popular method of sales promotion today that most businesses are inundated with unsolicited mailings. Therefore, you must ensure that your own mailers are well thought out, well prepared, professional in appearance, and designed to get attention. Typically, the most likely mailings to be opened are personally addressed, hand-stamped ones that appear to be announcements, personal or greeting cards, or invitations. Certainly, there are many other types of mailers that attract attention, but personalization, attentive preparation, and attractiveness are primary considerations in mailing piece design.

Although there are no guarantees that a mailing piece will be opened or read, you can increase a mailer's effectiveness by controlling its distribution and by following up the mailing with phone calls to the recipients. Telephoning recipients accomplishes several things. A phone call confirms the receipt of your mailer or, if it has not been received or has been discarded, it gives you the opportunity to send another. You also increase the chances of a prospect's reading your material if you speak to him or her about it. Furthermore, calling a prospect with a specific purpose—in this case, following up on a mailer—affords a greater probability of getting through during an initial prospecting call.

Mailers themselves can be designed to serve many different purposes. Simple pieces such as postcards or flyers are inexpensive ways to announce new products, new services, or special promotions. They can also serve as general reminders. Periodic mailings keep your name in the customer's mind and reinforce your sales efforts. As a general rule, written material, letters, and informational pieces are more effective when they are direct and to the point.

A business letter's opening statement should quickly illustrate the purpose for writing and highlight the benefit to the recipient, such as:

"We are financing specialists in the printing industry and have capital available for the purchase of printing equipment."

"We provide equipment leasing and financing and inventory financing."

"We have financing available for businesses in the plastics industry."

The body of the letter or mailing piece can then go on to include specific information about how your leasing or financing program works.

Prescreening the recipients increases the probability that your mailing piece will be read. You can call prospects before sending a mailing to inquire about their specific business operations and to determine the name and title of the person to whom the mailer should be sent. Prescreening also gives you some basic information about your prospect's business before you send a mailing piece, so you may be able to send specific information about the products and services you provide either by itself or with the general mailing piece.

Although direct mail is a cost-effective method of reaching a large number of prospects, and using a combination of mail and telephone increases the effectiveness of mailings, the telephone itself is a powerful marketing tool.

Telemarketing

Telemarketing—personal selling by telephone—is the fastest way to reach everyone on your prospect list, the quickest way to introduce yourself to prospects, and one of the most popular methods of selling leasing services. It would be impossible to personally visit, qualify, and close every potential customer. Telemarketing lets you qualify situations more quickly and less expensively than a personal visit. Telemarketing makes it possible for you to sell in a large market without being a large organization. With an efficient telemarketing process, you can contact many prospects, regardless of where they are located. Both general equipment leasing salespeople and specialists can benefit from telemarketing.

Telemarketing can also be used to research new markets, introduce new products, and gather feedback in order to measure potential. This creates the chance to start small while thinking big. For lessors, it eliminates the expense and risk of building a sales infrastructure before determining the extent of the return. For salespeople, valuable time and effort can be saved while researching a new market.

Because equipment leasing is such an immense industry, even seasoned professionals find it a challenge to become totally familiar with all the lease types and services in existence. Furthermore, leasing companies frequently change, improve, and adjust their services in response to changes in the economy, tax laws, equipment markets, and end-user customer preferences. The best way to make sure that you have all the information you need to effectively telemarket is to use a script.

Scripts

A script is a written outline that covers the key points you are most likely to need during your telemarketing calls. A script may be devised to address specific products, services, operations, processes, or features of your leasing specialties. Sometimes simple index cards are sufficient reminders; more complex circumstances may require more detailed scripts.

Scripts can be developed to address particular situations, such as the products or services offered by competitors and the key points to mention when talking to their customers. New plans and programs can be scripted to ensure that you cover all the benefits and details of their use. Terms and conditions of doing business can be listed so that you can answer particular questions about how your company operates. Lease documentation language may be scripted as well, to make sure that you offer consistent and accurate explanations of what the various contract clauses mean and how they are interpreted.

Scripts can be staged by organizing them in progressive or cross-referenced order. An introductory page, for example, that deals with generalities of your products and services may help identify the prospect's specific needs. Information regarding particular items of interest can be listed separately, in more detail. Moving from reference form to reference form supplies the information you need and keeps the sales discussion going.

Scripting processes can be automated by putting them into a computerized database. This gives you immediate access to cross-referenced material. The scripts can be detailed according to the depth of information you expect to be called on to provide in your telemarketing activity.

Telemarketing scripts can also be designed only to identify likely prospects, who will then be followed up later. Some scripts call for qualification of the prospect and determination of specific needs. Still others can handle the entire selling process, including maintenance of the customer relationship. In this case, the telephone totally replaces field sales activity. No matter how many scripts are created or to what extent they go, however, there are some pointers to remember when using them.

Personalize the Script

Even after the information you need is organized and readily available, you still have to communicate—and you can't sound like a recorded message. You want to build a rapport with the listener, and you accomplish this by being well-informed and personable. You can enhance your presentation and assure conversational professionalism by writing several versions of the same script, using language and style that fit you. During the calls, you can edit the material as you go along, listening for the best delivery of your messages. New ideas can be tested to see if you can improve your performance.

The prospect's reactions are the best indicator of how well your scripted approach works. The prospect may comment on your style or on the quality of the information you are delivering. Use this feedback to perfect your technique in order to get the most favorable results. Keep the things that work in your presentation and discard or replace those that don't.

Ordinarily, people who sell have particular characteristics, such as an outgoing personality, good communication skills, the ability to think and react quickly, and a strong desire to succeed. Don't lose the value of those qualities by "canning" your approach on the telephone. Scripts help you locate and use information, organize your calls, and indicate direction. But just as viewers sense intent or attitude through body language, listeners sense the same through tone of voice. Be certain that listeners hear you smile on the phone. Take advantage of your innate selling skills and inject them into your conversations.

Prepare

Advance preparation maximizes the productivity of your telemarketing activities. For example, before you begin your calls, review prospect lists and sort them by industry, product, vendor or customer type, geographic location, or any other criterion. It is simpler to use scripts when your prospects are sorted by common interests.

Organizing prospect lists also maximizes your time, allowing you to go from call to call without pausing to find reference information or telephone numbers. There will be common questions and objections from grouped prospects; your answers can be scripted by category, allowing for a quick response.

Time Your Calls

There are times of the day and week that are more productive for telemarketing than others. These times vary according to the prospect's job function. For example, sales managers may be easier to reach very early in the morning or late in the day and at the beginning of the month. Their schedules and time demands affect their availability. Experience will reveal the best calling patterns.

During the time you schedule for telemarketing, it is critical that you're able to work without interruption. Nothing should distract your attention. You might want to post your telemarketing time schedules so that others know that you won't be available for other activities. And, because your attitude comes through over the telephone, you shouldn't attempt to telemarket if, for any reason, your mood, tone, or delivery will be negative.

Obstacles

Although the telephone has many advantages over other forms of prospect contact, it presents significant obstacles too (Exhibit 3). Sixty-five percent of a sales visit is visual perception. In a personal sales visit, your audience responds more to your personal image, style, delivery, attitude, and professionalism than to the materials you present. The items you bring with you support your presentation; they don't make your presentation. When you telemarket, you lose that advantage. You now have only 35 percent of your in-person firepower, so you have to impress your listener verbally. Remember

Exhibit 3. Telemarketing obstacles.

- 65 percent of a sales presentation is visual.
- The phone is in the control of the prospect/customer.
- It is very easy to hang up. It is very hard to ask a visitor to leave.
- The prospect can exaggerate more easily during a "cold" phone call.
- Attitude can be "heard."
- You have fifteen seconds to make an impression.
- Good screeners are paid to get rid of you.

that your attitude is audible. If you sound like you are running down a prospect list hoping to find a nibble, your probability of success is greatly diminished.

Making your job even harder is the fact that the phone is in the total control of the person who answers it. It is easy for even the most well-mannered person to hang up, but that same person would probably not throw you out of his or her office. In telemarketing, you have approximately fifteen to thirty seconds to make a positive impression. Check your watch. It is certainly ample time, but good screeners are paid to get rid of you during that time. Practically every telemarketing call you make will pit you against a screener of some sort. Receptionists, secretaries, assistants, administrators, or other subordinates are your initial hurdle. The decision maker you are looking for rarely answers your first call. The larger the prospective customer, the deeper the screening process. In fact, you may have to go through several layers in a large company, dealing with new screeners at each stage.

Because of the popularity of telemarketing, screeners are deluged with calls not only from your competition but also from a countless number of other sources. They receive so much sales attention by telephone that they don't always listen to the subject. All that registers is that there is another salesperson on the phone, and you get a quick "we don't need any." The objective, then, is to take the screener out of the equation.

There are ways to bypass a screener, quickly and effectively. One of the best approaches is to create a scenario that the screener is not qualified to handle. You can accomplish this by immediately presenting an opportunity or benefit that the listener is not empowered to reject. Similarly, you can introduce comments that affect the operation of the business and are beyond the authority of the screener. Here are a few examples:

"I want to purchase $______ worth of your equipment."
"I want to save your company some money."
"I want to talk to someone about increasing your sales."
"I want to be your biggest customer."
"I want to speak to someone about your competition."

If you're met by resistance, you can politely inquire whether the screener is the person in charge of sales, marketing, or order entry or is the CEO, treasurer, controller, president, or other title.

The implication is that the benefit you offer requires the attention of someone of the rank you are seeking for that particular call.

Regardless of your introductory comments, you must be able to follow them up with additional information. Often, screeners are inclined to let you reach your target but want to hear more about the subject before connecting you. Since screening is part of their responsibility, their superiors judge them by whom they allow through the screen. Your reply to their requests for more information must be presented so that a determination of its value requires an authorized listener.

"I want to save your company some money," for example, might be followed by: "I know that equipment price discounts to your customers can cost companies like yours as much as 40 percent per sale. By simply adjusting your selling prices through discount-based financing, the cash purchase prices can be increased. If I can help you market this program, the financing structure will save you some, or perhaps all, of what your business may be losing. Our program has produced excellent results in your industry, and I would like to speak to your sales manager about it." This approach allows you to quickly differentiate your company.

Differentiation

Differentiation sets you and your company apart from competitors who are calling the same prospect. Leasing companies come in all shapes and sizes. By quickly establishing a specific purpose for your call, you distinguish yourself from the others as well as disqualifying the screener from evaluating the subject you introduced. The screener would be taking a risk by simply dismissing you and hanging up.

Differentiation can be implemented in a variety of ways. You may have a specialty that immediately sets you apart from alternatives. Examples include equipment leased, equipment cost ranges financed, customer type, lease structures, special plans, seasonal structures, company size, geography serviced, sales method, or any other characteristic that focuses your expertise.

The differentiating features of your sales approach can be scripted to the prospects you are calling. Several scripts can be designed to promote programs for different prospect types. For instance, you may be introducing a new lease structure for particular equipment. That message about your new program must be delivered immediately in your presentation. "Hello, my name is Mike

Berke. I represent QuotaButer. We are introducing a program that is designed to give your customers significant reductions in their cash outlay for acquiring your equipment. Would your sales manager or your chief financial officer be the person most interested in speaking with me?" Or, "We are specialists in medical equipment leasing. Changes in reimbursement regulations have affected the ability of hospitals to acquire equipment. Our new program helps prevent lost equipment sales by making compliance simpler. I would like to speak with your sales manager about increasing your sales!"

Whatever the case, the scripts, written in language that is comfortable for you, should list the subjects you want to present; they are the guides you follow in your telephone conversation.

Introductions

The most effective way to reach a decision maker is to have a specific reason for calling a particular company. Specific reasons for the call, professionally stated, bypass screeners. Asking for a specific person by name bypasses screeners. Referrals from recognized others bypass screeners. Recommendations from others bypass screeners. And, expertise bypasses screeners.

The Sales Presentation

Once you have reached the decision maker, you conduct your sales presentation. Although you are not physically present, your sales objective is the same as if you were. You must now qualify the prospect, sell your product or service, and complete your targeted goal.

Qualification is more difficult because you can't learn through observation. You have to ask more questions to fill in what you can't see. A plus for telephone communication is that people enjoy talking about their business. If you keep the conversation interesting, you can guide the discussion and learn about particular aspects of the business.

One of your scripts can be a checklist containing the categories of information you're seeking. But rather than running down the list as if it were a questionnaire, you should adopt a conversational approach. With vendors, rather than inquiring about equipment sold specifically by item, your question might be: "Can you tell me about your equipment?" As information is provided, you simply enter the data on your checklist sheet. The technique is more suited to telemarketing than an in-person interview across a desk. If you don't derive enough information from the vendor's responses, you can lead the discussion into new areas with further inquiries.

Questions can be structured to address each of the areas called for by the situation and arranged as a checklist.

Checklist of Vendor Telemarketing Questions

- ☐ How long has your company been in business?
- ☐ What is your annual sales volume?
- ☐ How do you sell your product? [Inside sales/outside sales/ directly to the end-user customer/indirectly through dealers or distributors?]
- ☐ Are you a manufacturer, distributor, or dealer?
- ☐ Can you tell me about your customers?
- ☐ What geographic territory do you cover? Are most of your customers from within the territory?
  [*If not*] Where are they located? Why?
- ☐ What is the trend of your business?
- ☐ What are the price ranges of your equipment?
- ☐ Is equipment sales your primary business?
  [*If not*] What is?
- ☐ Do you use an equipment leasing program now? How?
  [*If not*] Why not?
- ☐ Are you pleased with your lessor? Why?
  [*If not*] Why not?
- ☐ What is your current leasing volume?
- ☐ Is your equipment all hardware?
  [*If not*] What are the software, installation, delivery, and training costs?
- ☐ How many salespeople do you employ [locally/regionally/nationally]?
- ☐ How is your sales force organized?
- ☐ Do you service the equipment? Do you supply parts or replacements?
  [*If not*] Who does?

Depending on the size and type of vendor you're seeking, checklists can be tailored to identify the qualities that are important to you.

This same approach can be taken with a prospective end-user customer. The lease application you use to qualify end-user customers can also be used as a script. Here again, open-ended questions often result in detailed answers from prospects. As you hear items mentioned that are application questions, simply write in the details as you go along. This approach makes prospects more comfortable with you on the phone and doesn't give the impression that you're reading from a list of questions that will run on forever. Professional interest in a customer's business operation results in equally sincere answers, sometimes giving you more information than you actually need. But you can always use that information later on.

Credit reviewers sometimes need more information than that contained in lease applications. Ordinarily, reviewer's questions focus on prospect responses that are out of line with normal conditions for that business type. By using a conversational telemarketing approach with your prospects, you can enter the additional information you gather in your interview as comments or notes to the leasing application. Frequently these comments address the reviewer's additional questions, gaining you three advantages in the process: You appear professional to the reviewer, you won't have to recall the prospect, and you have accelerated the credit decision.

Telemarketing advantages are gained through listening. Prospective vendors or lessees mention the areas of most interest to them while speaking with you. Your job is to respond to these "hot buttons." Specific problems or needs mentioned by the person on the other end of the line are opportunities for you to provide solutions.

Preparing a variety of scripts on lease structures that can solve vendors' common equipment sales problems and as counters to particular competitive leasing programs equips you to respond immediately and accurately, when necessary. You can dissuade competitive pressure or offer solutions for selling slow-moving items by introducing specific lease structures. You can suggest methods for accelerating the vendor's invoice payment for equipment that takes a long time to install or encounters delays during the start-up phase. A vendor sales representative's apprehension about leasing can be offset by offers of training, field support, and written instruction.

When prospective end-user customers mention equipment acquisition problems caused by limited budgets, the continuing cost of existing equipment, or their organization's internal procedure for justifying equipment acquisitions, you point out how leasing's manageable periodic payments can help. First, you have to hear the problem; then you offer the solution that your organization can provide. Because you are conducting your sales by phone, you have to give careful, clear explanations. If you hear

Hesitation about leasing:	Explain how leasing works.
Hesitation about leasing documents:	Explain them and their purpose.
Hesitation about loss of equipment ownership:	Provide the details.

As you improve your listening skills, your opportunities will increase. Everything you hear is a clue to a prospect's needs. Prospects who sense that you are paying attention are more willing to talk. When you invite their questions, you make them more comfortable. You solve problems or objections as they arise and move on with the call.

It is critical to consider just how many sales calls a day your listener is subjected to and to quickly differentiate yourself from the rest of the pack by your sincere interest and desire to hear and understand their requirements. Professionalism and sincerity dispel doubts and concern.

Objections

As a telemarketer, you have to expect the prospect to object to your offerings. People never immediately agree to begin working with a leasing company without some hesitation. However, objections aren't no's; they can be used to your advantage. Objections are opportunities!

Objections allow you to fully explain what you do and why you do it your way. They permit you to clarify misunderstandings or miscommunications. An objection may be raised because you were not clear in your presentation. The chances of confusion are increased simply because you are communicating by phone. Objections also indicate problems, and problems generally have solutions. You must clearly identify the problem and work to resolve it.

Objections may also be stalling tactics or smoke screens put up by the prospect to divert you from some other factor. To identify the real hurdle and overcome it, it's mandatory that you keep up your questioning. Perhaps the person you're dealing with doesn't have the authority to commit to your program and doesn't want to disclose that fact. There may be competition that the prospect prefers not to mention. There may have been an unsatisfactory leasing experience in the past. A competitor may be serving the account at present, making the prospect uncomfortable discussing alternatives. Unfamiliarity with leasing may make the listener wary or unsure.

As you continue the discussion, probing for information and direction in overcoming objections, you gain the benefit of the time invested by your listener. Time is a valuable resource for busy people. The more time they are willing to spend conversing with you, the higher your probability of success. It is unlikely that a prospect has the time or inclination to repeatedly discuss the details required to develop a framework for a leasing program. If you can keep the communication with the prospect moving toward a positive result, you limit your competitors' chances and increase your own. (Common questions and objections are covered in more detail in Chapter 12.)

Prospects feel more at ease if they sense that you are focused on their needs. Despite the value of telemarketing in reaching a large number of prospects quickly and conveniently, each individual you call must be made to feel important. Your sales presentation must be directed to them as individuals. You can't allow your listener to feel that he or she is only one of many to be contacted and that you're eager to get on to the next call. Each of your targets is a potential sale requiring your full concentration.

Closure

The objective of telemarketing is to achieve a specific result. It may be to identify opportunities to be followed up by others, to qualify prospects as vendors or customers, or to close leasing business by phone. Whatever your goal is, you must focus on it throughout the call and complete your objective by obtaining agreement.

Agreement is acknowledged by the prospect's acceptance of your proposed close, and a close is the execution of the action that was the purpose of the call. For example, if the call's purpose was to identify opportunities for others, the close may be the prospect's agreement to have a salesperson visit. A close to qualify an end-user customer may be the prospect's agreement to send financial information and equipment lists for credit approval. A vendor business close may be the submission of a lease application for processing. Regardless of your purpose in calling, a successful closing is required.

Scripts can be written to include closing statements. At the point in the conversation when you perceive that the prospect is willing to agree, you must ask for the order: "Then we agree, Mr. Jones, that you will . . .

"See me at 8 A.M. on Monday at your office."
"Send me a lease application this afternoon."
"Speak to me again on Wednesday, after you have reviewed my material."
"Allow me thirty minutes on the twenty-second to meet and train your salespeople."
"Include my lease alternatives in all your written proposals."

Reaching closure with an account signals the time to thank the prospect and move on. You've attained your objective and don't want to reopen negotiation. You must, of course, now be certain that whatever you agreed to and promised is fulfilled.

Follow-Up

Follow-up to ensure customer satisfaction is critical to all sales success, but it is especially important in telemarketing. You don't always meet the people with whom you speak, because many telemarketing relationships are handled exclusively by phone. Sometimes the only customer contact you have is remote communication, leaving no margin for error in delivering what you promised. You can't run out to the car for an extra copy of material not received by the customer, as you could in a personal visit.

Since diligence in follow-up is not always practiced by your competition, it may be one of the strongest selling points you have to offer. Furthermore, it makes no business sense to exert all the effort that telemarketing requires and then neglect to complete the task.

During your telemarketing activity, you'll learn a great deal about the companies you contact. This gives you reference data for the future, which should be kept up-to-date in a vendor or customer file.

Customer or Vendor Reference Files

A vendor or customer file containing the information you have gathered is used for working with qualified prospects, for follow-up guidance, and for account maintenance. It includes information about the types of businesses these prospects conduct, their industries, typical characteristics, and common interests. It documents opportunities that are not of interest today but may be in the future. Telemarketing allows you to speak to a large number of companies, and the information you gather can grow into a valuable reference source for later use.

Typical files contain basic information such as prospect names, addresses, phone numbers, and individual contact names. The files also hold specific items about the particular business transaction in which you are engaged, financial data about a prospective customer, or type of equipment leased for a vendor. Files can be expanded, however, to have more than current utility.

The database can include complete listings of vendor product lines, all equipment sold (whether you currently lease it or not), price lists, models, and brochures. It can list all sales outlets, whether or not your organization presently services those areas. It can give a description of the entire vendor sales structure, including notes on parent offices, if you service branches, or the manufacturer, if you service dealers. Names of individuals such as company presidents, sales executives, financial officers, and sales personnel can be listed for future use.

Valuable information about your competitors can be gathered by questioning dissatisfied customers. As much if not more can be learned from those who are satisfied. Your files should include competitive rates, terms, and conditions; literature; sales material; and any other items that can be gathered from prospect and customer contacts.

The database should include a complete current listing of leasing volume, quality, and performance, as well as a historical summary of the account relationship, for reference when speaking to a vendor or customer. Active vendor files must contain comparisons of production to projection, to allow for monitoring of activity and for accuracy when discussing account status. The more information you collect and the more telephone experience you gain, the greater your opportunity for growth.

Telemarketing is a cost-effective way to reach a large population of prospects. It saves time, money, and effort. Even for full-time field salespeople, organized and focused telemarketing increases effectiveness and efficiency. Drawbacks are inherent in the process, because the advantages of image and style that are part of a personal visit are lost. But with practice, you will be able to project those same advantages over the telephone and read body language by ear.

The use of scripts that list the key points you want to cover during telemarketing sales calls enhances your style, pace, and professionalism. Rehearsal and practice polish your delivery. Add to this your product, company, and industry knowledge and telemarketing success is a sure thing.

Personal Visits

Depending on the leasing products and services you sell, personal visits are also an effective sales method. Personal visits are common in larger middle-market leasing transactions; in big-ticket leasing transactions; in complex leasing arrangements, such as tax-oriented leases; in large true and operating leases; and for the structuring of major financings. Personal visits are often called for because of the size and complexity of the transactions themselves, and because prospects who are entertaining the idea of arranging a lease for costly equipment generally want to meet the people they will be dealing with face-to-face. Although personal visits are commonly called for after opportunities to transact business have been identified, they are not as popular as telemarketing for initially soliciting prospects.

Personal sales calls are expensive and time-consuming, and they have a low probability of success in terms of a salesperson's ability to find sales opportunities through "cold" sales calls. Ten or fifteen years ago, it was customary for leasing salespeople to visit industrial parks, office complexes, and other areas with a concentration of commercial businesses and to knock on doors. At that time, however, leasing had not reached today's level of popularity, and leasing competitors were fewer in number and less sophisticated in their sales strategies. Because most leasing companies formerly used personal cold-calling as a sales strategy, prospects were not inundated with promotional material, direct mail, and telemarketing campaigns, and they were more likely to listen to what a visiting leasing salesperson had to say. Today, that is not the case. Leasing information is readily available and is distributed via mail, advertising, fax, and telephone.

Personal cold-calling has some other drawbacks too. Prospects are more inclined to entertain the idea of listening to a leasing sales presentation when they are actively engaged in acquiring equipment. When salespeople make unqualified personal calls, they have no idea whether a particular business is currently acquiring equipment. This means that even if salespeople are successful in obtaining an audience, their listeners may have no immediate need for leasing services.

Since personal cold-calling takes time, is expensive compared with other methods of reaching prospects, and is a totally unqualified method of selling, personal visitation should be limited to prospects that have been prescreened to determine that they are now, or soon will be, acquiring equipment.

Cold-calling on vendors, however, can make economic sense. Visiting vendor locations, branch offices, and sales outlets provides the opportunity to meet individual salespeople and sales management. Most vendors are willing to give visiting leasing salespeople an audience and will often listen to unsolicited leasing sales presentations. Nevertheless, leasing salespeople are generally better off arranging appointments in advance and doing some homework before the visit.

Whenever you visit a prospect personally, preparation for the meeting is critical. Because you are not at your own location, you must bring all the materials you need with you. If you normally use scripts and supporting information when you speak with prospects by phone, it is helpful to bring the same information with you when you visit. A good way to carry your sales presentation material, scripts, checklists, or any other information is to arrange the material in a binder or portfolio. This allows you to refer to needed information during your meeting, appearing organized and professional as you deliver your sales presentation.

Whatever method or combination of methods you use to solicit your prospects, the purpose of your solicitation is to identify the prospect's leasing needs.

Chapter 10

Stage 4—Identifying the Prospect's Needs

You identify a prospect's leasing needs by probing for information. Probing begins with the person you initially encounter when you contact a prospect for the first time. No matter how you perform your initial attempt to contact an unknown prospect, the first person you speak with at the prospect's place of business is probably not going to be the person you want to deal with. Typically, whether you are contacting a prospect by phone or in person, the first individual you encounter is a receptionist, secretary, administrative person, or someone else who is neither the decision maker nor the one responsible for the business's equipment acquisition plans. Your first objective, then, is to find out who is responsible for equipment acquisition.

The Decision-Making Process

Depending on the size and organizational structure of the prospect's business, a number of different people might be responsible for equipment acquisition decisions. In small privately owned and operated businesses, the owners ordinarily decide what equipment will be acquired, when it will be acquired, and how it will be paid for. Larger organizations, whether publicly or privately owned, generally separate the functions of the business into individual departments. In some departmentally structured organizations, equipment acquisition decisions are instituted by an individual within the department that needs the equipment itself, but the determination of how the equipment will be paid for is made by an individual within the accounting, finance, or budgeting department. In other departmentally structured businesses, financial decision makers control the entire equipment acquisition process. An equipment acquisition is rarely totally controlled by an individual within an operating department. Exceptions may occur, however, when a data processing manager has the authority to lease certain types of computer equipment, when a departmental employee can commit to a lease for small-ticket items up to a certain equipment cost, or when a departmental employee can commit to a short-term equipment rental up to a certain monthly rental charge.

Regardless of how many people are involved in the decision to acquire equipment or who they are, money is always a consideration.

The Budget

As a rule, large businesses establish a capital budget for each fiscal year. This budget determines how much money will be made available for equipment purchases. In some cases, the capital budget also allows for equipment leasing and financing and allocates funds to be used specifically for financing or leasing payments. It is also common for businesses to find that they need equipment that has not been projected in their capital budgets.

Many businesses establish departmental operating budgets in order to allocate the income and expenses specifically applicable to individual departments. If corporate capital budget funds are not sufficient to pay for needed equipment, or when there is an unexpected equipment requirement, funds can sometimes be made available from an individual departmental operating budget. Often, departmentally allocated funds permit equipment to be leased but not purchased, because the available funds are rarely sufficient to fully pay for costly equipment. When businesses lease equipment with funds from an operating budget, it's common for them to prefer true or operating lease structures. They want to arrange true or operating leases so that the lease payments can be treated as operating expenses. This way, the operating expense can be charged directly to the department that uses the leased equipment.

Because an individual business's internal budgeting and equipment acquisition process can be so complex, and because there is no standard way for businesses to make their equipment acquisition decisions, accuracy in your initial probing for information about who is responsible for making equipment acquisition decisions is critical. You must identify the authorized decision maker—and sometimes, more than one.

Outside Input

When you reach an authorized decision maker, it is a good practice to find out how the entire equipment acquisition process is conducted within the decision maker's particular business. You may find that the owner of a small business selects the equipment to be acquired, negotiates the equipment purchase price with the equipment supplier, and asks you to provide specific terms and conditions for a leasing transaction. A business owner's actions can lead you to believe that the owner makes a unilateral decision regarding your lease offering, and many times, that is precisely the case. Yet business owners frequently consult with others, such as outside accountants or attorneys, before making a final decision regarding a leasing transaction. If you aren't aware from the beginning that others may be involved in the decision-making process, you are subject to unpleasant surprises later on. The further you proceed into serious business discussions, the harder it is to adjust or amend what you have already proposed. The worst case is when a prospect's third-party consultant, whom you were unaware of, raises a last-minute question or problem that can't be resolved simply—or sometimes can't be resolved at all—after you have moved considerably far along in the leasing process.

The more you know about the specifics of the decision-making process, the better off you are.

Equipment Selection vs. Equipment Financing

In some businesses, the entire equipment shopping process is completed before the decision how to pay for it is made. This means that comparative methods of financing are not reviewed until after the equipment has been selected. In other businesses, the financing alternatives are reviewed before the equipment selection process begins, to determine whether the business can afford the acquisition. In still other businesses, the equipment selection process and the review of financing alternatives are conducted simultaneously. Therefore, when you are soliciting prospects, it is critical for you to learn as quickly as possible who initially decides that equipment will be acquired and who ultimately decides how payment for the equipment will be arranged. Often, these two functions—equipment selection and equipment financing—are separate, especially in businesses in which the equipment is a major concern to the individuals responsible for its operation. As a general rule, the more technical the equipment is, the more common it is for the individuals responsible for its operation to influence, or to actually determine, which equipment will be acquired. Pressroom managers, for example, strongly influence the selection of printing presses for printing companies; radiologists strongly influence the selection of x-ray units for hospitals and clinics; data processing managers influence the selection of computers and peripheral equipment for large businesses. However, an individual's ability to influence the equipment selection process and to ultimately decide what equipment will be acquired does not necessarily mean that the same individual decides how payment or financing will be arranged.

Although the primary focus of your solicitation is the individuals responsible for making financial decisions, you can't ignore the individuals who select the equipment. Quite often, especially in large businesses, people who use equipment shop for new items despite the fact that funds have not been allocated for the acquisition. Equipment users constantly research the market for newer, faster models that can help them be more productive. Equipment users also attend trade shows and demonstrations where they learn of advanced technology in the equipment types they use. What's more, equipment users are continually pursued by equipment sellers who inform them of new product introductions and try to convince them to add equipment or replace an existing model with a newer version.

Frequently, when equipment users believe that new or additional equipment should be acquired, they face barriers to the acquisition from others in their own organizations. Financial decision makers, who are responsible for a business's spending but are not responsible for the performance of equipment, often try to prohibit or delay equipment acquisitions that they think will stretch or encumber the business's capital budget. When financial decision makers are unable or unwilling to allocate funds for the outright purchase of equipment, leasing can often be the solution to obtaining the equipment.

But not all equipment users are familiar with the leasing solution, so you must educate them. In cases in which equipment users stimulate the leasing process, the user ordinarily submits a leasing proposal along with an internal requisition for the purchase of new equipment. This way, the user informs financial decision makers that leasing is available as an alternative to outright cash purchase.

If you are able to help equipment users by teaching them how to obtain equipment that costs more than capital budgets allow, and if you are able to help them prepare leasing requisitions for submission to financial decision makers, you gain several significant competitive advantages. You gain by providing a convenient acquisition alternative. You will also gain the advantage of an internal recommendation, by virtue of the equipment user's submission of your leasing information to financial decision makers. And you gain the advantage of potentially eliminating competitors, if your lease offering is attractive enough to the financial decision makers.

Additionally, when you assist equipment users by facilitating equipment acquisition, you are providing help that may not be available elsewhere. Equipment users are not necessarily financial experts, but they may be expected to justify the acquisition of equipment financially. That's where you come in. You can lend assistance by helping to write up a cost-justification analysis of the equipment and by demonstrating on paper how lease payments conserve cash, fit into operating budgets, and provide equipment that saves money or increases productivity today while being paid for in the future.

Part of your sales solicitation objective, therefore, is to obtain enough information about the internal operating functions of the business to enable you to determine how to proceed. If you don't touch all the bases within a prospect's business, you can waste significant amounts of time and perhaps lose the chance to close business. You may be dealing with the wrong people, or you may find out too late that there are other decision makers beyond those with whom you are dealing.

The smaller the businesses you solicit, the fewer decision makers there will ordinarily be. Because a business is small, however, does not mean that there is only one decision maker. In some partnerships, you may need to solicit two or more partners to determine whether any of them are contemplating an equipment acquisition. In professional practices, such as a medical or dental office, the practitioners may select professional equipment and an office manager may select business equipment. Many local manufacturing and service businesses are owner-operated; others are not. Soliciting a business's owner may reveal no plans for equipment additions, but soliciting the same business's operators can uncover a different plan.

The keys to successful prospecting are persistence and diligence when you solicit prospective customers so that you reach all the individuals who may decide on or influence the acquisition of equipment. When your prospect solicitation reveals a present or future equipment need, your next step is to identify specifically what equipment is needed.

The Stages of Equipment Acquisition

If you represent a general equipment leasing company, you may find that the prospects you solicit have various equipment needs that you can fulfill. As a generalist, you can provide leasing services to a wide variety of businesses. If, however, you represent a company that specializes in particular equipment types, lease structures, or end-user customer types, you must target your prospect solicitations more specifically. Regardless of your leasing capabilities, when you discover through your prospect solicitations that a business is presently acquiring equipment or will be in the foreseeable future, you must identify the acquisition needs of that particular prospect.

You can encounter several different circumstances when a prospect indicates that an equipment acquisition is currently taking place or soon will be. The prospect may be planning to shop for equipment; may be shopping currently; may have already selected the equipment but not yet ordered the item; may have already ordered the item but not yet finalized how to pay for it; or may have ordered the item and made plans for payment. The best circumstances for you are when prospects are in the process of obtaining equipment, especially if they have not yet decided how to pay for it. When prospects are currently ordering equipment or soon will be, that gives you enough time to plan and organize a well-thought-out sales strategy. You should also have the time to pace your sales process in a controlled fashion. However, when you encounter prospects that are farther along in the equipment acquisition process or have already ordered equipment, you must be prepared to perform quickly.

The most difficult sales circumstances are those in which you encounter a prospect that has not only ordered equipment but also made other plans for payment or financing. But as long as the equipment's cost has not actually been paid, you can still propose a leasing alternative. Prospects that are unaware of leasing's benefits or have not considered leasing for a particular acquisition, or those that intend to use a bank line of credit to pay for equipment or have simply decided to pay cash because it is expedient, can often be persuaded to lease equipment, even though the leasing alternative was suggested to them at the last minute.

Specific Equipment Information

Whatever situation your prospecting efforts disclose, you must obtain a complete and accurate description of the equipment to be acquired. If the prospect is acquiring more than one item of equipment, you must gather the same information for each item. The information you require is as follows:

1. The equipment type.
2. The equipment manufacturer.
3. The model type and/or model number (the serial number, if available).
4. Whether the equipment is new or used.
5. A listing of any additional features, accessories, software, connection cabling, peripheral equipment, initial and/or future supplies, or other items to be included in the equipment acquisition price.
6. A listing of any additional charges to be paid, such as delivery charges, transportation charges, transportation insurance, installation costs, operator training, installation/operating manuals.
7. The exact address where the equipment will be located.
8. Whether the site where the equipment will be located is owned, leased, or rented by the prospect. If the premises are leased or rented, the landlord must be identified, and details must be included indicating how long the lease or rental of the premises will remain in effect.
9. Whether the equipment attaches to the building in which it will be located or attaches to any other equipment, or whether the equipment can simply be removed.
10. What type of insurance coverage the prospect maintains in the event of casualty damage or loss of the equipment, including the name of the insurance carrier and the prospect's insurance policy number.
11. The exact name and type of the equipment supplier. (Is the equipment being purchased directly from the manufacturer, a distributor, a dealer, an agent, a manufacturer's

representative, or, in the case of used equipment, another end user?)

12. The address and phone number of the equipment supplier.
13. The name of the individual contact at the equipment supplier.
14. The exact terms of payment required by the equipment supplier.
15. A listing of any taxes (sales, use, state, county, city, personal property, other) applicable to the acquisition and to whom the taxes are payable.
16. Whether a purchase order has already been issued to the equipment supplier.
17. Whether any money, down payments, progress payments, or any other form of payment has already been made to the equipment supplier.
18. Whether any equipment has been traded in against the new equipment acquisition.
19. Whether the equipment is replacing existing equipment.
20. How any equipment to be replaced is or was financed.
21. Whether a discount of any type has been obtained from the equipment supplier against the equipment purchase.
22. How long the prospect anticipates using the equipment.
23. What specific function the equipment performs.
24. Why the equipment is being acquired.
25. The anticipated equipment delivery date.
26. The anticipated date on which the equipment will be accepted for use.

Obtaining the above information serves several different purposes. The first is simply that, sooner or later, you will need the information in order to propose, structure, and, ultimately, document the proper lease agreement for the prospect. The second purpose is to remind or illustrate to the prospect that an equipment acquisition is a complex undertaking that you can facilitate. Third, any one of the answers you receive from the prospect can trigger ideas for you to pursue because of your special expertise or capability when particular equipment acquisition conditions exist.

You must use some judgment when you ask the prospect about the acquisition, because your list of questions is long. Depending on your prospect's responsiveness to your inquiries and willingness to divulge information, you may decide to stage your questions over a period of time. In this case, if when the circumstances and your sales judgment indicate that you have the time to control the order and timing of your questions—that is, the equipment acquisition isn't imminent—you may decide to gather only the key information about an impending equipment acquistion. Key information generally includes the equipment type, cost, vendor, delivery date, projected use, and estimated useful life of the equipment. It also includes whether the equipment is new or used and whether there are any additional soft costs, such as software, delivery, or installation, or any other costs over and above the cost of the equipment itself. Time, however, is of the essence in every leasing sale, and you must always gather as much information as you can as quickly as possible. While you are probing for information, though, you should avoid appearing too pushy.

The Proposed Leasing Structure

The preliminary input you gather about the acquisition provides you with enough information to begin developing a proposed leasing structure. You can then present the structure as a preliminary lease quotation. If the prospect is satisfied with your proposed lease structure, you can move ahead with the rest of the leasing process. If, however, the prospect doesn't accept your proposal or wants you to present other alternatives or make adjustments, you can consider fine-tuning your offering. Fine-tuning or adjusting preliminary lease proposals, however, should be done only after you have obtained additional details about the acquisition.

Preliminary lease quotations are commonly called ballpark estimates and are used to give prospects a general idea of the lease term, the lease payments, and other terms and conditions of a proposed leasing transaction. Ballpark quotations are often requested by prospects that want to consider how a lease might be applicable to their needs or by prospects that want to "guesstimate" the costs of adding equipment through leasing. A key to eventual success in closing leases is to gather enough information to provide a reasonably accurate ballpark estimate. Despite the fact that estimates are, by definition, only approximations of what the terms of a final leasing transaction might be, you must be careful when giving ballpark quotes to prospects. It is not unusual for information discovered later about a prospect or a proposed transaction to rightfully preclude you from producing a leasing arrangement that is the same as or even reasonably close to the terms you originally quoted. Even when the circumstances clearly illustrate that the estimates stated in your ballpark quotation are undeliverable, prospects can sometimes become upset enough by your "misquotation" to seek leasing services elsewhere.

The Pitfalls

Because the successful completion of a leasing agreement is dependent on so many different circumstances regarding individual prospects themselves, and because so many outside factors can also influence a leasing transaction, diligence and care on your part are always required during the need-identification process. Leasing salespeople—regardless of their years of experience—often lay the groundwork for their own pitfalls.

Sometimes, salespeople create problems for themselves. Self-inflicted problems often arise when a salesperson confuses selling with accommodation, or when a salesperson uses an I-can-do-anything-you-want approach to the customer. The worst case is when a salesperson takes the prospect's side, urging his or her own organization to meet the prospect's demands, even though they are not warranted.

There are several reasons that these problem scenarios take place. First of all, sales is a tough business, and there are always competitors that a salesperson must outsell. Second, some salespeople fear that prospects might become upset if a pleasant, helpful sales-type person asks them to answer hard questions. And, last, but certainly not least, leasing salespeople sometimes go overboard in believing their own company's promotional material, advertising slogans, and public-relations information. Although it is true that leasing services are accommodative, flexible, convenient, competitively priced, user-friendly, quick, and simple to use, there is a significant difference between a salespersons' provision of an array of user-friendly services for a fair price and a salesperson's bending over backwards to give the services away.

When salespeople are not diligent in the need-identification process, they sometimes fall victim to "selective hearing." When they are probing for information from prospects about equipment acquisitions, selective hearing can cause them to hear only some things said by the prospect and not others. For example, a salesperson may hear only the equipment's cost, not its type. Costly equipment can mean that long lease terms are applicable, because some types of costly equipment can operate for a long time before becoming obsolete. If the equipment in question is a top-of-the-line standard machine tool or production machine, the leasing company is probably well protected against the equipment becoming obsolete; but if the equipment is actualy a state-of-the-art computer mainframe, the company's protection against obsolescence may not be good at all. A high probability of equipment devaluation over time generally precludes leasing companies from providing longer-term leases, because they don't want to risk having to repossess obsolete equipment. When salespeople hear only the cost and not the specific type of the equipment, there is a considerable chance that the salesperson may propose a lease term that doesn't apply to the equipment; a lease structure that doesn't apply to the equipment; or, in the worst case, a leasing structure that decreases the chances of obtaining credit approval for the prospective customer.

The same type of mistake can occur when a salesperson hears only the general type of equipment to be acquired and does not inquire as to the specific kind. For example, if a prospect indicates an interest in printing equipment, the salesperson may proceed as if the unit in question were a long-lived printing press, only to find out later that the acquisition is to be computerized typesetting equipment, which generally calls for different leasing terms and conditions because of its tendency toward obsolescence.

Credit analysts commonly ask salespeople why a prospect needs particular equipment. But for some reason, many salespeople don't ask prospects what purpose the new equipment will serve. A salesperson's failure to find out why a business needs additional equipment can delay the credit decision-making process or result in credit rejection. Had the information been available, the transaction might have been approved.

Perhaps salespeople neglect to ask relatively routine questions because of their desire to show the prospect how quickly they can perform. This is similar to the problem of selective hearing. Some salespeople stress the importance of performing speedily but ignore the importance of performing thoroughly. When leasing salespeople attempt to impress prospects with how simple and painless the leasing process can be by rushing through the need-identification process, they run the risk of failing to obtain the answers to critical questions and encountering fatal surprises when the information is finally obtained.

Another potential consequence of being too hasty in identifying prospects' needs is appearing unprofessional in the eyes of the prospect and in the eyes of one's own organization. This can happen when prospects express interest in arranging an equipment lease and rightfully expect the salesperson to manage the leasing process for them. But when a salesperson's desire to perform quickly results in an inadequate evaluation of the prospect's needs, or when haste causes the salesperson to neglect to obtain critical information, an unsatisfactory leasing arrangement will result. What's worse is that the salesperson's organization has reviewed and acted upon erroneous information. If the information submitted by the salesperson is incorrect or inadequate, the time spent by everyone involved in performing the evaluation is wasted. The salesperson, the organization, and the prospect have all lost time.

If the leasing contract that the salesperson ultimately presents is unsatisfactory to the prospect, and the dissatisfaction is the result of the salesperson's haste, neglect, or misunderstanding, the prospect rightfully becomes disturbed. The level of the prospect's disturbance generally depends on the closeness of the equipment's anticipated delivery date: The closer the equipment's impending delivery date, the more disturbed a dissatisfied prospect will be. In fact, if the prospect cannot make other arrangements to pay for the equipment, and there is no other source of financing available quickly enough to meet an equipment delivery deadline, the prospect may face the complete loss of the opportunity to acquire the equipment.

Even when leasing salespeople are able to correct errors caused by haste, and even when they are able to eventually provide a prospect with a satisfactory leasing arrangement, damage to the relationship has already been done. It is critical, therefore, for salespeople to ensure that they identify their prospects' needs accurately and adequately despite pressures created by time limitations.

When a prospect's needs have been properly and thoroughly identified, the next step in the sales process is the sales presentation itself.

Chapter 11

Stage 5—Making the Sales Presentation

A sales presentation is the description and demonstration of the products or services that you know or believe to apply to a particular prospect. Each step that you have taken to this point in the sales process has been designed to locate and identify those prospects that are most likely to need what you have to sell. When you were charting your personal prospecting plan—listing the products and services that your organization provides and its operating method—you prepared an inventory of items that you have for sale. Your sales presentation begins with your selecting the item or items that you believe are applicable to a particular prospect, based on your need-identification inquiries. Ordinarily, you deliver a sales presentation after the prospect has indicated that an equipment acquisition is or will be taking place, or when your prospecting data lead you to suspect that your services might apply to a particular prospect, although no specific need has been identified.

Presenting Your Organization and Yourself

Most often, your sales presentation includes some general information about leasing, some background or historical information about your company, and a description of the leasing products and services that your company provides. Depending on the type of prospect you are addressing and the type of equipment to be acquired, the introductory information about your company can be presented to highlight certain features that apply to the particular situation.

As a rule, businesspeople feel more comfortable conducting business with those they have something in common with. Therefore, it is a good practice to present information that establishes a common interest between you and your company and the prospect and his or her business early in your introductory comments. For example, you might say:

> "We have been leasing equipment to businesses in this area for twenty years."
> "We are specialists in leasing and financing hospital and medical equipment."
> "We lease all types of printing equipment."
> "We have financing available for high-technology businesses."
> "I am a member of your industry association."

Such statements serve to inform the prospect about what you do as well as establish a specific relationship with the prospect and his or her business.

When you are describing your organization, you should highlight the particular benefits that your organization can provide. If you represent a large, full-service general equipment lessor, for example, you might want to stress your company's size and financial capability when you are presenting to a major corporation. If you represent a national lessor, you might want to stress your ability to conduct business across the country when you are addressing prospects whose businesses are large or have many locations. If you represent a leasing broker, you might want to stress personalized service, which permits hands-on attention to local businesses. Throughout the presentation of your company description, you must select those items from your inventory that specifically meet the needs of individual prospects.

During the presentation, you must try to avoid "tripping" over features of your company that might disqualify you in the eyes of your prospect. If, for instance, you work for a small, local leasing broker, a representative of a major corporation might fear that your operation can't provide adequate services to meet his or her corporation's needs. In this case, if the resources exist, you can stress the relationships your company has with major banks and funding sources. Your capability to arrange a variety of leases and financings with many different types of qualified sources may, in fact, be an advantage to a major corporation. It's possible that, as a leasing broker, you may be able to arrange larger credit lines and provide a wider variety of services for a major company than any one leasing source could provide by itself, regardless of size.

Conversely, if you represent a large, full-service national lessor and stress your company's size and strength to smaller prospects, you might intimidate them. They may fear that they are too small to merit a major leasing company's concern. A smaller prospect's fear of large financial service providers is not always evident. Consequently, representatives of large leasing companies must be certain to make smaller prospects feel comfortable and to assure them that their business is important to the leasing company. One way of doing this is to demonstrate that the company has satisfied customers of the same size and type as the prospect's business. Another way to assuage doubts is to demonstrate that although the salesperson's company may be large, the salesperson is personally responsible for working with the prospect and values his or her business.

Whatever size prospects may be, they are all important, and a good method of enhancing a sales presentation is to illustrate third-party proofs of performance. Proofs of performance are endorsements, validations, or testimonials from customers supporting the claims and promises that salespeople present. They include letters, citations, recommendations, and other acknowledgments that have been sent to the salesperson or the salesperson's company and demonstrate customers' pleasure or satisfaction. Praise or acknowledgment that comes from customers and businesses in the same industry or of the same size as the prospect ordinarily carry the most weight in supporting a salesperson's claims.

In some cases, a salesperson may suggest that a prospect contact a satisfied customer directly. Naturally, the salesperson should obtain permission from the customer in question before suggesting the reference call. A written endorsement should also be preapproved by its writer before it is shown to prospects.

The best customer endorsements of all occur when a satisfied customer refers the salesperson to another prospect. Customer referrals usually eliminate much of the salesperson's work, because the salesperson receives information about the new prospect's decision makers from the existing customer. The salesperson's need to present his or her company's credentials is also lessened because, by virtue of the customer's referral, the credentials have already been basically established. Since referrals from satisfied customers are so valuable in identifying new sales opportunities and can significantly expedite the sales process, it is always a good idea to ask your satisfied customers whether they know anyone else who might also need your services.

Presenting the Benefits of Leasing

When you have satisfactorily established your company's credentials for a prospect, the next step in the sales presentation is to illustrate the benefits of leasing. There are two aspects to address: the general benefits the prospect can derive from using leasing as a financial tool, and the specific leasing benefits the prospect can derive by using your particular products and services.

General Benefits

What you have learned about the prospect so far can help ensure that you address only the aspects of equipment leasing that apply to the particular prospect and that you don't indicate leasing benefits that the prospect may not be able to gain. The general benefits of leasing include:

- 100 percent financing
- No down payments on the equipment's purchase price
- Off-balance-sheet financing
- Cash-flow maximization
- Cash or working capital conservation
- Preservation of existing bank lines of credit
- Possible tax savings
- Ability to overcome budget restrictions
- Avoidance of restrictive loan covenants
- Establishment of an alternative line of credit
- Individually tailored payment schedules
- Long-term financing
- Various purchase options
- Flexibility in lease structure
- Ability to upgrade or trade in equipment
- Protection against equipment obsolescence
- Protection against inflation

Not all these benefits apply to every prospect or to every type of equipment, however. Consequently, when you present the benefits of leasing, you must be careful to avoid highlighting *all* leasing benefits, and particularly avoid stressing leasing benefits that you know or suspect will not apply to a particular prospect's situation. If you know, for example, that you will be able to provide the prospect with only full-payout financing, you should not stress the fact that leasing offers off-balance-sheet financing. Full-payout finance leases can't be treated as off-balance-sheet financings for accounting purposes, and such leases don't necessarily provide any tax savings to the customer either.

You also have to defuse inquiries about leasing benefits that the prospect can't gain by explaining why the benefits are not available. There is usually a valid reason that certain benefits are not available, often because of the prospect's business or the equipment itself. In cases in which certain leasing benefits would or might be available to the prospect but your company can't provide them, you must be prepared to counter a prospect's questions with valid points to demonstrate why the alternative that you can provide is a better one.

Questions from prospects about leases that offer off-balance-sheet financing or preferential tax treatment, for example, arise fairly often. Although certain true or operating lease structures for certain types of equipment can provide off-balance-sheet financing or preferential tax treatment, these same leases can also result in the highest total cost. The lessee's high total cost to ultimately own the equipment is caused by the lease structures themselves. True or operating leases either provide no option for the lessee to acquire the equipment or, at best, include an option to purchase the equipment for its fair market value at the end of the lease term. If equipment will have a considerable value when the lease term expires and the customer plans to purchase the equipment, the total sum of the payments paid during the lease term, plus the equipment's residual value, may add up to more than the total cost of a full-payout lease. Full-payout leases, although typically having higher lease payments than true or operating leases, permit the lessee to purchase the equipment for a "bargain" price that may be as low as one dollar.

It is a good practice to calculate the total costs of true or operating leases and compare them against the total costs of a finance lease to determine how much the prospect will have to pay to eventually own the equipment. Knowing the prospect's total cost to eventually acquire the leased equipment can be useful when a prospect is considering the merits of different lease structures. When you know the full cost to eventually own the equipment for different lease types (when you can offer a variety of lease types) and you sense that the prospect is likely to select the lease type that offers the lowest total cost to acquire the equipment, you will be able to show the prospect exactly what the total cost of acquisition will be for each lease type.

Leasing salespeople don't always bother to add up and compare total leasing costs, concentrating instead on the size of the payments or the purchase option amount as the only factors to be considered. Failure to at least determine the total cost of various types of leases, even if the information will not necessarily be presented to the prospect, precludes the salesperson from having valuable information available should it become necessary.

Calculating the total cost of eventual equipment acquisition is especially important if you are unable to provide a true or operating lease but can provide a finance lease. Unless the prospect insists on employing a true or operating lease or can't use any other type of lease structure, you can point out the comparative costs of eventual equipment acquisition to the prospect. Ordinarily, the total finance lease costs should be lower than total costs of the true or operating lease in respect to eventual equipment ownership. Before you address the total cost issue with a prospect, it's a good idea to gather as much information as possible about the competitive alternatives so that you can present a valid comparison.

You won't always succeed in winning a prospect over to a finance lease with an equipment acquisition cost comparison, because there are other aspects of alternative lease structures that the prospect will probably consider. True and operating leases, for example, are treated differently for accounting and tax purposes than are finance leases. Furthermore, the payments called for in a true or operating lease may be significantly lower than those in a finance lease, thereby permitting the prospect to gain some cash-flow advantages during the lease term. If, however, a prospect looks only at the total cost of one lease structure versus another, a finance lease may prove to be the best alternative for eventually purchasing the equipment.

Certainly, there are many lease structures available, and many leasing companies offer a wide variety of leasing types from which prospects can choose. There may be circumstances within a prospect's business that cause one lease structure to be more favorable than another. There will be other circumstances when, unless you can provide a particular lease structure, you can't satisfy the prospect's requirements. The point is that unless you are precluded from providing what the prospect needs, you must be certain to direct your prospect's interest to the benefits of leasing that you can deliver.

There are some leasing benefits that apply to virtually all businesses, and all leases provide these benefits. Ordinarily, these benefits are the ones that most businesses need.

Leasing vs. Cash Purchase

All leases conserve capital. By simple virtue of the fact that leases provide term financing—whether the lease term is six months or many years—the customer does not have to pay cash for the full purchase price of the equipment. The customer's ability to conserve capital may be the most important benefit of leasing. Cash is a valuable asset to any business. Available cash permits a business to pay its bills, obtain discounts from suppliers, hire employees, purchase inventory, advertise, promote sales, expand, pay the costs of research and development of new products, reserve for emergencies, and perhaps even acquire other businesses. Generating cash creates a direct cost to a business, however, and spending cash involves hidden costs.

The most common way for a commercial business to obtain cash is to earn it. A business generates its cash from the income earned in its operation, and the business must pay taxes on the income that it earns. If, for example, a business pays 50 percent in combined taxes (federal and state income taxes, alternative minimum taxes, county taxes, city taxes, and whatever other taxes are applicable), the business must earn two dollars in order to keep one dollar. Therefore, for every dollar that the business spends on equipment, it must earn two dollars to replace the cash spent.

The total tax obligations of businesses vary, and many businesses pay far less than 50 percent of their revenue in taxes. Tax liability depends on the location, size, and organization of the business. States, counties, and even municipalities assess different types of taxes and establish different tax rates. It is a good idea to familiarize yourself with what taxes apply where you do business. When you are familiar with your prospect's tax obligations, you have the ammunition available to demonstrate the impact of taxes as a cost of capital when those prospects are considering paying cash for equipment.

Once spent, cash is no longer available to be used for business opportunities that might present themselves. Opportunities might include the ability to take advantage of inventory promotions offered by suppliers, hire additional employees, introduce new products, expand the business, add more space, relocate, purchase another business, or cover the cost of any other expenditure that could help the business. Available cash also permits a business to react quickly when events occur that would otherwise require borrowing money.

Businesses can also raise cash in other ways aside from earning the money. Some businesses sell equity to private investors or in the public market or raise capital by issuing bonds, debentures, or other debt instruments. Here too, however, the cash raised by the business is not free of cost. Certainly, leasing is not always the least expensive nor always the best way to acquire equipment, and each prospect's situation must be evaluated individually to compare the costs of financing. But when businesses borrow capital for equipment acquisition, all the costs of borrowing must be considered.

Leasing vs. Bank Borrowing

Another leasing benefit that applies to virtually all businesses relates to the merits of leasing versus bank borrowing for the acquisition of equipment. Next to its own cash, a business's most ready source of capital is the money that can be borrowed from banks. Banks lend money to their customers in two basic ways: secured loans or unsecured loans. Secured loans are collateralized by the business's ability to repay and by a specific lien against, or establishment of, the lender's interest in a particular asset or group of assets owned by the borrower. Unsecured loans are advanced only against the borrower's ability to repay.

When businesses have arranged unsecured lines of credit with a bank, the funds are generally available to the business at any time. The immediate availability of the funds provides the business with the freedom to use the funds whenever and for whatever purpose the business chooses. Aside from the additional cost attributable to the loan, a business is in essentially the same position as if it had had the borrowed cash on hand. Consequently, unsecured bank lines of credit are a valuable and expedient resource by which businesses can obtain cash for almost any purpose. Unsecured lines of credit provide the insurance of having funds available to take advantage of opportunities or to be used in emergencies. But if businesses use unsecured bank lines of credit to acquire equipment or any other fixed asset, the freedom and flexibility in borrowing are gone. Leasing keeps a business's unsecured bank lines of credit open and available for other purposes.

A business's ability to borrow from banks on a secured basis can also provide some flexibility in comparison to other types of secured borrowing. Banks are not necessarily expert in the relative value of one asset versus another, and they don't want to take all the risks of repossessing and reselling assets in the event that a borrower defaults on a loan agreement. In order to protect themselves against the potential loss that might be incurred should a borrower default, banks typically lend a lower amount than the secured assets are worth. (Other assets that a business can pledge as security for bank loans include accounts receivable, inventory, and marketable securities, for example.) Although this means that the borrower may not be able to borrow the full value of assets pledged as collateral, a substantial amount of the collateral's value can be borrowed. A business that has the ability to arrange secured loans with a bank has the insurance of available funds for a variety of purposes. Once a secured line of credit has been used, however, the funds are no longer available until the loans have been paid back.

Leasing provides specific equipment to a business and does not affect the business's existing lines of credit or the other assets possessed by the business. In this way, leasing provides a business with an additional line of credit for the acquisition of equipment and leaves open other lines of credit for other purposes. The conclusion, therefore, is that a borrower's secured and unsecured bank lines of credit provide the borrower with the ability to obtain funds quickly when needed and protect against the borrower's being caught short of funds in emergencies. However, once the funds have been borrowed, the protection is gone.

Leased Equipment Pays for Itself

A third benefit of leasing that applies to virtually all businesses is leasing's ability to permit the customer to pay for equipment as it performs. When cash is spent to acquire equipment, the entire cost of the purchase is paid out immediately. Long-term lease payments are small percentages of the equipment's cost, paid periodically over the term of the lease. Most businesses acquire equipment to earn or to save money. New production equipment, for example, is acquired to produce new or more products, which a business will sell to earn additional income. Automation, such as a computer system, ordinarily saves a business money by reducing expenses. When cash is used to acquire equipment, the money is spent today, but the additional income or savings are gained in the future. Leasing permits a business to spread the cost of equipment acquisition over the period in which the equipment operates, thereby allowing the equipment to pay for itself.

Beyond the general benefits that apply to most businesses, there are additional advantages of leasing that ordinarily apply only in particular circumstances.

Specific Benefits

When you have completed your general description of leasing's benefits, you have arrived at the stage of your sales presentation where you present the specific leasing products and services that you have to offer. You must now focus your sales presentation on the products and services that apply to the prospect. Here again, you must use what you already know about the prospect to guide you in your presentation. If you simply present an array of leasing services to a particular prospect without regard to what you know about him or her, it is possible that you will present products or services that don't apply to the prospect's needs or that the prospect is not qualified to obtain.

It's common, for example, for a leasing salesperson to get carried away while describing the ability of his or her organization to arrange a wide variety of different types of leasing structures, provide a wide variety of value-added services, or be flexible in accommodating a prospect's requirements. What's more, some salespeople believe that the best way to demonstrate how extensive their services are and to impress the prospect is to rattle off an unqualified list of available products and services. Several problems can be created, though, when a salesperson presents a prospect with an unedited list of alternatives from which to select.

You must remember that not all prospects are able to meet the requirements called for by all lease structures, and not all prospects will measure up to the criteria established by your organization for users of some of its leasing services. When you present an unqualified list of available leasing products and services, prospects may select an alternative for which they are unqualified. They may select an alternative that doesn't apply to the equipment being acquired. Or they may choose products or services that are wrong for a particular situation. When you present specific leasing products and services, you must select only one, or perhaps two or three, of the alternatives available from your inventory list.

Focusing Your Lease Offering

Your initial presentation of a limited number of alternatives begins to lead your discussion with the prospect in a particular direction. Limiting the alternatives in the beginning also tends to reduce the possibility of confusion or misunderstanding on the prospect's part. It is important that you suggest lease alternatives methodically—after making some preliminary decisions about what type of lease you think will suit a particular prospect best, what type of lease the particular prospect can qualify for, what type of lease the equipment can qualify for, and what type of lease you can deliver under the particular circumstances.

If your original suggestions are not accepted by the customer, you commence a leasing negotiation. Your position in the negotiation is bounded by your ability to deliver only those leasing products and services provided by your company and by your company's operating guidelines for customer acceptance. Your objective in the lease negotiation is to satisfy your prospect's needs while remaining within your boundaries.

One of your advantages in a leasing negotiation is that you ordinarily have enough flexibility in leasing products and services to satisfy the needs of most prospects. The exception is leasing salespeople whose services are so specialized that they apply to only certain types of equipment, certain types of customers, or both. But if you have a lot of flexibility in the leasing alternatives you can provide, you can begin negotiating with your prospect by offering a leasing suggestion and then modifying or changing your suggestion later on, if necessary.

Modifying Your Lease Offering

The need to modify your initial leasing suggestion is a result of your prospect's negative reaction. Any changes in or additions to your initial offering need not be drastic, however. You might, for example, suggest that a three-year finance lease is the appropriate leasing structure for the type of equipment the prospect is acquiring. If the prospect then indicates that the proposed lease payments are too high, you don't have to introduce an entirely different type of lease structure. There are several ways to reduce the size of the payments. One way would be to employ a true lease structure as an alternative to a finance lease structure, because true lease payments are generally lower. If, however, a true lease structure would be less desirable to your company because of the equipment in question, your suggested alternative might expose you to the possible rejection of the transaction by your company. You might be able to satisfy the prospect's desire for lower lease payments by extending the lease term to four or five years while still providing a finance lease. You might also suggest a lease with quarterly payments, which reduces the payment size by accelerating the payment schedule, or even suggest a prepaid purchase option or down payment. You do not, however, have to modify your suggestion by immediately lowering the price or including extra benefits at no additional cost to the prospect. When prospects indicate that an alternative is too expensive, they are not necessarily stating that the price is unfair, but merely that it is too costly for their particular circumstances.

When prospects ask price or structural questions about your leasing suggestions, your objective is to find out why the prospect raised the question. Some salespeople weaken their own negotiating positions immediately by intimating that they can, or actually will, reduce the price simply because a prospect hesitates or implies that leasing payments are higher than expected. The best way to respond to prospects who react negatively is to clearly establish and justify why you suggested a particular alternative in the first place.

If you have done a thorough job of identifying the characteristics typical of the prospect you are addressing, and if you have selected the prospect because of the prospect's business type, equipment needs, and demographic criteria, your leasing alternatives should already be matched to the prospect's needs. Your leasing inventory itself is composed of leasing alternatives that have been designed for businesses that are similar to your prospect's business and whose needs are similar to your prospect's needs. You can now take what you know about the prospect's business in general, combined with what you have learned about the particular prospect, and use that information to support your leasing suggestions. For example, if you are presenting a finance lease structure to a small business and detect hesitation on the prospect's part, you might inform the prospect that you suggested a finance lease because of the business's size. Although some lease structures might offer lower payments, they would require a large purchase option at the end of the lease term. Leasing companies are not always willing to bear both the risk of leasing equipment whose full cost will not be repaid during the initial lease term and the credit risk inherent in small businesses. If creditworthiness is a potential problem, as it can be when dealing with small businesses, one way to reduce lease payments and to offer your company a more palatable transaction is to have the prospect prepay a purchase option or remit a down payment in the amount of 10, 15, or 20 percent of the equipment cost.

Conversely, if you have suggested a true or operating lease for a large business and learn that your prospect is concerned about the possibility of a large purchase option price at the end of the lease term, you have to be certain that your prospect understands how the leasing structure functions. Ordinarily, large businesses lease equipment because they want to use operating budget funds to pay for the leasing expenditure. You must ensure that your prospect understands that high purchase option prices are inherent in true and operating leases because of the criteria that qualify those leasing structures for advantageous accounting treatment. In effect, the prospect can't have it both ways—by treating an equipment lease as an operating expense and paying a minimal option price to purchase the equipment.

Unless you are limited by the services your company provides or restricted to particular prospect and equipment types, you will encounter a wide variety of leasing needs among the prospects you contact. Because leasing is such a flexible financial tool, however, you should be able to fulfill a significant number of the leasing needs you encounter. Much of leasing's flexibility derives from its ability to be adapted to the customer's financial situation. Quite often, the customer's financial requirements boil down to acquiring equipment in such a way that the cost incurred or the leasing payments fit the customer's budget. There are many ways to structure leasing transactions to meet the customer's needs.

Lease Structuring by Management

Your degree of flexibility in lease structuring depends on your organization's policies regarding how and by whom transactions can be formulated. In some leasing organizations, the formulation of leasing structures can be conducted only at the senior or middle management level, and salespeople are not authorized to adjust or modify the leasing structures prescribed by management. Most often, management adjusts leasing structures from time to time in order to adapt the structures to changes in the money market or other economic conditions, or when the managers believe that the circumstances of an individual leasing situation call for an adjustment.

Differences in transaction size, lease type, and even customer quality can be accommodated by management's establishment of a variety of leasing plans. This can be achieved by putting alternative lease term periods, equipment cost ranges, and purchase options into separate categories. By categorizing its lease structures, a company can provide considerable flexibility in its lease offerings while still maintaining its pricing policy objectives. Although the rates, terms, and conditions for leasing transactions are predetermined by management, a selection of leasing alternatives is available. A prospect may still choose a particular lease term, a particular end-of-term option for purchasing the equipment, and, in some cases, the number and type of advance payments (if any are required).

Managerially established standards for leasing rates, terms, and conditions are common in small-ticket leasing. The low cost of the equipment in a typical small-ticket lease reduces or eliminates the need to structure leasing transactions individually.

Rate Charts

The most common way for a small-ticket leasing company to furnish its salespeople with current rates, terms, and conditions is to provide them with cards, sheets, or charts that contain the company's standard leasing plans. Many leasing companies also provide pricing information for equipment vendors in a similar manner so that vendors can quote leasing prices to prospective customers.

The information contained in rate charts is based on the categories that the leasing company uses as its standard rates, terms, and conditions for various types of leasing transactions. The rate chart is laid out in a matrix format (Exhibit 4). Each of the vertical columns in the matrix is headed by a particular lease term category (e.g., 12 months, 24 months, 36 months); the various equipment cost range categories are listed down the left side of the matrix. The rate factor is found by selecting the appropriate lease terms and equipment cost range from those displayed; the rate factor is located in the box where the lease term column and equipment cost range row meet. The monthly lease payment is then calculated by multiplying the actual cost of the equipment to be leased by the applicable rate factor.

The rate chart also contains any additional terms and conditions for various lease structures, including the number of advance pay-

Exhibit 4. Rate chart: monthly lease payment calculator.

	Lease Term			
Equipment Cost	24 Months	36 Months	48 Months	60 Months
$0000-0000	.0000	.0000	.0000	.0000
$0000-0000	.0000	.0000	.0000	.0000
$0000-0000	.0000	.0000	.0000	.0000
$0000-0000	.0000	.0000	.0000	.0000
$0000-0000	.0000	.0000	.0000	.0000
$0000-0000	.0000	.0000	.0000	.0000
$0000 plus	.0000	.0000	.0000	.0000

ments required (if any) and the prospect's purchase options. A leasing company can prepare an individual rate chart for each type of leasing structure offered. Salespeople then use the rate charts to determine the lease payments, purchase options, and any other criteria that apply to the various types of leasing transactions.

Rate Factors

The most common way for leasing companies to establish standard lease payment calculations is by formulating rate factors. A lease rate factor is a percentage of the equipment's cost, applicable to the leasing rate and term over which the equipment will be leased. This percentage, when multiplied by the equipment's cost, results in the lease payment. A rate factor also takes into consideration any other criteria that are applicable to the specific lease structure, such as the number of advance lease payments, the amount of any security deposits, and the amount and type of purchase options (if any). Rate factors are expressed as decimals, representing the equipment's cost per period of the leasing transaction calculated to as many places as necessary.

Leasing companies use rate factors to calculate lease payments because they are simple to work with and provide a constant method of deriving a lease payment, even though the cost of equipment may vary. Rate factors generally apply to a range of equipment costs (e.g., $15,000–$25,000), and the same rate factor can be applied to any equipment cost within that range. Therefore, if the rate factor applicable to a sixty-month lease for equipment costing $25,000 is .0250, the lease payment can be calculated by multiplying $25,000 by .0250, for a payment of $625 a month. If the equipment cost were to change, let's say to $23,198, the .0250 rate factor would still be appropriate because the cost is still within the $15,000–$25,000 range. Multiplying $23,198 × .0250 produces a new lease payment—$579.95 a month—quickly and simply.

Lease Structuring by Salespeople

Not all leasing companies prescribe their exact rates, terms, and conditions. Some leasing organizations establish certain criteria and allow salespeople to formulate lease structures within those guidelines. Leasing company criteria for formulating lease structures generally include the establishment of minimum rates and/or yields and guidelines for advance payment minimums, purchase options, lease terms, and equipment cost ranges.

The structuring of leasing transactions by salespeople is more common in upper middle-market and big-ticket leasing, because such leasing transactions must often be individually tailored. In order to be able to do that, however, salespeople must first have a thorough understanding of the financial formulations of leasing and how the components of a leasing transaction affect one another.

Interaction of Lease Components

In an example used earlier, it was pointed out that one way to reduce the size of lease payments is simply to provide a longer lease term. Another way to adjust payment size is to obtain some sort of prepayment from the customer, such as a prepaid purchase option or a down payment. Still another way to reduce the size of lease payments is to include or increase the size of an option to purchase the equipment. Therefore, by adjusting one or more individual components of a leasing structure, salespeople can create different lease payments without changing the rate or yield of a leasing transaction.

The rate in an equipment leasing transaction is the price charged to the customer. The yield of an equipment lease is the total financial return earned by the lessor, less the cost of the equipment to be leased and any other expenses incurred in the transaction by the lessor, expressed as a rate of interest. The yield is a function of six things:

1. The number of lease payments
2. The value of the lease payments themselves
3. The value of a purchase option (if any)
4. The value of any advance payments, down payments, prepayments, or security deposits of any kind received from the customer
5. The value of any discounts to the lessor (if any) to be subtracted from the purchase price of the equipment
6. The value of any other income received by the lessor as part of the leasing transaction

Present-Value Theory

Leasing rates and yields are generally calculated by determining the present value of all the components of a leasing transaction. A present-value calculation determines the value of money today (the value of the money paid to a vendor for equipment) and the value of the dollars to be collected in the future (the payments and/or purchase option received from a customer) using a particular rate of interest. Present value is the most commonly used method of calculating lease payments, lease rates, and lease yields. In order to calculate a lease payment (net of any taxes or other charges) using the present-value method, you must know:

1. *The lease term.* The number of payment periods—weeks, months, quarters, years.

2. *The sum of any amounts to be received from the customer in advance.* The number and amount of any advance payments, nonrefundable security deposits, prepaid options, or down payments, for example.

3. *The rate to be used for calculation purposes.* This rate can be the leasing rate that will be charged to customer, the rate that the lessor pays for funds, or some other rate, depending on the purpose of the calculation. The rate must also be consistent with the number of payment periods in the leasing transaction. For example, if you are calculating a monthly lease payment, you must use a monthly rate for calculation purposes; if you are calculating an annual lease payment, you must use an annual rate for calculation purposes; and so on.

4. *The present value of the amount to be financed, plus the amount to be paid for any other expenses.* This amount is generally the actual net price paid by the lessor to acquire the equipment.

5. *The future value of the equipment.* This is the amount that will be paid by the customer to acquire the equipment at the end of the lease term or the estimated value of the equipment's future worth at the end of the lease term, if the final purchase price is not known today.

Adjusting the Lease Components

Since rates and yields are based on the values of the components that make up a leasing transaction, changing the value of any one component changes the values of others as well. If, for example, you determined the payment amount in a leasing transaction calculated at a particular rate and then wanted to reduce the size of the payment, you could:

1. Lengthen the lease term.
2. Increase the amount to be prepaid by adding advance payments, a down payment, or a prepaid purchase option.
3. Reduce the amount to be paid for the equipment.
4. Increase the amount of the purchase option.
5. Decrease the leasing rate.

It is this ability to change the values of the components in a leasing structure that permits leasing companies to design leases that not only meet the needs of the customer but also meet the criteria of the leasing company. In fact, the values of five of the six leasing components can be changed without the company having to reduce its leasing rate.

Example of the Five Components of a Leasing Transaction

1. The lease term is 36 months.
2. The lease rate charged to the customer is 16 percent.
3. No advance payments of any kind are to be received from the customer, and the lease payments are due at the end of the month (in arrears).
4. The equipment cost is $10,000.
5. The purchase option amount is $1.

In this example, the lease payment, calculated by the present-value method, is $351.57 a month.

This same leasing transaction is calculated seven different ways to come up with seven different lease payments, while the equipment cost and leasing rate remain the same:

1. If you change the lease term to 48 months, the payment becomes $283.40.
2. If you change the lease term to 60 months, the payment becomes $243.18.
3. If you leave all the other components of the leasing transaction the same but require the payments to be made at the beginning of the month (in advance), the payment becomes $346.94.
4. If you leave all the other components of the leasing transaction the same but require an additional payment to be made in advance (that is, you will receive the first and the last payments in advance), the lease payment becomes $342.54.
5. If you leave all the other components of the leasing transaction the same but require two additional payments to be made in advance (that is, you will receive the first and the last two payments in advance), the lease payment becomes $338.33.
6. If you leave all the other components of the leasing transaction the same but change the purchase option from $1 to 5 percent of the equipment cost, the lease payment becomes $340.66.
7. If you leave all the other components of the leasing transaction the same but change the purchase option from $1 to 10 percent of the equipment cost, the lease payment becomes $329.75.

The calculations themselves are not the important issue; they are simply financial arithmetic. The purpose of the above example is to illustrate how much flexibility can be gained by adjusting the various components in a leasing structure, and how wide a variety of leasing solutions can be offered as a result. Theoretically, there are an infinite number of structures that can be created for any given leasing situation. The only limitations are the criteria established by a leasing company as to the minimum and maximum values that can be assigned to any leasing component.

Lease Payment Calculation Tools

You can calculate lease payments on a financial calculator, such as the Texas Instruments Business Manager or MBA models and the Hewlett-Packard model 12C, 17B, or 19B. You can use printed residual rate tables such as those produced by Financial Publishing Company of Boston, Massachusetts, to select leasing structures, or you can use computer programs that are designed to formulate leasing structures.

If you structure leasing transactions, your leasing arithmetic must be correct and accurate. However, the most important aspect of the numbers in leasing isn't necessarily your ability to calculate them. With some training and experience, virtually any salesperson can input numbers into a financial calculator or a computer program or look the numbers up in a rate table. The most important aspect of leasing arithmetic is how well you understand the theory behind the arithmetic. Your ability to preserve the rate and yield in a leasing structure by adjusting the value of one or more other components permits you to design leases that meet a wide variety of prospective customers' needs.

Salable Lease Structures

Although the lease structurer can adjust the size of lease payments by assigning more or less value to the other components in the structure, what must also be considered is that changing any leasing component may change the basic structure of the leasing transaction itself. The structure that results may not be salable to the prospect or acceptable to the leasing organization. For example, if a prospect indicates that a proposed three-year lease term results in payments that are too high, the salesperson could extend the lease term to five years in order to lower the payments and maintain the lease rate. But with a five-year lease term, the equipment and perhaps the credit condition of the prospect become much more significant aspects of the leasing transaction. Most leasing companies agree that almost any type of equipment can be leased for three years, but many might be concerned about leasing certain types of equipment for five years. Therefore, despite the fact that your financial calculator or rate chart can help you provide prospects with more attractive leasing structures, you must be certain that the alternatives you provide are acceptable to your company.

Most often, your primary objective in designing a lease structure is to achieve a desired rate or yield. However, a properly designed lease structure must also apply to both the equipment and the customer. You must ensure that the values you assign to the individual components that make up the structure do not result in leasing transactions that are unsalable to the customer or unacceptable to your own organization.

Lease Structure Pitfalls

Problems in lease structure design generally occur because of the structurer's desire to offer attractive lease payments and a minimal number of advance payments while producing rates or yields that meet company objectives. Low lease payments are generally strived for so that the lease appears competitive in the market and compares favorably with other financing alternatives. Efforts to minimize any type of advance payment usually stem from salespeople's concern about customer objections to paying more than a small sum of money at the beginning of the lease.

When lease structures focus on minimizing both lease payments and front-end advances from the customer, the relative values of four lease components are immediately reduced as to their ability to contribute to the rate or yield. The lease payments and advance payments can't contribute any more to the rate or yield than the values assigned to them by the lease structurer; the rate or yield is predetermined because it is the targeted return from the lease on which the lease structure calculation is based; and the cost of the equipment itself is predetermined. The only remaining components that can help reach a desired rate or yield, because their values have not yet been determined, are the lease term and the residual value of the equipment (the equipment's value at the end of the lease term).

In lease structure calculation, a lease term can be determined by formulating the assigned values of the lease payment and advance payment amounts, the equipment cost, the leasing rate, and the residual value of the equipment and then solving for the lease term. Depending on the values assigned to each of the known leasing components and the desired rate or yield to be earned, the calculation could produce an acceptable lease term. If, however, the values assigned to the known leasing components are too low, the resulting lease term might be too long. When lease rate calculations produce lease terms that are too long, the residual value of the equipment can be adjusted. By increasing the residual value, the term of a lease can be shortened; the additional residual value compensates for the absent payments.

The rub is that when the lease term and/or the residual value of equipment is increased to cover shortages in yield or rate because the values assigned to other leasing components are too low, the resulting structure may be unacceptable. The lease term may be too long, or residual value may be too high for the equipment in question; the structure may be unacceptable because company policy dictates that lease terms and residuals cannot exceed certain limits; or the structure may simply be unsalable to the customer.

But even when lease structures are acceptable to both the leasing company and the prospect, there can be hidden pitfalls that result from the emphasis placed on longer lease terms and/or higher residual values. The most prevalent pitfall is a leasing application being denied because a particular prospect's financial condition precludes a longer lease term or a higher purchase option value. Specific equipment types might preclude either a longer lease term or a higher residual. Still another pitfall involves a prospect that wishes to use the same lease structure to lease more than one type of equipment—some of which is acceptable for a longer lease term and/or higher residual treatment and some of which is not. In other cases, there may be add-on or ancillary equipment that doesn't qualify for a longer lease term or higher residual value assessment.

One way to satisfy prospects that are acquiring equipment that includes unqualified accessories or attachments is to "blend" the lease payment. Blending a lease payment can be accomplished by calculating a residual-based lease payment for the qualified equipment and then calculating a full-payout lease payment for the nonqualified items. The two lease payments can then be added together to form a single lease payment. Although blending lease payments does not result in a total payment that is as low as one applicable to fully qualified equipment, a blended lease payment may be acceptable to the prospect.

Anticipating Long-Term Lease Structure Problems

Longer lease terms and higher residual assessments can also cause problems over the long haul.

Many customers lease equipment today that will be traded in or upgraded during the original lease term, but all leasing structure calculations assume that the total value assigned to each of the components will eventually be collected. In order for a leasing company to earn the rate or yield established in a leasing structure, all the frontend payments, the lease payments, the residual value assigned to the equipment, and any other income originally projected to be earned from the lease must be collected. Consequently, if a customer wishes to terminate an agreement early in order to acquire new or upgraded equipment, the customer must fully satisfy any unpaid balance due on the existing lease. Most often, the balance consists of the future lease payments applicable to the period between the early termination date and the original lease expiration date (plus any unpaid charges, such as late fees). If, however, there is a residual value included in the lease that was to be paid by the customer at the end of the lease term, the residual value must also be paid upon early lease termination—even if the customer had an option to purchase the equipment at the end of the original lease term but was not required to do so. This is the case because in an upgrade or trade-in situation, the original equipment is no longer available to the lessor; it is returned to either the original vendor or another vendor, whichever is providing the upgraded equipment.

Since a leasing company must collect the total income that was anticipated to be earned from a lease, longer lease terms and high residual values translate into high buy-out costs for a customer that wants to upgrade equipment before a lease term expires. A leasing company's willingness to accommodate a customer by permitting an early buy-out of an existing lease may be overshadowed by the high cost. In fact, high buy-out costs may actually dissuade customers from upgrading equipment, and the leasing salesperson, the leasing company, and the vendor all lose the opportunity to close a new sale.

Salespeople have to explain to prospects and vendors exactly how the arithmetic of a lease buy-out works. After the numbers have been explained, a prospect may decide to accept higher lease payments rather than being precluded from acquiring upgraded equipment later on. Vendors that are aware of the hidden costs of equipment upgrades may choose to work with informed leasing salespeople to help design programs that are structured with future equipment sales in mind. But even when low front-end cost is the key issue for prospects or vendors, the advance warning about potential pitfalls should help defuse any future disappointment.

Competitive Lease Structures

At times, especially in highly competitive situations, it may be necessary to reduce payment size or make front-end adjustments.

At other times, however, price accommodation requests from prospects or vendors can be handled in other ways. Salespeople must take a broad look at lease pricing if they are to meet the rate and yield objectives of their own organizations and satisfy the desires of their prospective customers.

If a leasing salesperson has done an effective job in matching his or her inventory of products and services to the typical needs of the prospects he or she solicits, and if the needs of those prospects have been properly identified before a salesperson quotes the rates, terms, and conditions for doing business, the salesperson's pricing should fit the prospect's budget and the prospect's expectations. Most often, when salespeople find that they are not price competitive, it turns out that they are either competing against a type of leasing company that is different from their own or soliciting prospects they have not properly qualified.

Leasing Company Types

Significant price discrepancies may exist between general equipment leasing companies and leasing specialists. Leasing specialists often allow for residual values that are significantly higher than those that a generalist can reasonably assess. Specialists understand the equipment they lease and the specific equipment market; they themselves may be buyers and sellers of the equipment they offer for lease. A leasing generalist might be taking a huge risk in assessing a sufficient residual value to equal or better the lease payments offered by a specialist, but the specialist may be taking minimal or no risk.

Captive leasing companies also can have significant pricing advantages over competing lessors. Captive leasing operations may buy equipment at a discount from the parent company, and they have a built-in facility to remarket returned equipment. They are sometimes financially subsidized by the parent. Leasing salespeople who find significant price discrepancies between their offerings and those of a captive may be competing against the captive's ability to assume high residual values for equipment, its internally negotiated equipment pricing arrangement with its parent, and other related advantages that an outsider can't effectively compete with. Furthermore, some captive leasing companies are viewed by their parents as being in the business of facilitating the parent's equipment sales, not as stand-alone profit centers. When a captive leasing company is treated by its parent as an adjunct to the parent's business, it may not have to earn the same margin of income as the competition.

Master Leases

Another situation in which it is difficult to compete is when a master lease already exists between the prospect and another leasing company. In such an arrangement, a leasing company generally provides a lease line of credit to cover the customer's projected leasing needs over a period of time. If the leasing company takes into account the total cost of the equipment that will eventually be added to the master lease, the leasing company may provide a volume-related price concession to the customer.

Other leasing companies generally can't compete with the price concessions in a master lease because their prices are based on an individual leasing transaction, whereas the master lease price is based on the customer's total leasing volume. Rarely is the price for a single transaction comparable to master lease pricing, unless the size of the single transaction is in the same range as the total master lease volume, or unless the leasing entity (a leasing captive or specialist) can provide certain types of equipment at highly competitive prices.

Pricing Capabilities

Salespeople often willingly enter lease pricing or structuring competitions where they don't belong. Leasing salespeople tend to try to win high-volume or major business accounts that are beyond the capabilities of their organization. This situation occurs because most leasing salespeople earn their income based on the volume of leasing business they produce. Leasing volume ordinarily amounts to the total cost of the equipment that a salesperson is responsible for placing on lease; therefore, the larger the transactions, the greater the volume. Salespeople may chase leasing transactions because of the high cost of the equipment involved, the potential leasing volume of an individual prospect, or both. The tendency to try to compete for the big deal often goes a step further when salespeople try to compete for the business produced by major equipment vendors, whether the salesperson's organization is capable of handling the vendor's leasing production or not.

Unfortunately, if the resources of the salesperson's organization are not adequate to satisfy the needs of the major prospect, the major individual transaction, or the major vendor, the salesperson's time and effort will be wasted. What's worse, the time of credit analysts, lease structurers, documentation personnel, and a number of others can also be wasted when salespeople solicit leasing situations that are out of their league. Sales managers may realize when a salesperson is trying to compete where he or she shouldn't be and will either assist the salesperson or require the salesperson to walk away from the situation.

Comparing Competitive Alternatives

When proposing leasing structures to prospects, salespeople must listen carefully to the prospect's responses and gather information about what, if any, financing alternatives are available to the prospect. A salesperson who knows what other alternatives are being considered by a prospect can present the features of his or her own offerings in the best competitive light. For example, if a salesperson suggests a finance lease to a prospect and a true or operating lease has been proposed by a competitor, the lease payments in the salesperson's proposal are likely to be significantly higher than those in the competitor's. A prospect who is unaware of the differences between finance, true, and operating leases may simply choose the lower lease payments without requesting further information about the differences in lease structure. A salesperson who knows about the competitor's proposal can level the playing field by pointing out that the two lease structures are based on different terms and conditions.

A prospect may tell you that a competitor's proposed leasing structure is priced at a particular "rate." Leases, however, are not loans, and leasing companies are not banks. Banks are required by law to inform borrowers of the specific annual percentage rate applicable to a loan, but leasing companies do not have to make the same disclosure. Some leasing companies and some leasing salespeople do quote lease prices by stating the lease rate or may inform a prospect of the rate in a proposed transaction when requested to do so. The problem is that, since leasing companies are not required to provide the specific rate in a leasing transaction in a regulated format, there is no standard by which all leasing rates are quoted or to which all leasing companies must conform. Therefore, different leasing companies and different leasing salespeople may quote rates differently. To be told by a prospect that a competitor's rate is *x* percent is essentially useless, because you don't know how the competitor calculated the rate.

Inexperienced salespeople can sometimes be knowingly or inadvertently misled by a prospect into believing that a competitor has quoted a significantly lower leasing rate than the particular prospect, lease type, or equipment merits or a rate that is lower than those generally available in the market for similar situations. There are several reasons for the apparent discrepancy.

Many prospects are not financial or leasing experts, so they may not fully understand how a leasing rate was derived. Some leasing companies calculate and quote the rate for leasing the equipment during the lease term but do not quote a total rate, which includes the eventual equipment acquisition by the customer. Therefore, the rate in a true lease, for example, is sometimes quoted as the rate that applies only to the lease payments themselves; it does not include the purchase option price. Sometimes leasing rates are quoted that do not include the value of any advance payments. The key point is that when your leasing rate is apparently higher than the rate of a competitor, you must obtain all the parameters of the competing lease structure for comparison purposes:

1. The exact equipment cost.
2. The exact lease payment in dollars.
3. The exact number of lease payments to be made by the customer.
4. The exact number, type, and amount of any prepayments to be made by the customer (advance lease payments, refundable or nonrefundable security deposits, down payments, prepaid purchase options, commitment fees, etc.).
5. The exact timing of the lease payments (monthly, quarterly, semiannually, annually).
6. The exact terms and conditions of any arrangement to purchase the equipment. (Some equipment purchase arrangements are actually *puts*, or requirements that the customer purchase the equipment for a predetermined amount of money. Under such an agreement, the leasing company can sometimes assume a higher residual value, because the risk of equipment devaluation is offset by the customer's guarantee of purchase.)

The reason for obtaining the lease payment amount in dollars is that prospects sometimes round off rate factors. In leasing situations involving costly equipment, a minor variance in a rate factor can have a significant effect on a lease rate. A rate factor, for example, that is described as .035 of the equipment cost per month for three years, but that is in reality .0355 of the equipment cost per month, can result in a lease rate that is actually one percent higher, depending on the other components in the competitive leasing structure. When you obtain the exact lease payment amount in dollars, you can then input actual values into your comparative calculation, or you can calculate the actual competitive lease rate factor for yourself. Lease rate factors can be determined by dividing the lease payment amount by the equipment cost amount (e.g., $625/$25,000 = .025). It is often said that major leasing transactions are negotiated down to rate factors that are calculated eight digits to the right of the decimal point.

Sometimes, a prospect will show you, or perhaps actually give you, a copy of a written proposal from a competing leasing company. When you are able to read the information in a competitive proposal, you can, of course, then determine the exact rates, terms, and conditions of a competitive leasing transaction. You may be asked to provide leasing proposals as well.

Writing Lease Proposals

Quite often, prospects want you to confirm your leasing proposal in writing. Written leasing proposals are common in middle-market and big-ticket leasing and for leasing arrangements proposed by specialists. Prospects use proposals to analyze the financial aspects of a leasing transaction, to discuss the proposal with others in the operation or with outside advisors, and to compare leasing competitors' offerings.

Written proposals are also used by many leasing companies. Large leasing contracts can't necessarily be completed immediately, even when prospects agree to go ahead with verbal proposals. In fact, many leasing companies don't want to begin credit checks, documentation preparation, or the administrative processes involved in a leasing agreement until after a prospect signs and accepts a formal leasing proposal and remits a commitment fee of some type. This assures the leasing company that the prospect is serious about entering a leasing agreement and that the proposed leasing transaction is acceptable to the prospect, subject to final approval by the leasing company. Furthermore, proposals that have been signed and accepted by prospects imply that the transaction has been "taken off the street," meaning that the prospect will ordinarily stop shopping for other financing.

Leasing proposals contain a detailed written description of the suggested leasing transaction. Some leasing companies allow salespeople to prepare the proposal paperwork. As a rule, however, leasing companies prefer not to propose a leasing transaction in writing until after they have obtained as much information as possible from or about a prospective customer. Reviewing information about a prospect in advance allows the leasing company to determine how to structure a mutually acceptable transaction; the leasing company or leasing salesperson is then better equipped to prepare an accurate proposal that states the leasing terms and conditions that can realistically be provided to a prospect.

Leasing Bids

When the prospect is a large public corporation; an institution such as a hospital, college, university, or school; a not-for-profit organization; a municipality; or a government agency or government-related business, all leasing or financing proposals may be required to be submitted in a written format because financing alternatives are selected through a bidding process. Salespeople can lose some or all of their ability to sell the prospect on the merits of their organization, products, or services when a bidding process is used, because the bid alone determines which leasing source will be selected. When prospects establish rigid criteria for a leasing structure and request a leasing source to submit a price for providing that particular structure, there is not much the bidder can do except comply with the request as instructed or decline to bid.

Most often, leasing specialists—such as those leasing companies that provide certain types of equipment or specialize in leasing to particular types of municipal, government, or government-related entities—become expert in responding to requests for bids. Equipment-related leasing specialists are often successful in winning bid-based pricing competitions because they are able to structure leases for equipment that they not only lease but also buy and sell. Municipal and government leasing specialists generally establish their prices to include the benefit of favorable borrowing costs, which can include consideration of tax incentives available to lessors that lease to municipalities and governments. Because many bids require the expertise of specialists, and other leasing contracts are awarded based only on the price competitiveness of a bid, many general equipment leasing companies prefer not to compete in bidding situations.

Exceptions to the above situations can be found when a general equipment lessor wants to accommodate an equipment vendor in competition for a bid-based equipment sale that must include leasing or financing availability. Sometimes, when a vendor and leasing company work together to structure a competitive bid, both parties can be successful. The ability to win a bid that is based on both the equipment and its financing cost can sometimes be enhanced by incorporating vendor discounts on the equipment cost, a leasing company's reduction in price to accommodate a valued vendor, or a combination of both.

Typical Written Proposals

The majority of lease proposals are not rigid bids in the context of the bidding process described above, but they are nonetheless formal written offerings describing the terms and conditions of a proposed leasing transaction. There is certain information that is generally included in all proposals and a standard procedure for writing them, frequently amended by the particular style of individual leasing companies. All written proposals, however, should include the following:

Dear Mr. or Ms. Prospect:
We are pleased to submit the following proposal covering the terms and conditions of a leasing agreement for an XYZ machine costing $75,000 to be leased for a term of five years. Suggested terms and conditions are as follows:

<u>Lessor:</u> Best Leasing Corporation
123 Easy Way
Yourtown, NY 10000

<u>Lessee:</u> Top-Rated Performance Company
55 Profit Drive
Theirtown, NY 10001

<u>Guarantor:</u> [*The exact legal name of any individual(s) or business(es) required as guarantors of the leasing transaction.*]

Vendor:	Goodsale's Machine Co. 1000 Deal Place Yourtown, NY 10000
Equipment:	[*A specific description of the exact equipment to be leased, including the make, model, accessories, attachments, serial number if available, and any other information regarding the item(s). If there are many items of equipment to be leased, a separate schedule can be prepared and attached to the proposal, with the notation:*] as listed in Schedule A, attached, written in this section of the proposal.
Equipment cost:	[*The exact equipment cost. If the customer is to receive a discount from the vendor, value for equipment traded in, or any other reduction in the price of the equipment, such details should be described here.*]
Lease Term:	[*The specific period for which the equipment will be leased; for example:*] 60 months.
Lease Payment:	[*The specific periodic lease payment; for example:*] $1,875.00 per month, net of taxes, insurance, maintenance, service, or any other charges for the use, operation, repair, or servicing of the equipment.
Advance Payment:	[*The specific number and type of any advance payments to be paid by the customer; for example:*] The first and last months' lease payments are payable in advance. [*Any security deposit(s), down payment, or other type of advance payment required from the customer is also listed in this section.*]
Purchase Option:	[*A description of any option provided for the customer's acquisition of the equipment at the expiration of the original lease term; for example:*] The equipment may be purchased at the end of the original lease term for its then fair market value, provided that the lessee has satisfied the terms and conditions of the lease agreement, and provided that no event of default has occurred. [*Similar language may be used to describe the particu-*

lar type of purchase available to the customer and the specific terms and conditions under which the customer can exercise the option to purchase the equipment.]

Since written proposals ordinarily define the specific terms and conditions of a leasing agreement and often contain the information on which a final contract is based, proposals should always be written in strict accordance with the policies of the leasing company offering the proposal. In some cases, especially for proposals covering costly equipment or complex leasing transactions, leasing companies require that proposals be drafted by or with the advice of legal counsel, authorized credit personnel, or authorized contract administrators.

Standard Formats

When salespeople or sales administrators are authorized to prepare and submit proposals to prospects, it is common practice for them to use a standard proposal form designed by their company. This is a model containing the leasing company's terms and conditions for conducting business laid out in a proposal format. Within the model, areas are provided for the insertion of specific information relative to a particular leasing transaction. Some leasing companies list the terms and conditions for writing proposals in a manual or guide, some enter model leasing proposal language into a word processor or on a computer disc, and others preprint proposals on paper. This way, the proposal preparer can simply copy or print out a model proposal and then fill in specific information for a particular prospect. Spaces can be provided for the entry of the prospect's name and address, the equipment description, the lease term, the lease payment, and so on. Standardized proposal forms are usually developed with the assistance or advice of legal counsel. Some leasing companies may require authorized individuals to review proposals before they are submitted to prospects.

Specifying Commitment Fees

The use of preprinted proposals can offer a slight advantage when it comes to collecting commitment fees upon the prospect's acceptance of a proposal. Some prospects may object to remitting a fee;

some may want to negotiate the size of the fee. Fee requirements that are listed in a proposal in a predetermined, standard fee schedule, or fee requirements listed by equipment cost range, can often eliminate or minimize prospect objections. An example of a fee schedule follows:

Example of a Commitment Fee Schedule

> x% of the equipment cost for equipment costing $50,000–$100,000.
> y% of the equipment cost for equipment costing $100,000–$250,000.

When fee schedules are included in a proposal in such a way that they appear to apply to all prospects, and not just to the prospect in question, they tend to be more palatable.

The scheduling of fees as part of a standard preprinted proposal format works best when the leasing transactions proposed are more or less standard themselves. When proposals that cover complex transactions are individually designed to address unique circumstances, the commitment fee should also be individually established. It is not a good idea to submit a proposal on a preprinted form that has been adapted by adding or changing language. This can imply to a prospect that the leasing company did less work than was actually performed. It can also give the prospect the impression that it is acceptable to negotiate not only the amount of a commitment fee but also other terms, including the price of the leasing transaction itself.

A key to presenting written proposals is not only to present prospects with the best leasing alternative but also to present that alternative in its best light. Some thought before putting a leasing proposal together can give you a significant advantage when you must ultimately convince a prospect to accept your proposed terms and conditions and also when you must obtain a commitment fee.

Leaving Room for Adjustments

A prospect may or may not act on a proposal immediately. Some proposals are subject to delay because of the time it takes to complete an actual leasing agreement; sometimes the prospect needs time to complete the proposal review process or to receive and review alternative proposals from competitors. Because the prospect may not immediately act on the proposal, and because proposals contain terms and conditions that the prospect expects a leasing company to comply with, the details listed in proposals must be considered and written very carefully.

A proposal is exactly that: a proposal. It is not a commitment on a leasing company's part to unequivocally provide a leasing agreement exactly as stated in a proposal. Although the final transaction agreed on may be exactly as described in a proposal, the proposal stage is generally too early in the leasing process for a firm written commitment on the final leasing rates, terms, and conditions. Consequently, proposal letters must clearly state that the leasing company's writing is a *proposed* offering of leasing or financing terms and conditions. Proposals must contain language that provides for adjustments based on items or circumstances that are subject to change.

Protecting the Lease Rate

Lease rates may change between the time a proposal is submitted to and accepted by a prospect. Therefore, all leasing proposals must contain an expiration date to protect the leasing company against increases in its cost of funds. Another way for leasing companies to protect themselves is to include a formula designed to adjust the lease rate in the event that the leasing company's cost of funds increases. A leasing cost adjustment can be accomplished by basing the proposed lease rate on an acceptable rate indicator or rate base.

For example, lease rates can be based on the prime rate of interest charged by banks or some other indicator, such as the Treasury bill rate. This does not mean that the rate in the leasing agreement *is* the prime rate or the Treasury bill rate. It means only that if a change occurs in the rate used as the indicator, the rate in the lease proposal will be changed accordingly.

Ordinarily, leasing companies include a formulation that addresses only increases in the cost of money, as determined by changes in the indicator rate. If the prime rate, for example, is the indicator, the lease rate rises in direct proportion to any rise in the prime rate. But interest rates can decrease as well. Generally, the availability of a proportional rate decrease depends on the particular pricing policy of the leasing company. Most often, leasing companies determine whether or not to provide a prospect with the benefit of a rate reduction on an individual transaction basis. The leasing company generally considers the rate at which interest rates themselves are falling, the overall credit quality of the prospect's business, the competitive alternatives open to the prospect, and whether or not the leasing company itself will be able to obtain funding at a reduced rate.

Prospects do not always understand the difference between short- and long-term interest rates. The prime rate of interest charged by banks, the federal discount rate, and the Treasury bill rate are all short-term interest rates. Equipment leasing rates are long-term rates. Leasing companies generally do not borrow at the prime lending rate but at a higher rate that banks establish for longer-term loans. The long-term rate is higher because the risk is greater in long-term loans than short-term loans. Therefore, the prime rate is ordinarily the rate charged by banks to their most creditworthy customers for loans of thirty days or less. Depending on the credit quality of a particular business, the business's relationship with the bank, the overall makeup of the money market at the time the loan is arranged, and the term of the loan itself, businesses usually arrange long-term bank loans at some percentage above the prime rate. It is common to hear businesspeople describe their bank borrowing rates as being one, two, three, five, or some other percentage over prime.

Since the prime lending rate is a short-term interest rate, it can be volatile. When economic conditions cause the supply of money to shrink or the bank's costs of borrowing to increase, interest rates can rise rapidly. When money is readily available or when the borrowing costs of banks decline, interest rates generally decrease. When interest rates move in either direction, the change can be rapid or slow, depending on the overall conditions of the money market at the time. Consequently, long-term interest rates do not always move in direct proportion to short-term interest rates. If there is a slow-moving trend toward higher rates, the prime rate may adjust at a faster pace than long-term rates. By adjusting the prime rate often, banks can allow for increases in their own short-term costs of money—on a daily basis, if need be—while maintaining a more gradual pace for adjusting long-term rates. Whereas the prime rate is generally directly proportional to a bank's cost of daily funds, long-term interest rates provide a greater margin for banks to absorb small fluctuations in their cost of borrowing.

Banks borrow from other banks, primarily the Federal Reserve System. The "Fed" lends to banks on a short-term basis and establishes a basic interest rate for borrowing known as the federal discount rate. Depending on the type of equipment you lease and the type of prospects you solicit, you ordinarily will not be called upon to discuss the federal reserve banking system or the borrowing activities of banks themselves. You will, however, be better prepared to work with your prospects if you know how the banking system works. Your ability to negotiate with prospects and to make value judgments about competitive alternatives will be enhanced if you understand the overall condition of the money market itself, the banking community, and the current policies of the federal banking system. This information can be found in the business sections of newspapers, in business magazines, and in the business news broadcasts on radio and television.

You do not have to become an economist or an expert in banking practices to succeed in equipment leasing. But negotiating with prospects will be easier if you understand in a broad sense what is reasonable and unreasonable for a prospect to expect or request of you, based on overall money market conditions. If, for example, a prospect at a small business informs you that long-term funds are available at an incredibly low bank rate for the prospect's circumstances, you can use your knowledge to tell the prospect why the bank rate seems unreasonable rather than trying to compete blindly. Conversely, if you know that funds are readily available at low bank rates, because that is the trend you have observed from your own information gathering, you can prepare yourself to deal with those circumstances.

Handling Equipment Changes

Sometimes a prospect wants to add items or accessories to equipment or may decide to acquire a different or more expensive unit altogether. If the cost of accessories or the price of a different item is considerably greater than the equipment on which the proposal was based, the proposed leasing terms and conditions may no longer apply. The addition or substitution of costly items may necessitate the leasing company's request for additional information about the equipment or additional credit information from the prospect, or it may necessitate changes in the leasing terms and conditions.

Leasing companies often include in written proposals a provision allowing for a change in the equipment cost of plus or minus a certain percent. If the added equipment is within the permissible range, the terms and conditions of a leasing proposal remain the same. If the cost increases, however, the lease payment must change as well. Leasing companies can provide for a change in the lease payment by including a statement in the proposal, such as: "In the event that the equipment cost shall change, in an amount not to exceed x percent of the cost of the equipment described herein, the lease payment will be adjusted proportionally."

By including provisions for rate adjustments to cover possible increases in borrowing costs and providing for possible changes in the cost of equipment, leasing companies can protect themselves against possible loss exposure. An even more critical consideration is for leasing companies to avoid committing in writing to a prospect that a leasing transaction is acceptable before a final credit approval has been granted.

Establishing Credit Criteria

The majority of leasing proposals are presented to prospects before the leasing company has completed a final review of the prospect's credit condition. Many proposals are used simply to provide the prospect with written information about a suggested leasing alternative. What's more, many proposals are presented to prospects who are still in the early stages of shopping for equipment. In many cases, the leasing company has not received any of the prospect's financial information before the proposal is prepared. In other cases, the leasing company may not even want to review a prospect's financial condition until after the prospect has indicated that the terms and conditions of a proposed leasing transaction are acceptable. Therefore, leasing proposals must contain specific language stating that the proposal is subject to final approval by the leasing company. To address this contingency, written proposals often include a description of the leasing company's policy on credit requirements. For example:

Credit Policy Statement

This proposal is subject to the receipt and satisfactory review of pertinent financial information regarding Prospect Corporation. Final acceptance of this transaction is predicated on the approval of the credit committee of XYZ Leasing Corp., in its sole discretion. The financial information required includes, but is not limited to, the following:

1. Last two year-end financial statements. [*In some*

cases, leasing companies may accept federal income tax returns in place of audited or accountant-prepared financial statements, and some leasing companies may require statements for more than two years of operation.]

2. A recent interim financial statement if the year-end financial statement is more than six months old.

3. A complete description and listing of the equipment to be leased.

4. Bank reference(s), including the branch, person to contact, account number, bank address, and telephone number.

5. Trade reference(s), including person to contact, account number, address, and telephone number. [*Not all leasing companies require trade reference information, nor are trade references required for all leasing transactions. Upper middle-market and big-ticket lessors and certain specialists lease to businesses whose superior credit ratings make the need for trade references unnecessary. Although trade references are almost always required in small-ticket leasing, exceptionally strong prospects may not be asked to supply trade references.*]

6. Current personal financial statements for any individuals who are guarantors of the leasing transaction (if applicable). [*If the guarantor is a business, the leasing company would require the financial information listed in items 1–5 regarding the guarantor.*]

Depending on the circumstances, a leasing company might require additional information about the prospect, a guarantor, the equipment, or some other aspect of the prospect's business. In this case, the additional items would be added to the credit policy statement.

Naturally, the more advanced the sales process is when a proposal is drafted, the more definitive the list of required financial information will be. If, for example, a proposal is being sent to an existing customer, the only requirements might be an updated financial statement, an equipment list, and a confirmation that the reference contact information is still accurate. Regardless of the particular information that might be required for credit review, the key is for the leasing company to protect itself against a prospect's ability to enforce a leasing proposal as if the writer were committing to accept a proposed transaction.

Establishing Documentation Requirements

Similar to the need to approve a prospect's credit before committing to a proposed transaction, a leasing company must also be able to properly document an agreed-upon leasing transaction between itself and the prospect. Leasing companies do not ordinarily prepare documentation until after the terms and conditions of a final transaction have been accepted in principle by both the leasing company and the prospective customer. Therefore, a leasing proposal must contain a provision stating that the finally agreed-upon transaction must be documented in a form and substance that is satisfactory to the leasing company and/or its legal counsel. Some prospects may request that the proposal state that the final documentation must be acceptable to both parties—the leasing company and the prospect. This might allow the prospect to obtain reimbursement of any fees paid to the leasing company in the event that the prospect finds terms and conditions of the leasing documentation to be unacceptable and refuses to execute the contract.

Any other protections that a leasing company requires, and any other aspects of a leasing proposal that are subject to change or adjustment, must also be addressed in the written proposal.

The point of highlighting some of the potential exposures to leasing companies is to demonstrate that proposals should not be treated as merely quickly written quotations to be presented to prospective customers. Leasing salespeople and leasing companies must guard against the fact that prospects sometimes take for granted what has been quoted to them by leasing companies, especially when the quotation is presented in writing. If prospects assume from the way a proposal is written that a leasing company is fully prepared to commit to the terms in the proposal without further qualification, the leasing company can find itself in a very difficult position. Proposals, therefore, must be carefully thought out before being reduced to writing, and it must be ensured that what is written does not create risks that the company is unwilling to take. These risks can include the potential loss of income and the exposure to disputes (perhaps even lawsuits).

By the time your sales presentation reaches the ballpark quotation or written proposal stage, you are well on your way to the possible closing of a leasing transaction. But your proposals can be met by either agreement or objections.

Chapter 12

Stage 6—Overcoming Objections

Objections from prospects are to be expected in sales. Rarely will a prospect who is shopping for any costly item simply sign an order without an objection of some sort. Some objections, though, are more serious than others, and some objections may only appear to be objections. The first step in overcoming objections is to determine whether the prospect's reaction to your offering is truly an objection or merely a question.

Many salespeople assume that any question a prospect asks about a proposed leasing transaction is in fact an objection. This assumption may stem from the salesperson's expectation that there will be objections to particular aspects of a proposed leasing transaction. When salespeople prime themselves to expect an objection about a particular issue, they may also tend to become defensive as soon as the subject is brought up by a prospect. A common cause for this defensiveness is the salesperson's concern about his or her ability to provide an acceptable answer or concern that a prospect's objection might be justified. Once a salesperson takes the defensive, his or her ability to answer a prospect's question or overcome a real objection without having to offer some sort of concession is greatly reduced. A salesperson must therefore be fully prepared to answer prospects' questions clearly, accurately, and confidently and to support those answers with hard information.

The most common questions and objections from prospects typically concern:

1. The cost of leasing
2. The credit review process—specifically the amount of information required and the amount of time required for approval
3. The specific terms and conditions of leasing transactions

Cost Objections

Ordinarily, a prospect's first questions involve the cost of leasing. Certainly, questions about cost should be expected. But leasing salespeople can create problems for themselves when they respond to price questions with a story rather than a direct answer. Their belief that a story is called for often arises from their expectation that the prospect will object to the answer.

For example, a prospect asks, "What is the rate in this transaction?" If the salesperson fears that a direct answer will lead to an objection, the salesperson might respond as follows: "We're competitive in the market," or "We aren't a bank, so our rates will naturally be higher than your bank's might be, but we provide many other benefits," or "We're very flexible," or "We have many customers in your business, and they all find our rates to be competitive." These answers all evade the price issue and generally make prospects wonder why the salesperson is unwilling to state a rate directly. Although all of these responses may be true, the time for a salesperson to make these statements is not in response to a direct price question. A simple, direct answer to a question about price is better: "The lease payment is $1,422 a month for 36 months" or "The leasing rate is 15 percent." By stating the price without hesitation and by appearing to expect the prospect's agreement, a salesperson establishes the premise that the leasing price is proper for the transaction in question.

When leasing salespeople qualify their answers to prospects' price questions with explanations of why the leasing cost is whatever it happens to be, the answer can appear evasive or inconclusive. As a consequence, the price quoted by the salesperson can appear to be incorrect, high, or negotiable. By attempting to explain or justify a price, the salesperson may in fact be providing a prospect with cause to turn a price question into a price objection.

Certainly, even a direct, clear, and confident statement of leasing costs is not going to meet with the approval of every prospective customer. Regardless of how accurately and properly a leasing transaction is priced, there is still a good chance that a prospect's initial reaction to a price quotation will be objection. It is when a prospect actually objects to a price quotation that the salesperson must provide an explanation of leasing costs.

When price objections are raised, it is always a good practice for the salesperson to restate all the terms and conditions of the proposed leasing transaction. A restatement can confirm that the prospect understands exactly what is being offered. For example, a salesperson might respond to a prospect's price objection by saying, "Ms. Prospect, our leasing transaction covers a three-year term, calls for a small advance payment, allows you to acquire the equipment at the end of the lease term, and requires a payment of only $1,500 per month." The other features of the lease offering, such as a minimal advance payment, the option to purchase the equipment, and a three-year payment period, may remind the prospect of the advantages of the lease. Furthermore, restating each component of a proposed leasing transaction permits the salesperson to focus the prospect's objection on a specific area of the transaction, as opposed to treating an objection as being applicable to the entire offering.

Lease Payment

A lease payment can be adjusted in many different ways. Therefore, if the prospect's objection is to the size of the payment, the salesperson can offer a longer lease term and lower payment while still preserving the transaction's rate or yield. A salesperson can overcome objections to the size of a leasing payment by adjusting the values of the remaining lease components or by restructuring a quoted lease offering. When prospects object to the rates that have been quoted, however, the situation is somewhat different.

Lease Rate

Prospects' objections to lease rates leave less room for adjustment. No matter how a lease offering is restructured, the rate itself normally remains the same. Therefore, when the lease rate is the prospect's reason for objection, a salesperson doesn't have many alternatives other than justifying why a particular rate is appropriate for the prospect's circumstances.

Since rate objections can ordinarily be overcome only by comparing the cost of other financing alternatives, the first step in overcoming a lease rate objection is to find out why the prospect raised the objection. Sometimes it is because a prospect is not aware of long-term financing rates in general. Prospects who seldom arrange significant financings may not be familiar with the typical costs of long-term financing. This is frequently the case among prospects who operate service businesses (consultancies, agencies, and professional practices) that don't acquire costly equipment often. When your prospects are unfamiliar with the costs associated with term financing, educating them about the differences between short-term and long-term rates may help overcome a rate objection.

Leasing Costs vs. Cash Purchase

Some prospects who indicate that leasing rates sound high may believe that cash purchase is more advantageous. Here again, you can educate them about the value of cash generated within their own businesses. A good way to demonstrate the "cost" of income generated by a business is to perform a calculation for the prospect. By extracting some information from the business's financial statement, you can calculate the "return" earned by the business. If leasing costs are lower than the return generated by the business, leasing is the better equipment acquisition alternative.

There are several calculations that you can perform to illustrate a business's return. For example, income can be calculated as a percentage of stockholders' equity, as a percentage of sales, or as a percentage of inventory. These calculations illustrate that for every dollar of equity in the business, every dollar of sales, or every dollar's worth of inventory, the business earned so many dollars. What the calculations ultimately demonstrate is that once those dollars are spent on equipment, the business can no longer immediately earn from them. Depending on the type of business, every dollar invested in sales, inventory, or equity should return income at the rate derived from the calculation.

Even if the cost of leasing is somewhat higher than the prospect's internal cost of capital, however, leasing may still be a better alternative than cash purchase, because the capital itself provides the prospect with more financial flexibility, the ability to deal with financial emergencies, and the ability to take advantage of opportunities that may arise. In this case, a salesperson can demonstrate the prospect's reduced ability to generate capital internally, based on the prospect's own financial information. Presenting the actual costs, supported by arithmetic, has a greater impact than the mere suggestion that spending cash costs more than a prospect might think.

You can get a significant amount of information about the typical income, expenses, and financial makeup of a variety of businesses, organized by size, type, and industry, by reviewing the *RMA Annual Statement Studies*, published by Robert Morris Associates, Philadelphia, Pennsylvania. The publication is used by many credit analysts to determine whether a particular business fits the profile of similar businesses of the same size and type. The publication can also be used, however, for sales purposes; familiarity with the financial makeup of different types and sizes of businesses in different industries can help you determine what a prospect's typical financial condition might be. Understanding how various businesses ordinarily operate financially can also help you focus your prospects not only on what their cash costs but also on where their cash can best be utilized. Some businesses are best served by investing in inventory, others may be best served by investing in sales support, and still others may be best served by building stockholder equity.

Leasing Costs vs. Bank Loans

Some prospects compare leasing costs to bank borrowing. On the surface, leasing costs are rarely lower than the borrowing charges imposed by a prospect's own bank. Although leasing specialists may be able to offer leasing costs that compare very favorably with bank borrowing costs for the original period of a true or operating lease, rarely will the total acquisition cost of leased equipment be lower than that of a comparable bank loan.

Leasing should not ordinarily be compared to a bank loan on surface information alone. First of all, there are often additional costs in bank loans that do not appear on the surface. Second, there are transactional elements to bank loans that can be less favorable than a comparative lease.

Compensating Balances

Many banks require their borrowers to maintain compensating balances against the amounts borrowed. Compensating balances are cash amounts that the borrower is required to keep on account with the lending bank. Compensating balances are not ordinarily included as part of a lending agreement between a bank and a borrower but are treated as "side arrangements" or sometimes as additional covenants to loan agreements. Compensating balance accounts occasionally pay interest to the borrower, but most do not. In either case, however, the borrower does not always receive the full cash benefit of the bank loan, because the compensating balance offsets the amount of money the business receives. Despite the fact that a bank advances the total amount of a loan, the borrower does not have the use of the offsetting funds held by the bank in a compensating account.

A way to determine the cost of bank borrowing is to deduct the amount of any required non-interest-bearing compensating balances from the total loan proceeds and then calculate what the interest rate would be if the borrower were to receive the loan proceeds less the amount held in the compensating account. This formulation illustrates that although the borrower appears to receive the full loan amount, the borrower is actually paying interest on money that it provides to the bank. Naturally, if a borrower were to pay a bank on the total amount of a loan agreement and lose the benefit of the money held on account by the bank, the borrower's rate would be significantly higher than the apparent loan rate.

Even when a borrower earns interest on compensating balance accounts, there is a hidden cost: the difference between the rate the borrower pays on borrowed funds and the rate the borrower earns from the compensating balance account. Although this arrangement is less expensive to the borrower and more complex to analyze, the bank still has the use of the borrower's funds at a lower rate than it is charging to the borrower for a portion of the total loan advanced.

Many large businesses ordinarily maintain bank accounts in excess of the minimum balances required to offset loans. Therefore, a compensating balance requirement may not appear to be detrimental to the borrower's business because the money would be left in the bank account anyway. In these situations, the only thing salespeople can do is create what-if scenarios for prospects, such as:

"What if you had to use the money in your compensating balance account? Would the bank simply permit you to withdraw the amount you need?"

"What if you withdrew an amount that reduced your bank balance below the required level? Would the bank impose a penalty charge?"

"If you withdrew an amount that reduced your bank balance below the required level, would that cause a real or technical default in your loan agreement?"

"If you withdrew an amount that reduced your bank balance below the required amount, would your company be listed as a problem account, perhaps jeopardizing your overall banking relationship?"

"What if the bank did not impose a severe penalty for your withdrawal of funds from a compensating balance account but did list your business as a problem account? Would that harm your business if the bank were to provide reference information about your business to other creditors, investors, or suppliers?"

Restrictive Covenants

The above scenarios are intended to illustrate to prospects that the rate in a bank lending agreement is not the only thing to be considered when comparing loans to other forms of financing. Beyond the existence of possible hidden costs in loan agreements, there may be other aspects of bank borrowing that a prospect should consider. Banks often include language in loan agreements that requires a business to meet or maintain particular standards. For example, loan agreements may contain requirements that a business maintain a net worth above a particular amount, maintain its cash flow above a certain minimum, maintain working capital at or above a particular ratio (the working capital ratio is the ratio of current assets to current liabilities), or maintain a particular ratio of debt to equity or net worth. These additional requirements included in bank loan agreements are referred to as restrictive covenants.

By including restrictuve covenants in a loan agreement, a bank helps protect a loan by prohibiting a borrower from exceeding certain financial limitations that, if exceeded, might prevent a business from repaying a loan as agreed. By including restrictions in a loan agreement, however, a bank may also be restricting a business from conducting its financial affairs freely under certain circumstances. One such circumstance might arise, for example, if a business wished to arrange additional financing from another source. Even if the borrowing would not jeopardize the business's ability to repay its bank loan, restrictive covenants might prevent it from borrowing if the restrictions imposed by the bank would be exceeded.

Aside from limitations on additional borrowings, bank loans may include other requirements. Banks sometimes secure themselves with assets worth more than the amount borrowed. Banks secure their interest in assets pledged to collateralize a loan by perfecting a lien against those assets. In this way, a bank may secure a lien against specific assets, such as a business's inventory, accounts receivable, machinery, or equipment, or it may secure a blanket lien against all a business's assets. When an asset is specifically secured by a bank—or any other party, for that matter—a business can't unilaterally dispose of that asset until the lien is released. Consequently, banks may establish a degree of control over a business's other operating functions.

A bank's inclusion of restrictive covenants or the requirement that assets be pledged to secure loans may or may not hamper a borrower's business operation. Large businesses might be unaffected by a bank's lending criteria and find that bank demands are relatively simple to comply with. Smaller businesses, however, might find that the restrictions imposed on them by bank loan agreements prohibit freedom in financial or operational decision making. In contrast, leases do not include restrictive covenants, they do not require liens against other assets, and they do not place limitations on where or how a business arranges other financings. Depending on the size and type of a prospect's business, and on the prospect's relationship with a bank lender, the evaluation of a lease versus a bank loan must go beyond a simple comparison of rates.

Credit Review Objections

Amount of Information

Generally, a prospect's objection to providing information relates to the size of the prospect's business. Public companies and large privately held businesses ordinarily have prepared financial information readily at hand, but many smaller businesses do not.

Prospects who have little or no exposure to the leasing process frequently question or object to the request to submit thorough financial information. If you look at the information-gathering process from their perspective, you can understand why: A complete stranger from a leasing company is requesting financial information and details that many businesspeople consider to be confidential. Therefore, salespeople must be aware that some prospects are hesitant or reluctant to discuss this confidential information with a stranger and must do their best to make the prospect more comfortable.

What matters most often when financial information is unavailable is *why* it is not available. In some instances, a prospect's financial information simply hasn't been prepared yet. In other cases, prospects may not want to take the time to gather all the required paperwork; they decide that leasing is just too cumbersome.

The first step in dealing with prospects who object to submitting financial information is to find out the cause for the objection. Unfortunately, if the required financial information has not been prepared yet, you will have to wait until the paperwork is completed, or you may even have to pass on the transaction. You can, however, explain to a prospect why you need the financial information and ask the prospect how you might go about obtaining it. There may be a banker who can provide detailed information about a prospect's business and loan history. There may be a possible guarantor who was otherwise unknown to you. There may be a pending public offering that precludes the release of financial information to outsiders. In these cases, the answers may be unacceptable, but you won't know until you ask.

If your prospect merely thinks that too much information is required for credit review purposes, you can volunteer to help gather the paperwork. You can suggest that you call the business's outside accountant or gather the bank and trade contact information from someone in the prospect's accounting or bookkeeping area. You can offer to speak directly to the vendor to obtain information about the equipment or talk to an equipment operator within the prospect's business itself. Furthermore, you can handle your probing for financial information in a painless conversational approach, listing the information as you hear it, rather than presenting the prospect with a long checklist for completion.

Amount of Time

Similar to prospects who feel that gathering financial information is too cumbersome are prospects who question or object to how long the lease approval process takes. Except for small-ticket leasing, most leasing applications require financial statement review. For the most part, however, the turnaround time or time required for credit decision making is not long.

A typical credit decision can be made reasonably quickly, provided the credit decision maker has all required information. Therefore, if the information received from an applicant is complete and accurate, the decision-making process is accelerated and simplified. If you stress the need for completeness and accuracy of names, addresses, and phone numbers, you help the prospect expedite the credit review process. The same is true of financial statements. If prospects submit complete financial statements or federal income tax returns in the first place, the credit reviewer will not have to waste time requesting additional pieces of information later on.

Salespeople themselves are key factors in determining how expeditiously the credit review process is performed. When salespeople appear to be informed, professional, and confident, prospects generally are more willing to trust the salesperson's ability to help them. After making a prospect feel comfortable, however, the salesperson must be certain to do a thorough and professional job of obtaining the required financial information, submitting the same for credit review, and following up to ensure that the credit decision is made expeditiously.

Objections to Lease Terms and Conditions

When prospects acquire costly equipment, the equipment itself is ordinarily the most important aspect of the acquisition. The equipment will earn or save a business money, and in some cases the equipment is the most important factor in a business's operation. If the equipment isn't available, some businesses can't produce at all. For this reason, many businesspeople, especially those operating smaller businesses, are very concerned about contracts they enter into that could cause their businesses to lose their equipment.

Many objections to lease terms and conditions arise because prospects don't know what risks they may encounter when leasing from unknown leasing companies. Leases themselves are typically written in fine print, which in and of itself can be intimidating to those who are unfamiliar with leasing documentation. Unfortunately, many leasing salespeople create further concern because they are not necessarily legal experts and sometimes gloss over important points. It is not uncommon for leasing salespeople to tell a concerned prospect, "Don't worry about the fine print; it's just a standard lease" or "Its OK, Mr. Prospect, every customer signs the same agreement" or "If you don't sign the contract, we can't lease you the equipment."

Look at the situation from the prospect's perspective: A complete stranger asks the businessperson to submit confidential financial information and then implies that when the contract is ultimately executed, the businessperson will not be given an adequate explanation of what the fine print actually means. This scenario is all too common and probably causes the loss of many leasing transactions, simply because some leasing salespeople do not take the time to empathize with the prospect's situation.

Leasing documents are, in fact, legal contracts. The purpose of a leasing contract is to establish and protect the lessor's rights according to the specific terms and conditions of a particular agreement. Most leasing contracts, however, are not onerous and don't disadvantage the customer (lessee). Although a customer can incur penalties and, in extreme cases, can even lose the equipment as a result of default of the contract, as long as the customer performs as agreed there is no real exposure to penalty or loss.

There are, however, many leasing companies and many types of leasing contracts. Most leasing companies use their own documentation and enforce contracts in their own fashion. Whatever the types of documents used and whatever the methods used to enforce them, salespeople are generally the ones who present leasing paperwork to prospects. It is in a salesperson's best interest to thoroughly understand what each document says and what each document means and to explain the same to his or her prospects.

As a rule, even overly concerned prospects are made to feel more comfortable when they receive clear, knowledgeable answers to questions concerning lease terms and conditions. Sometimes, if salespeople are well informed and are perceived to be knowledgeable by prospects, sending documents out for legal review can be avoided. But a salesperson's lack of understanding, appearance of uncertainty, or attempts to dismiss a prospect's concerned questions generally serve to heighten any anxieties on the prospect's part.

It is critical, therefore, for salespeople to be able to answer prospects' questions and objections in a professional and competent manner. As a rule, if prospects have been properly qualified in the first place, a leasing company's products and services have been specifically designed to meet the typical requirements of those prospects. Since that is usually the case, questions and objections can be answered through illustration, education, and demonstration. Once a prospect's questions or objections have been satisfied, the next step in the sales process is to close the leasing sale.

Chapter 13

Stage 7—Closing the Leasing Sale

Interestingly, although closing the leasing sale is the most important step in the sales process, sometimes the close itself can be an anticlimax. After all, every stage of the sales process has been designed to lead to the closing of a lease, but by the time the point of closure is reached, most of the work has already been done. You prospected and solicited businesses to find sales opportunities. You identified a prospect's specific needs to determine which of your products or services was called for. You delivered sales presentations to inform, educate, and demonstrate how leasing could apply to a particular prospect's equipment acquisition situation. You presented written or verbal proposals to suggest a specific leasing alternative. Throughout the sales process, you have been building toward the eventual consummation of a leasing sale. All that remains to be done is to ask for the order.

Asking for the Order

In small-ticket leasing, asking for the order may be presenting a completed lease form and asking the prospect to sign the paperwork and give you a check for any required advance payments. For middle-market and big-ticket leasing transactions, the close may be asking the prospect to sign a commitment letter prior to the preparation of final lease documentation. In other middle-market or big-ticket cases, the close may be asking the prospect to execute the final documents. Whatever the closing process is, however, once you have reached the point of closure, you must ask for the order.

Not all prospects immediately comply when they are asked for an order (Exhibit 5). If they don't agree to go ahead, you may have

Exhibit 5. Reasons for rejection.

Four Common Reasons for Prospects Not to Do Business With You:

1. The prospect is not convinced that you can deliver.

2. There is no need for your services, or the need has not been identified yet.

3. The prospect thinks that the service is not worth the cost.

4. There is no hurry to go ahead with you.

to ask for the order more than once. Your attempts to obtain an order are called trial closes.

Trial Closes

Similar to your presentation of the rates, terms, and conditions of a proposed leasing transaction, your trial closes result in the prospect's either agreeing to go ahead with your lease offering or declining to do so. If the prospect declines your lease offering, you must identify and overcome the objection. Therefore, a trial close is an attempt to determine if the prospect is ready to go ahead with the leasing transaction or if you will have to sell harder or clarify or modify your offering. The difference between proposals and trial closes is that proposals are only preliminary leasing suggestions and trial closes are direct attempts to obtain an order.

Although it is true that a leasing proposal might be accepted by a prospect—making the proposal a trial close in a sense—proposals are more often used as a basis for negotiation than as a closing tool. Trial closes are attempted when a salesperson believes or suspects that a prospect might be prepared to accept a lease offering. If that is the case, you must clearly confirm your thoughts by making a closing statement.

Closing Statements

Closing statements are comments that clearly demonstrate to a prospect that you expect to obtain an order, such as:

"Now that all of your questions have been answered, Ms. Prospect, if you will please sign the leasing documents we can order your equipment."

"We're pleased that you have decided to go ahead with XYZ Financial Services; please indicate your acceptance by signing this commitment letter."

"The leasing documents contain the terms and conditions that we agreed upon; please sign them for me so that we can go ahead."

Naturally, your closing statement should reflect your agreement with a particular prospect, but it should also confirm that the prospect is prepared to go ahead with you.

Despite the fact that lease closings can be anticlimactic, they can contain several pitfalls—some of which are caused by salespeople themselves. In some cases, since the closing is the last step in the sales process, some salespeople don't ask for the order after agreement on a leasing transaction has been reached. They complete the sales process, including overcoming a prospect's objections, and then don't confirm a prospect's agreement. This may be a result of their fear that the prospect might still say no. Neglecting to take the last step has many possible ramifications.

Obviously, failure to obtain closure leaves the situation open to competition. A prospect may also decide to pursue other alternatives for obtaining equipment. Had the transaction been closed, the prospect would more than likely have considered the matter a done deal. Instead, the equipment's financing is left open, and the equipment vendor may lose the order to a competitor.

Leasing Paperwork

Similar to a salesperson's neglect to ask for an order is a salesperson's assumption that a leasing transaction has been closed, without the prospect's written confirmation. This scenario can occur when salespeople don't immediately complete the closing process by obtaining signed documents, commitment letters, or any other type of required paperwork from the prospect. At times, salespeople neglect to complete the paperwork because they are busy with other tasks, or they may feel that they have plenty of time to handle the documents later. In other instances, they may not want to travel to a remote location or make other arrangements to ensure closure of a distant account.

Oddly enough, for some salespeople, neglecting to follow up on completed paperwork from a prospect may have to do with the anticlimactic aspects of the closing process itself. For some salespeople, the challenge of leasing sales is identifying viable prospects, identifying and fulfilling prospects' needs, negotiating leasing transactions, overcoming prospects' objections, and obtaining prospects' agreement to do business. For these salespeople, once these challenges are met, the excitement of the leasing sales process is ended. They consider the actual closing process to be merely paperwork.

Leasing paperwork, however, is the lifeblood of the leasing business. Leasing companies have nothing, nor do salespeople, if the paperwork is not complete, accurate, and enforceable. Leasing paperwork can cause the "unclosing" of many leasing situations. Although leasing salespeople sometimes look at leasing contracts as necessary evils, without properly executed documents there is no deal. A leasing company must be able to collect its income from its customers and control the equipment that it places on lease. Leasing documents are the instruments that ensure the lessor's rights.

Consequently, salespeople must be prepared to assist, comfort, and educate prospects when documents must be executed. Many prospects' objections to leasing documents are caused by their unfamiliarity with the documents themselves. It is critical, therefore, for salespeople to understand the language, intent, and meaning of each required document. A salesperson's clear, understandable, and accurate explanations of the language in contracts can go a long way toward making prospects feel more comfortable with what they are being asked to sign. Although it is not necessary for leasing salespeople to be legal experts, the more they know about what leasing documents say and mean, the better their ability to get prospects to sign them.

Salespeople have latitude in determining how much they want to learn about leasing documents. Many questions that prospects ask about documents are routine and arise frequently; other questions are less common. Salespeople do not have to know the answers to every question, because assistance is usually available from legal or documentation experts. It is not unprofessional to seek help from experts on some questions, but time can be wasted, a closing can be interrupted, or a transaction can be left unsigned until a salesperson obtains an answer. And time can be a pitfall to lease closings.

Furthermore, when a salesperson doesn't know the answer to a documentation question, a concerned prospect may feel that the salesperson doesn't want to answer the question. If a salesperson has to seek legal advice, an otherwise comfortable prospect may feel that he or she should seek legal counsel too. What's more, although a prospect's question may not be routine for the salesperson, it may be routine for the prospect. If the prospect thinks that a salesperson is unprofessional because the answer to a routine question is unknown, he or she may have second thoughts about doing business with the salesperson.

Since there may be direct or indirect exposure to the loss of business because of an inability to make prospects feel at ease, it is critical for salespeople to be fully conversant in their own contracts. One way to do this is to obtain an interpretation of all the "legalese" in every required leasing form. By carrying a "translation" of the contractual meaning of each document, form, clause, and codicil, salespeople can quickly refer to the meaning of the language in each form they use.

Beyond explaining the meaning of leasing documentation, salespeople can also help themselves by thoroughly reviewing every required documentation package before presenting the paperwork to the prospect. A listing of each document and form required, how many of each form are required, and the name or title of the required signatory can also help facilitate lease closings.

Documentation Checklists

Even the most skilled leasing salespeople can be helped by using a documentation checklist (Exhibit 6). A checklist helps because salespeople can sometimes become sidetracked during a lease closing. Forms may be moved around a conference table, sent into another area for review, sent to be copied, or inadvertently misplaced during the closing process. Even if missing documents can be signed later or lost documents can be replaced, time will be lost, equipment purchase orders can be detained, or, in the worst case, leasing transactions can be reconsidered by a prospect when closings are not completed.

A documentation checklist should include a listing of every document and form that must be executed by the customer, a notation of how many copies of each document and form are required, and the name and/or title of each individual who must sign the paperwork. If some documents require the affixing of a

Exhibit 6. Documentation checklist.

Document/Form	Number of copies required	Name of signatory
☐ Equipment lease	______	______________
☐ Equipment schedule	______	______________
☐ Personal guaranty	______	______________
☐ Corporate guaranty	______	______________
☐ UCC-I financing statement	______	______________
☐ Delivery/acceptance certificate	______	______________
☐ Corporate resolution/ certificate of secretary	______	______________
☐ Landlord waiver	______	______________
☐ Other	______	______________

corporate seal or must be attested to by a notary public, that requirement should also be noted on the checklist. Checklists help organize and formalize a lease closing and make the process more professional in appearance. They also ensure that you bring or send all the required paperwork for the lease closing.

Despite the fact that most individuals who are responsible for preparing lease documentation are thorough and attentive to details by virtue of their responsibility, people do occasionally make errors. If you have documentation prepared for you by another person, it is always a good idea to review the documentation with the preparer. This way, you can be certain that you have all the paperwork you need and that there will be no surprises when the lease is executed.

Closing is not an anticlimax to the sales process. Closing is a critical step that confirms a prospect's agreement to enter a leasing agreement with your organization. Despite the fact that closing takes place at the point where a prospect is ready to do business with you, there must be confirmation of that agreement. The confirmation of a prospect's agreement to do business is evidenced by the execution of leasing documentation.

Once you have reached the point of closure and the necessary paperwork has been executed by the prospect, the time has come to thank the prospect for the business transaction and move on. By the time you reach closure, all the prospect's questions have been answered, the prospect has been made to feel comfortable in agreeing to do business with you and your organization, and documentation has been executed. If the prospect has further concerns or questions, of course you must answer them. If, however, there is nothing further to be done regarding the particular transaction, you should thank the prospect and leave.

Your departure should be courteous and brief. Although there may be no real danger of reopening a closed transaction, you don't want to continue discussions, rehash the situation, or cause the prospect to have second thoughts about a leasing agreement that has been completed. Once the equipment has been delivered and installed, paid for, and the lease has started, you can then pursue the customer for additional business referrals and recommendations.

PART IV
THE COMPETITIVE ARENA

Competition is the word that probably causes the greatest concern among leasing salespeople. The leasing market is a highly competitive arena and will continue to be so. Therefore, you must prepare yourself to deal with competitors every day.

Competitors are not the insurmountable obstacle to leasing success that some salespeople perceive them to be. If they were, there would be no reason for any but a few leasing companies to try to compete. In fact, there are innumerable competitors in the leasing industry, and more of them are entering regularly. Competition, then, is not something to be feared; it is simply a business condition that must be respected and understood.

Much like the other aspects of leasing sales, competition must be approached in an orderly and thoughtful way. The most common mistake—and probably the worst approach that leasing salespeople can take to competitors—is to react impulsively when faced with a competitor's offering. Salespeople often erroneously assume that the presence of a competitor requires an immediate reduction in their own price, an accommodation in leasing terms and conditions, or some other concession to a prospective customer. Sometimes these measures may eventually be called for. But there are many other options before a salesperson should resort to "giving away the store."

What if the prospect has not disclosed the full terms and conditions of a competitor's apparently more attractive offering? What if a competing salesperson has presented a prospect with an unauthorized or undeliverable proposal? What if a competitor has not fully qualified a prospect and therefore may not be able to deliver a leasing structure as preliminarily quoted? Scenarios such as these are possible and actually occur quite often. Consequently, a major part of dealing with the competition is considering the "what ifs." Knowing the most likely "what ifs," and understanding how to present them to a prospect goes a long way toward disqualifying competitors and winning leasing sales on your own terms. This part covers the competitive aspects of leasing sales and how to put yourself in the most advantageous position to close business in competitive situations.

Chapter 14

Dealing With the Competition

Regardless of how long people have been in leasing sales or how well they know the particular products and services they sell, a word that can cause them great apprehension is *competition*. This apprehension is understandable, and there are rarely leasing opportunities that don't involve some type of competition. Yet if there were no competitors, salespeople wouldn't have as great an opportunity to excel and wouldn't be rewarded as handsomely—monetarily, personally, or psychologically.

When facing the potential loss of business, salespeople certainly don't stop to thank their competitors for providing them with the opportunity to excel. Nonetheless, competition does exactly that. Because competition is not going to go away, and also because salespeople can be highly rewarded for closing business only in competitive arenas, the question for salespeople is "How can I excel in a highly competitive arena?"

Understanding the Competitive Situation

Assuming that salespeople have sales ability and product knowledge and also that they represent worthy competitors, the first step in competing is to understand the competition. Competition in the leasing business comes in all shapes and sizes. Salespeople compete with the outright cash purchasing power of prospective customers, with providers of other types of financing, with financing plans and programs offered by equipment vendors, with other sources of leasing, and even with the possibility that a prospective customer may decide not to acquire the equipment in question after all. Therefore, in every potential leasing situation, a salesperson must find out what alternatives a prospect is considering.

Sometimes, prospects readily reveal other alternatives that are being considered. It's not uncommon for a prospect to make statements such as: "I'm talking to my bank about this acquisition. Why would leasing be a better method of financing the equipment?" "I have leased before through XYZ Leasing and have asked them for a quotation for my new equipment." "The equipment vendor has offered a financing plan that we are reviewing." In these cases, you know who your competition is and can present your leasing alternative in its best light by comparison.

At other times, prospects won't tell you what alternatives they may be pursuing, so you'll have to either inquire or make an educated guess. Inquiring about competitive alternatives can be a ticklish issue. Some prospects might feel that a direct question about other competitors is rude or pushy on your part; other prospects may feel that it is perfectly acceptable for a salesperson to want to know. Consequently, when you inquire about competitive alternatives, it's important that you ask your questions at an appropriate time and that you inquire discreetly. A question such as "Are you considering other financing alternatives?" should not be upsetting to most businesspeople. If you don't receive a direct answer to your question, however, probing for more information may meet with a prospect's displeasure.

It can also be helpful to inquire whether a prospect has ever leased equipment before. If the answer is yes, you can then ask which leasing company or companies were used. However, even prior leasing experience may not reveal the nature of the current competition. This may be a new situation that does not fit the business parameters of the previous company. A business that has leased from a small-ticket leasing company may now be acquiring equipment that is too costly for that leasing company to consider. Or a business may have leased a computer or machinery from a specialist that doesn't handle the equipment the prospect presently wishes to lease.

If a prospect answers no to your question about having leased before, it is always a good idea to find out why. Some prospects may have never considered leasing before. Other prospects may have considered leasing but selected a different alternative. Still other prospects may have disliked something about the way a leasing alternative was presented to them or disliked the alternative itself. Any of these responses from a prospect can give you some insight into how to proceed.

When you encounter prospects who have never leased before, your strongest competition will most likely be a nonleasing alternative. Ask "How have you acquired equipment in the past?" to help determine the type of acquisition alternative you'll probably be competing against. When dealing with a prospect who has never leased before, you need to provide information about leasing's benefits somewhat more carefully and thoroughly than usual. Your description of how leasing works and what leasing offers must be presented at a pace that allows the prospect to absorb the information and permits you to fully answer any questions. Your presentation must also stress leasing's typical advantages over the types of financing the prospect has used in the past.

Prospects who are unfamiliar with leasing may have preconceived notions, unfounded concerns, or general fears about different sources of financing in general. In this case, if a salesperson moves quickly through a leasing presentation or appears to be unconcerned about a prospect's anxieties, the prospect's concerns often increase. Therefore, anxious prospects must be made to feel comfortable as well as informed by the presentation. It can be helpful for salespeople to assume the role of educator or consultant. In this role, a salesperson is better able to approach the discussion of equipment acquisition alternatives as an ally rather than the seller of an unfamiliar concept. The situation also calls for the presentation of proofs, endorsements, and evidence of the existence of satisfied customers whose businesses are the same as or similar to that of the prospect.

Focusing on a Competitive Alternative

When prospects inform you of another, or preferred, nonleasing method of acquiring equipment, your objective becomes more specific: You must compare leasing to that method. As discussed in Chapter 11, you must present specific information about why leasing is more beneficial than a cash purchase, bank borrowing, or other method of financing equipment. Here again, rather than using a hard-sell approach with prospects who are unfamiliar with leasing's benefits, you can often be more successful if you assume the role of a counselor. Many prospects do not have a financial background; other prospects may not be abreast of current money market conditions; and still other prospects may have never spent sufficient time analyzing the differences between alternative methods of equipment acquisition. In such cases, you may be providing a prospect with enlightening information when you illustrate the differences in the actual costs of financing alternatives.

If a cash purchase is being considered, your presentation of a leasing alternative can often be enhanced by actually working with a prospect's financial information. You can prepare cash-flow comparisons and calculations of the prospect's return on invested capital, return against sales, or return against inventory. Your comparative analysis may not be available to the prospect from anywhere else. In the case of prospects who are considering bank financing, educating them about the hidden costs of compensating balances and the potentially limiting effect of restrictive covenants in bank loan agreements may win the prospect's confidence.

For some prospects, an alternative might be acquiring the equipment through a vendor's leasing or financing plan. In this case, you must find out the exact terms and conditions of that plan. Some vendor plans are actually managed and operated by leasing companies, and others are handled by vendors themselves. If a third-party leasing company runs a vendor's leasing program, you may be competing head-to-head with the rates, terms, and conditions of a leasing program that is similar to yours. However, that is not always the case. Some vendor leasing plans are rigid in terms of the variety of leasing structures available. A vendor leasing program may not offer particular lease structures that you can provide—structures that might be more beneficial to a particular prospect. Additionally, although many vendor leasing plans are managed by third-party leasing companies, they are sold by vendor sales forces as a convenience for their customers. In many cases, an equipment salesperson is responsible for handling the leasing details for the prospect. As a rule, vendor salespeople are not experts in equipment leasing and therefore may not be able to provide as much support as you could to help the customer arrange a leasing transaction.

When prospects inform you that a vendor offers financing for equipment, you can anticipate a different set of circumstances. Many vendor financing plans require substantial down payments. As much as 20 or 25 percent of the equipment cost can be called for up front. Furthermore, vendor plans often limit the financing term to three or four years. When costly equipment is involved, both the down payment and a shorter repayment term may be less favorable to the prospect than a long-term lease.

Beyond the possible structural drawbacks to vendor leasing and financing plans are other factors that may permit you to prevail. In many cases, especially in the case of vendor financing plans, vendors offer the plans only to ensure obtaining an equipment order.

Since financing is not the primary purpose of the vendor's offering the plan to begin with, many vendors don't aggressively compete with other sources of financing. Therefore, although a vendor may appear to be working diligently to help a prospective customer arrange financing, the vendor may actually choose to benignly neglect the financing issue once another viable financing alternative presents itself.

A vendor's decision to allow another source to win the competition for arranging financing for an equipment purchase can be caused by several factors. Vendors may have to support financing arrangements for their customers by providing financial recourse for the transactions. Vendors may also have to report the financing transactions not only as a direct source of income but also as a contingent liability of the business. Contingent liability is incurred because a vendor may be called upon to compensate a leasing company that has been provided recourse against losses. When vendors are responsible for reporting financial recourse or the financing transactions themselves in their financial statements, the direct or contingent liability incurred may limit the vendor's ability to obtain other types of business financing. A bank or other lender, for example, may feel that although a vendor is only contingently liable for recourse against possible problem financing transactions with customers, the potential liability is enough to limit how much can be borrowed for other purposes. Therefore, while helping to accommodate customers and facilitate closing equipment orders, vendor financing plans can create financial management problems for the vendor.

Dealing With the Prospect's Decision Not to Proceed

Aside from direct competition from alternative leasing or financing plans, salespeople can "compete" with the possibility that a prospect may decide not to acquire equipment at all. Although not competition in the strictest sense, a prospect's decision not to go ahead with an acquisition nonetheless is a reason for losing a leasing sale. When prospects are uncertain about whether to acquire equipment, you have the opportunity to sell leasing.

Most often, vendors introduce you to prospects who are undecided about an equipment acquisition. Vendors frequently use leasing companies to qualify prospects for them; they may refer a prospective customer to a leasing company simply to find out whether the prospect is creditworthy. Sometimes vendors want to increase the probability of a sale by stressing the affordability of long-term leasing plans, or they may use leasing companies to smoke out hidden competitors for the equipment sale. Prospects are likely to inform a third-party leasing company about competitors that are being considered, even though they may not provide the same information to the vendor.

Vendors may also introduce third-party leasing companies to prospects in order to get a better idea of how serious their prospects are. Vendors become wary when prospects delay an equipment order for longer than a vendor believes is necessary for the circumstances, despite assurances that an order will be forthcoming. In this instance, many vendors choose to introduce a leasing salesperson directly to the prospect, especially when costly equipment is involved. The vendor's premise is that if the prospect hesitates about placing a direct purchase order and doesn't respond favorably to the idea of a leasing arrangement, the prospect is probably not immediately viable.

Vendors not only want to know how serious their prospective customers are about an equipment acquisition, they also want to know the timing of their prospects' planned acquisition. It is not uncommon for prospective equipment buyers to act as if a purchase is imminent even though the actual circumstances are quite different. First of all, it ordinarily doesn't cost a buyer anything to delay a purchase, unless prices are about to increase or equipment is specially sale priced for a limited time. Second, some buyers may be trying to obtain authorization for an equipment acquisition and encounter unforeseen internal obstacles. Furthermore, some equipment shoppers may not be authorized to acquire equipment at all and may be trying to convince an authorized individual to approve the acquisition. In these cases, a vendor can often obtain more accurate information about the actual circumstances within a prospect's business by introducing an unrelated third-party leasing company. Prospects often divulge more information, and may also be more responsive, to those who represent a source of money than to a supplier of equipment. From the vendor's viewpoint, introducing a leasing salesperson makes sense, because selling time is costly.

If a prospective customer informs a leasing salesperson that an acquisition will be delayed, the vendor is better able to determine how much time to spend pursuing the prospect. If the leasing salesperson finds hidden competition for the equipment sale, the vendor can determine how to counter the competitive offer accordingly. And if the individual representing the prospect is not a qualified decision maker or the equipment purchase has not been officially approved, the vendor can change the intensity on the pending sale by moving it from the front burner to the back burner.

Regardless of how you encounter prospects who are uncertain or procrastinating about an equipment acquisition, this situation can present you with the opportunity to sell leasing in its best light. Frequently, the cause for a prospect's uncertainty or procrastination about an equipment acquisition is "sticker shock." Sticker shock occurs when prospects realize that equipment is more expensive than they assumed. Unlike situations in which you encounter price differences between your offering and that of a competitor, in this situation you are competing only against a prospect's possible decision against acquiring equipment.

Sticker shock is found in shoppers who are simply dissuaded from acquiring equipment because the price is higher than they anticipated. Other shoppers find that the capital budget is not sufficient to cover the equipment's cost. Some prospects find that although an item of equipment can be afforded, a more advanced, more desirable, and therefore more costly model would be better. In such situations, the mere introduction of a leasing alternative may be enough to convert a shopper into a customer. Often, however, equipment shoppers perceive leasing to be simply a way of paying out a high cost over a long time. If the shopper is hesitant about paying the cost of an item to begin with, it is not unusual for the shopper to be reluctant to pay leasing costs as well.

Justifying the Equipment Acquisition

If a shopper who is confronted with a high sticker price is merely offered the opportunity to arrange for lease payments, the offer may make no real impression. In this case, you must go beyond simply presenting a leasing alternative by illustrating how leasing provides long-term financing. You must also demonstrate how leasing applies directly to the shopper's business.

Many shoppers do not do an adequate job of justifying an equipment purchase in advance. Although the shopper may have recognized a need or desire for new equipment, it is not until the shopper actually begins to look for equipment that the acquisition is seriously considered. If, in the early stages of shopping, the equipment price is found to be too high, the shopper may simply decide against the acquisition. This situation can occur because the shopper has not thoroughly analyzed either the benefits that can be gained from the acquisition or the costs.

When you encounter hesitant shoppers, therefore, it is reasonable to assume that you will have to do more than simply provide a leasing alternative to convince them that an equipment acquisition makes economic sense. One way to do this is to find out from the prospect why the equipment was being shopped for in the first place. If the equipment is to be used in production, what would the equipment produce? If the equipment is to be used for automation purposes, what functions would be simplified or replaced? Once you determine how the equipment is to be used, you can begin to expand your leasing solution by adding more detail.

Creating a Spreadsheet

Let's say, for example, that the equipment to be acquired produces particular items. By finding out the price for which the item sells, how many items the equipment can produce (per hour, shift, day, week, month, and/or year), and how many units can be sold in total, you can work with the shopper to determine the additional revenue that the equipment will create. The costs of operating the equipment can be determined in the same way. Operating costs may include materials, utilities, rent, maintenance, and other items. From the above information you can create a spreadsheet itemizing the revenue and expenses of the equipment by the hour, shift, day, week, month, and/or year, thereby helping the shopper to visualize the merits of the equipment's acquisition more clearly. What's more, you have reduced the presentation of your lease terms to a more realistic, and perhaps more attractive, level by breaking them down into smaller increments. Let's say, for example, that the lease payment for equipment costing $100,000 is $2,500 a month for five years: $2,500 a month equals $625 a week (4 weeks), $125 a day (5 days), or $15.62 an hour (8 hours).

If equipment is to be acquired to automate a process or operation, you can design the same type of justification spreadsheet to demonstrate the savings. The basic information needed to create a spreadsheet can often be obtained directly from an equipment vendor. Many equipment brochures or specification sheets contain estimated costs of operation for use by different businesses. Furthermore, many industry publications include articles and studies of the estimated revenues earned and costs incurred from operating particular types of equipment.

You do not have to create a perfect model, and you should not imply to shoppers that you are an expert in the operation of the equipment. What you are trying to do here is to stimulate the shopper to consider an equipment acquisition in more detail. You can gain several competitive benefits by developing a more detailed presentation regarding the costs of acquiring equipment:

- Your presentation may crystallize the decision-making process for the hesitant equipment shopper, thereby creating or accelerating a leasing transaction.
- Your presentation may salvage or accelerate a sale for the equipment vendor.
- Your presentation may positively differentiate you from competition in the eyes of the equipment shopper, helping to ensure a leasing sale.
- Your presentation may positively differentiate you from competitors in the eyes of the equipment vendor, leading to additional referrals to vendor customers.

Using the Law of Averages

The estimate that 80 percent of all products are sold by 20 percent of all salespeople may or not be accurate, but it is safe to assume that the vast majority of salespeople are not successful. For our purposes, it doesn't matter why so many salespeople fail, it only matters that they do.

Based on the above estimate, it can be assumed that the average vendor or your average competitor employs only one top producer out of every five salespeople. Therefore, the probability that a vendor or a prospective customer is working with a top-notch salesperson is relatively low. So if you do a professional and thorough job in selling to prospects, there is an 80 percent chance that you will outsell your leasing competitors. But there is also an 80 percent chance that you will do a better job of selling the vendor's equipment than the vendor's own salespeople.

Because the above scenario is apparently true, vendors tend to gravitate toward leasing salespeople who consistently help them sell equipment. When vendors rely on leasing salespeople to qualify prospects, both parties benefit because each has the chance to close a sale. But the vendor is often doing more than simply providing a salesperson with an opportunity to sell. The vendor is placing a great deal of responsibility on the leasing salesperson; the vendor will, to some extent, rely on the salesperson's evaluation of how to proceed with a sales strategy. Consequently, if leasing salespeople can earn a vendor's trust, to the degree that vendors want to work with them as partners, salespeople can put themselves in a strong competitive position.

Furthermore, once a salesperson becomes a valued resource to a vendor, the typical pressure to continually compete for a vendor's business tends to diminish. Vendors are more likely to let the leasing salesperson decide unilaterally what leasing plans should be offered to prospects, what leasing terms and conditions are appropriate, and how and when to introduce leasing to prospective customers. Although other leasing companies may be able to offer competitive rates, terms, and conditions, they cannot offer the one leasing salesperson that the vendor has come to trust and rely on.

Leasing is a highly competitive business. Competitors exist at virtually every level of the industry. Although there are apparently no real secrets to overcoming the competition every time, there are things leasing salespeople can do to increase their probability of winning.

Increasing Your Probability of Success

One way to increase the probability of winning business is to sell within the guidelines of your own organization. Since leasing companies design their products and services to meet the needs of particular equipment, vendor, or end-user customer types, the greatest chance of success lies within the boundaries of your organization's primary market. Concentrating on your organization's primary market has three advantages: The products fit the customers, the competition is known and has probably been considered in the design of the products and services, and the chances of facing unknown competition decrease. The first two considerations are more or less obvious, but the third may not be.

Considering the size and scope of the leasing market, there are leasing companies that fulfill a wide variety of leasing needs. When salespeople discover prospects with unqualified leasing needs and try to fill them, there is no assurance that the salesperson can deliver what the prospect desires. Prospects themselves may not understand enough about the differences between leasing alternatives to know that a salesperson is not competitive in comparison with another alternative. If, for example, a prospect is reviewing appropriate competitive lease structures for a particular purpose and a salesperson can't provide the structure that is ultimately chosen, the salesperson has wasted considerable time and effort only to find out that he or she was not qualified to compete in the first place.

Although the above scenario can happen even within known markets, a salesperson is more likely to do a better job of prospect qualification and competition identification within known markets. Known markets allow for a certain amount of consistency in leasing competition. Although the leasing market is vast and leasing providers are numerous, there tends to be only a limited number of competitors within each segment of the market. Experience and time spent within the same markets familiarize salespeople with the most common needs of vendors and end-user customers in those markets as well as with the most likely competitors. Competitors in a known market can then be categorized and ranked in an organized way.

Assessing the Competition

It is a good idea to keep thorough competitor files (Exhibit 7). Vendors and end-user customers frequently provide salespeople with literature, mailings, or rate charts from competitors. When you obtain competitive information, you should read and analyze it, highlighting the strengths and weaknesses of competitive offerings. Competitive leasing plans contain obvious information such as published leasing rates, terms, and conditions, but they can also provide you with other not so obvious insights.

Low Rates

Leasing competitors that offer very low rates may appear to be extremely competitive in the market, but they may also be unable to serve certain types of customers or certain types of vendors. Although some major leasing companies have the ability to obtain funds at lower cost than others, the cost of funds is only one part of the total cost of providing leasing services. Leasing companies must also cover their costs of personnel, operation, and overhead. Fur-

Exhibit 7. Contents of competitor information file.

What Do You Need to Know?

Their strengths

Their weaknesses

Their products

Their operational procedures

Their reputation

Their history

Their economics

thermore, leasing companies are in a high-risk business and must provide for possible losses or bad debts in their portfolios of leasing transactions. All things considered, then, a leasing company's ability to borrow favorably does not mean that lower rates are passed on to the customer. Low rates can also indicate that a leasing company must be extremely conservative in its credit policies, because the rates charged decrease its ability to reserve against bad debt. A low-rate competitor may not be able to service end-user customers that can't meet stringent credit criteria or to accommodate vendors that have less than the highest-quality customers. This does not mean that higher-rate leasing companies will or should take undue risks; it only means that higher rates can permit the building of larger bad-debt reserves, thereby increasing credit flexibility. As a rule, low-rate leasing providers are also likely to be more stringent in their documentation requirements, because more rigid contracts help minimize loss exposure.

When competing against low-rate lessors, you may find clear evidence that conservative policies exist through the credit criteria provided to prospective customers and vendors. In other cases, the policies may not be so apparent. Signs of conservatism can be searched for by questioning customers and vendors about how a low-rate provider handles lease applications. One sign of conservatism is a generally slow responsiveness or turnaround time. Conservative leasing companies tend to take a longer time to make decisions and may require significant additional information about prospects that do not have impeccable credit credentials.

Some conservative leasing companies try to appear aggressive while remaining cautious. By stating how flexible their policies are and by agreeing to look at virtually all lease applications, some conservative leasing companies try to create the image that they are, in fact, aggressive. As a practical matter, however, through long turnaround times, requests for significant amounts of additional credit information, and general procrastination in response to credit applicants they are unsure of, conservative leasing companies may simply stall until another leasing source approves the transaction.

Vendor Recourse

Because low rates can reduce a leasing company's ability to have flexible credit policies, low-rate providers sometimes offset their inability to adequately reserve against potential bad debt by requiring vendors to guarantee leasing transactions through the provision of recourse. Vendor recourse can be implemented in several ways. Full recourse requires a vendor to purchase defaulted leasing transactions after a certain period of time or under certain default conditions. Partial recourse provides for a sharing of losses incurred from lessee defaults between the vendor and the leasing company. Partial recourse is sometimes implemented by establishing a pool of funds; the leasing company holds back a certain amount of the vendor's proceeds from the leasing company's equipment purchases (typically 5 to 10 percent of the equipment cost) and applies the pool against the lessor's first losses incurred from defaulted leasing transactions. Sometimes vendor reserve pools are limited to a particular amount. Once the vendor has accrued sufficient funds in the pool, the leasing company pays the full cost for its equipment purchases until the reserves are decreased below the agreed-upon level.

Another way to arrange recourse is for the vendor to agree to guarantee leasing transactions and to purchase them outright in the event of lessee default, without the creation of a reserve. In this case, once a leasing transaction has been defaulted by the lessee, the vendor buys the transaction under prearranged terms and conditions established between the vendor and the leasing company.

Sometimes leasing companies allow vendors to replace a lessee who is in default of a contract with another acceptable customer. The new customer then takes the place of the original lessee for the remainder of the lease term. Ordinarily, a leasing company limits the amount of time the vendor has to find a new lessee to ninety days or less. If, by the end of the remarketing period, the vendor has not found an acceptable replacement lessee, the vendor is obligated to buy the leasing contract by paying the full unpaid balance.

Some leasing companies offer a variation of vendor recourse by establishing an ultimate net loss arrangement. Here, the vendor agrees to repay the leasing company for the specific loss incurred from a defaulted leasing transaction—after the leasing company has pursued all of its remedies against the lessee—within a certain period of time. Sometimes the ultimate net loss is not determined until after legal proceedings have been instituted against the lessee or the equipment has been resold. Since legal proceedings can take time to resolve, the vendor may have to reimburse the leasing company's losses before a final conclusion has been reached. However, once a situation has been concluded, the vendor may recover some money from the legal action against the lessee.

Vendor Remarketing

As an alternative to vendor recourse agreements, vendors may be required to remarket equipment repossessed by a leasing company as a result of lessee default. Remarketing agreements may be mandatory, wherein the vendor is obligated to resell repossessed equipment, or they may simply call for the vendor's best efforts to try to resell it. When a vendor is obligated to resell equipment, the equipment itself must be identified by the vendor as being for sale, and the vendor must demonstrate to the leasing company that an active effort is being made to accomplish the sale. Vendors do not have to apply the same amount of diligence in best-effort remarketing situations.

Vendor remarketing agreements fall far short of recourse protection for the lessor, because there is no guarantee that the equipment will ever be resold. And even if equipment is resold, there is no guarantee of the selling price and no guarantee of how much time will be needed to complete the resale. Furthermore, remarketing agreements do not necessarily guarantee that a vendor will attempt to sell repossessed equipment before pursuing new equipment sales. Therefore, although providing some support to leasing companies, remarketing agreements do not ordinarily permit them to take significant credit risks.

Vendor Risks

Although vendor recourse or remarketing agreements may help vendors sell equipment to customers with credit ratings below a leasing company's standards, vendors pay a premium for those sales. If the vendor is providing full or partial recourse, the vendor is guaranteeing the lease obligation of the customer to some extent. If the vendor is required to reserve against the leasing company's losses by contributing to a loss reserve, the vendor is receiving less money for each equipment purchase made by the leasing company. Even in the case of remarketing agreements, the vendor faces the potential responsibility of having to resell equipment.

Once leasing companies have obtained a vendor's financial guarantee, the vendor may incur hidden risks. The leasing company may, for example, approve questionable transactions that should not have been approved, even with recourse. The risk of questionable approvals exists simply because, as far as the leasing company is concerned, the vendor is ultimately responsible for payment of the leasing transaction.

Therefore, when you encounter lower-rate vendor leasing competition, you must pursue the recourse issue. Many higher-rate leasing companies are able to create adequate internal bad-debt reserves to give them more flexibility in credit decision making. If your vendor program can achieve a high ratio of lease approvals from the applications submitted without a vendor's having to provide recourse or remarketing guarantees, the vendor may be better served. If vendors are contributing to loss reserve pools through discounts, providing the same discount to a leasing company that does not require recourse can save the vendor from the potential liability of buying transactions back—and still lower the customer's lease payment.

Reasonableness

Because leasing company policies can be complex, and because the offerings leasing companies make to vendors and end-user customers can be so varied, it is never enough to simply react to the appearance of competitive offerings. A competitor's low rates or apparently unreasonable leasing terms and conditions may not be the whole story. At times, of course, you will encounter competitive offerings you can't compete with. Often, however, you'll be able to counter what appears to be a better offer if you do some digging.

The first test for a competitive offering is a check for reasonableness. Take a step back and ask yourself if a competitor's proposal sounds reasonable under the circumstances. If it does, you must then determine whether you can present a better alternative. Your alternative proposal must be based on the particular circumstances and must be within the guidelines of your organization. Perhaps you can present a different lease term or lease structure or introduce factors that a prospect has not considered. Therefore, in reasonable competitive situations, you must simply organize your resources to outsell a competitor. You will probably win some and lose some. That's what competition is all about.

If, however, competitive offerings are unreasonable, you must find out why. Leasing salespeople often panic and immediately search for ways to match or beat a competitor's quoted rates, terms, or conditions when they are confronted with a low rate or an extraordinarily attractive offering. When the leasing rate is the issue, it is not unusual for salespeople to try to convince their own managers to permit them to meet or beat a competitor's rate in order to get the deal, save the vendor, or beat the competition. At times, that approach may be necessary, but only if all else fails.

Before deciding to give up and meet or beat a competitor, it is more effective to spend some time determining why the competitor has made the seemingly unreasonable offer. A conservative leasing company may publish rates that are more attractive in comparison to yours, but perhaps the prospect can't meet the offerer's credit criteria. A specialist may have offered a leasing structure wherein the prospect must pay a significant amount of money to purchase the equipment at the end of the lease term. A bank may have offered extremely low rates but will contractually inhibit the prospect's financial flexibility. A vendor may be requiring a large down payment. A competitive leasing salesperson may have proposed an unauthorized offering that his or her management may not approve. These examples illustrate that you don't necessarily have to meet or beat a competitor's offering simply because it appears to be more favorable than your own.

It may be easier for some salespeople to plead with a sales manager for a lower rate, more flexible terms and conditions, or some other form of prospect accommodation than to convince a prospect that their leasing alternatives are as good as if not better than a competitor's. Salespeople sometimes forget where they should be directing their sales efforts. Assuming that most salespeople are articulate, personable, and knowledgeable and possess excellent communication and interpersonal skills, the only question is where those skills should be applied.

Selling Internally

Some salespeople choose to direct their arsenal of skills internally instead of externally. In these cases, salespeople may spend significant amounts of time trying to sell their own credit people on why a marginally acceptable prospect should be credit approved. They spend considerable time trying to convince contract administrators or attorneys to waive required documentation to prevent upsetting the customer or losing the deal. They try to cajole sales managers into accommodating vendors because a competitor is willing to approve weak credits.

The fact of the matter is that most salespeople who take the above approach achieve only temporary success. Leasing companies need business volume in order to grow and succeed. At times, poorly performing salespeople or the internal sales experts survive only because the organizational environment allows them to. Some leasing companies permit poor performers to survive because, in a growing industry such as equipment leasing, they simply need enough bodies in the field to support their sales activities.

The time will come, however, for real performance—valuable new account development, sales profitability, the payment performance of individual accounts—to be measured. Internal sales experts don't grow. Their external sales abilities normally don't improve; at best, they tend to improve at a slow pace as a result of "osmosis" rather than from any effort to achieve. Therefore, when leasing companies have to make hard decisions, internal sales experts are vulnerable. If leasing companies must cut the size of the sales force, internal sales experts will be the first to go. Promotions may be withheld or opportunities to gain more responsibility denied. Choice sales territories may be awarded to others with less seniority.

Internal sales experts leave themselves open to the perceptions of others because they have not proved their ability to achieve established goals and objectives. These salespeople are vulnerable to becoming the "victims" of a managerial perception that ordinarily can't be overcome; most managers have documentation to illustrate how and where salespeople failed to produce adequate results or performed at a loss to the organization. Although internal sales experts can lead themselves to believe that they are top-producing salespeople, the numbers will eventually prove them wrong.

Becoming a Top Producer

To become top sales producers, leasing salespeople must succeed not only in the outside world of leasing competitors but also within their own organizations. But because a salesperson's production capability derives from his or her abilities to achieve in the market, and not only from the capabilities of the organization he or she represents, it is reasonable to assume that a top producer can excel in a competitive market almost regardless of the organization represented. Top salespeople produce business profitably as a result of their individual abilities.

Top producers enjoy the benefits that result directly from their sales achievements, and they gain the additional advantage of being able to select the leasing organization they would prefer to represent. Although a top producer is not absolutely guaranteed employment with any leasing entity at any time, there is a high probability that this can be accomplished. Furthermore, there is a high probability that any organization that employs a top producer will make every effort to retain his or her services.

Reaching the top production levels takes time, education, training, and experience. Within the business itself, all the aspects of leasing sales must be mastered, but this is not enough. The knowledge and experience gained must be focused on the external market and applied diligently. Although salespeople are more likely to succeed if they have greater knowledge, competition must still be overcome.

A hurdle for top producers is that the better they become, the greater the sales challenges they are likely to encounter. Challenges become greater because a top producer's organization wants the best sales performers to handle the situations that offer the most opportunity. The organization is likely to give a top producer more sales responsibility and a larger production quota. What's more, top producers tend to apply additional pressure on themselves to reach personal goals.

Internal Competition

The above factors serve to increase the competitive challenge faced by those who desire to become top producers. Top producers must compete in the outside markets for sales production, and they must also compete within their organizations to outperform other salespeople. Top producers must retain their positions by leading the sales force in production, profitability, and any other measure by which an organization measures its salespeople. Even in organizations where there is no internal system for competition among salespeople, or where there are no other rewards or recognition for accomplishment beyond direct compensation, top producers tend to measure themselves against other salespeople. A top producer, then, generally desires to outcompete all challengers, whether there is a definitive measure or not.

Because top producers face competitive challenges in all phases of their endeavors, dealing with competition becomes a more significant factor for them. And the more they produce, the greater the challenges become. The greater the achievements of top producers, the less margin for error. Top producers are expected to compete successfully for larger, more important, higher-quality accounts, and it is reasonable to assume that the competition will also be deploying its own top producers. The more responsibility an organization places in the hands of top producers, the better they have to perform. As other salespeople in the organization grow and accomplish more, the challenge becomes even larger for top producers to outperform them. Because top producers derive their accomplishments from their ability to perform in the market, however, even internal challenges must be overcome in the outside market, not within the organization. Top producers are measured by their success in leasing sales. A top producer can't retain his or her status unless that status derives from business production.

Although there are no shortcuts to winning competitive battles, there are things that a salesperson can do to become or remain a top producer. Arriving at top production levels takes time and effort, but it also takes a realization that sales production does not happen by accident. Despite the fact that a salesperson can occasionally win an important account by being in the right place at the right time, top sales production is built on consistency.

Consistency in sales is achieved when salespeople continually meet or exceed the sales goals established by their organizations or themselves. As stressed throughout this book, the probability of sales success can be increased by analyzing and understanding the various aspects of the leasing environment and then focusing your efforts where you have the highest chance of closing sales.

External Competition

Selling the products and services that your organization can readily deliver makes sense, because it is with those products and services that you stand the best chance of satisfying a prospective customer. Understanding your own organization makes sense, because you have the highest chance for sales success when the opportunities you discover meet the organization's parameters for acceptability. Targeting your markets and focusing your sales efforts on the most viable candidates within those markets make sense, because the probability of finding viable prospects increases when you know where to look for them. The competitive market can be approached the same way.

You must understand and analyze your competitors in the same way that you do the other aspects of the business. There is a good chance that you will face the same competitors regularly, and competitive information can be obtained from vendors and end-user customers. This competitive information should be thoroughly analyzed to gain perspective on how a competitor operates in general. Examine all the competitor's plans and programs. Try to determine the competitor's philosophy for conducting business. A competitor's rate chart, for example, can indicate where the emphasis is placed for attracting customers. Many competitors that are active in a market segment must offer a wide range of leasing plans and programs in order to be a viable entity in that market. Yet a particular competitor may stress certain types of lease structures, as demonstrated by its offerings, while deemphasizing others. Therefore, an analysis of all a competitor's offerings may divulge weaknesses in the total program. Instead of focusing on the rates in a competitive proposal, read all the terms and conditions for lease approval. Sometimes you will discover through the analysis of a competitor's credit criteria how the rates came to be so low.

When given the chance, obtain and read competitors' documentation, contracts, lease applications, and supporting paperwork. A competitor's contractual leasing terms and conditions may give you the opportunity to demonstrate how your contracts better fit a prospect's needs. Uncovering competitive weaknesses in the fine print may win an extra sale or two.

Keep and organize all the information you obtain about your competitors, including information about competitors that you do not ordinarily encounter. Update your competitor files every time you acquire new information. Look for trends in competitive offerings. Note when a competitor's trends are out of line with the rest of the market. When a particular competitor acts aggressively where others do not, it may mean that a particular market is being sought through price penetration. This sign indicates that you must contact and stay close to vendors and customers in that market in order to protect your relationships. Trends in another direction—a competitor's price increase or tightening of policies, for example—may indicate that a market is being phased out or minimized in importance. This situation indicates opportunity for you in those markets.

Read leasing industry publications. Helpful and current information can be found in the articles and advertisements, but the personnel and announcement items can be even more useful. Which competitors are expanding? What new salespeople are in your territory? Which leasing companies have merged, been purchased, relocated, downsized?

Personal Evaluation

Aside from what you learn about your competitors, your efforts can be enhanced by things you are able to learn about yourself, your organization, and what you sell.

When a prospect decides to do business with you, ask why. After you have closed your business transaction, find a proper time to inquire about the reasons the customer or vendor decided to conduct business with you. The answers may surprise you, because perhaps you were simply in the right place at the right time. In other cases, you may find that there are things about your selling style that prospects appreciate, the importance of which you were unaware. Although it may be rude to fish for compliments, you are in a highly competitive business and need the information for professional purposes. Naturally, any information that relates directly to your organization and what it offers should be passed on to management.

Conversely, but just as important, you should try to find out why a prospect didn't do business with you when that happens. In this case, the things you hear may be painful, but at least you will know what needs to be corrected. You may have lost a sale, but you can gain valuable information. Some salespeople view the cost of losing a sale but learning how to become better at their jobs as the "tuition fee" for a professional leasing sales education. In fact, it is possible that you don't learn anything from a sales situation that went exactly as it should, simply because there was nothing to learn. The case where everything blows up in your face, however, can provide significant insight for future use, provided that the mistakes are remembered and not repeated.

A good way to enhance your skills is to ask a manager or associate to accompany you on sales calls or to listen to your telemarketing presentations. They will be able to point out strong and weak points that you might not recognize on your own. Because you are in a competitive business, however, you can't let them be hesitant about stating things that are negative. Your objective is to become as good as you can be, not to avoid getting your feelings hurt. You must learn everything you can about yourself that can help you succeed.

The same is true of your competition. Ask prospects why they chose a competitor; don't simply lick your wounds and walk away. Ask them what they liked about a competitor's offering and about the way that it was offered. Similarly, always ask why a prospect chose not to do business with a competitor. However, don't ask about competitors in a way that will reintroduce them as future contenders or reiterate points about the business you have closed. A simple question, such as "Why did you decide not to do business with XYZ Leasing?" will suffice. Don't say something like, "We've heard that XYZ Leasing is an excellent company; why did you select us?" In this way, you will be enhancing your skills and refining your technique based on the most important source of information: your prospects, your customers, and those who are in the best position to give you helpful, objective opinions.

Each step in the competitive process, then, is like the steps in the selling process. You identify the competition, probe for information, present your alternative, answer any questions, overcome any objections, and ask for the order.

Index